HELPING STUDENTS WRITE WELL

A Guide for Teachers in All Disciplines

HELPING STUDENTS WRITE WELL

A Guide for Teachers in All Disciplines

BARBARA E. FASSLER WALVOORD

THE MODERN LANGUAGE ASSOCIATION OF AMERICA
NEW YORK   1982

Library of Congress Cataloging in Publication Data

Walvoord, Barbara E. Fassler, 1941–
    Helping students write well.

    Bibliography: p.
    Includes index.
    1. English language—Rhetoric.   2. Universities
and colleges—Curricula.   I. Title.
PE1408.W31336   808'.042'071173   81-14166
ISBN 0-87352-096-3   AACR2

Published by The Modern Language Association of America
62 Fifth Avenue, New York, New York 10011

Fourth printing

TO JOHN ALLEN
1923–1980
my longtime colleague and friend

Acknowledgments

I am indebted to a large number of persons from various disciplines who read, and offered suggestions on, various parts of the manuscript or who helped me collect writing samples:

From Central College in Pella, Iowa: Arthur Johnson, John Miller, Donald Butler, John Allen, Mildred Steele, John Bowles, Thomas Kopecek, James Van Hoeven, Kenneth Tuinstra, Dorothy Bosch, Joyce Huizer, William Julian, Donald Racheter, David Crichton, James Graham, Allen Moen, Judith Lauber, Robert Schanke, Donald Huffman, Barbara Dieleman, Thomas Iverson, William Paul, Chad Ray, and Ronald Byers.

From Loyola College in Baltimore: Francis Xavier Trainor, Faith Gilroy, Frank Haig, S.J., Linda Spencer, F. Xavier Spiegel, John Jordan, Daniel Duffy, Jack Breihan, Nicholas Varga, Paula Scheye, Barbara Mallonee, Donald Wolfe, and Thomas J. Higgins, S.J.

From Towson State University in Towson, Maryland: Margaret Benner, Karen Toussaint, Deborah Shaller, Marion Hoffman, Gary Wood, Barbara Frankel, Anne Burley, Linda Mahin, Jim Kim, Filmore Dowling, Karl Larew, Frances Rothstein, Harvey Paul, and Dan Jones.

From West Chester State College in West Chester, Pennsylvania: Patricia Grasty, Phyllis Goetz, Betty Hasson, George Reed, Robert Green, J. Bernard Haviland, Laureen Meiswinkel, Anne Sessa, Robert Weiss, Nona Chern, and Judith Ray.

From George Mason University in Fairfax, Virginia: a group of faculty from various disciplines, among whom Robert Karlson, Emmett Holman, Gloria Fauth, and Linda Samuels offered especially helpful advice.

I also wish to thank Donald Gallo of Central Connecticut State College as well as W. R. Irwin and Richard Lloyd-Jones of the University of Iowa for their support and for their advice about the manuscript. Others who offered useful criticism are Richard Larson of the City University of New York, Christopher Thaiss of George Mason University, Virginia Steinhoff of the University of Maine at Orono, and Beverly Palmer of Pitzer College in Claremont, California.

I owe a debt of thanks to Reva Rydstrand and Evelyn Loynachan for typing the first complete manuscript.

The preparation of the manuscript was financially supported in part by Central College in Pella, Iowa; Towson State University in Towson, Maryland; and Loyola College in Baltimore.

B. E. F. W.

Contents

Introduction: Writing and Learning

This handbook is for the junior college, college, or graduate school instructor of economics, physical education, literature, biology, history, or what have you. It is for the tutor or the teaching assistant in any discipline and for the teacher-to-be. In short, it is meant to help any faculty member who must coach and evaluate students' writing.

The cry of many such teachers is "I already have more than I can do to cover my subject in a semester; I don't have time to teach writing." This handbook tries to be realistic about the time constraints all of us face. Throughout, it delineates levels of effort; if you can do only a little, the chapters suggest where you might best place your energies.

No matter how busy we are, however, most of us have to deal with student writing. One reason is that writing is a skill. Like other skills, it can be acquired only through practice. Students must write regularly throughout each semester of their educational careers. Students develop writing skills slowly; a semester or even a year of required composition is not enough. From an extensive body of linguistic evidence about how people learn to write, we discover that teaching students to write well requires an effort across the curriculum and involves teachers in the various disciplines as well as those who teach the writing classes.

But, you may hear from students and others, why is it necessary to worry that much about students' writing skills? Modern citizens don't need to do that much writing anyway. C. G. Enke, a Michigan State chemist, provides an answer for that one:

> It is difficult to overemphasize the importance of writing in the professional life of a scientist. The amount of time my colleagues and I spend writing is out of all proportion to the fraction of our training devoted to developing writing skills. "Publish or perish" is a cliché, but it carries the unmistakable implication that experimental work and elegant theories have no peer value until they have been put in manuscript form. I was shocked to find that the time and effort of

1

writing was often equal to that of the research work being described. . . . The tasks of writing fall heavily on industrial scientists
as well.[1]

Not only academics but also people working in other areas are aware
of the importance of writing in their lives. In one study, college graduates
working in many fields were asked to rank seventeen college disciplines
in order of importance to them as employed adults. The graduates put English right at the top, second only to business administration.[2]

An even more compelling reason why the amount of writing in college courses should not be decreased, no matter what the pressures, is that
writing is one of our most valuable tools for making learning take place.
Several studies support the important role verbalization plays in learning:
one sample showed that people who verbalized were superior in problem
solving to those who did not verbalize, especially as tasks grew more
complex.[3] In another study, college students showed greater command of
a subject they had written about than a subject they had only read or
heard about.[4]

Janet Emig, in a seminal study, proposed that writing is a uniquely
effective tool for learning because the two are strikingly parallel: learning
is multifaceted, as is writing, which uses eye, mind, and hand, right and
left brain. Learning profits from self-provided feedback—the kind available in writing, where the product takes gradual shape before the writer's
eyes and is then available for review and reflection. Learning serves an
analytical and connective function, as does writing, which organizes individual facts, images, and symbols into sentences, paragraphs, and whole
essays. Learning at its best is engaged, committed, and self-rhythmed, as
is the best writing.[5]

Other studies indicate that when an object is shown to children and
then removed, they can describe the absent object more accurately if,
while it was present, they talked or wrote about it.[6] Such findings lead us
to view writing as "the presence of things not seen"—as a way of freeing
students from enslavement to present physical reality and of allowing
their minds to abstract and conceptualize.

Another image of writing skills is that of a climbing rope whereby
students can hoist themselves to the next level of intellectual maturity.
Andrea Lunsford suggests that writing assignments can be structured to
help college students build and exercise the skills on the final rung of Piaget's ladder of intellectual development: the skills of abstracting, synthe-
sizing, and forming coherent, logical relations.[7]

We may never find the perfect paradigm for the complex relation of
writing to learning, but many of us know that the connection is there. We
believe that, until our students can express an idea with some sort of clarity on the page, they do not in fact really understand that idea. Along
with one science journal editor, we suspect that "Bad scientific writing

involves more than stylistic inelegance; it is often the outward and visible form of an inward confusion of thought."[8] Despite our rueful recognition of the time and effort needed to assign and respond to students' writing, we cannot escape a conviction that writing is the mother's milk of learning.

Like any other teaching technique, writing assignments can be handled with more or less skill, with better or poorer results, and with an efficient or a wasteful investment of time. In the following chapters I suggest how teachers in every discipline can make writing assignments meaningful, establish a wholesome and stimulating writing environment for their students, coach pupils in the writing process, respond accurately and specifically to student papers, communicate clearly with students about their writing successes and failures, and help students improve writing *as they learn* and *in order to learn* their sociology, biology, business, law, or engineering.

Part One

THE
WRITING PROCESS

Chapter One

Planning the Writing for Your Course

How Much Writing?

Merely increasing the amount of assigned writing does not by itself improve students' writing, or so the best available evidence suggests.[1] So if you are asking for four papers each semester, jacking the requirement up to eight papers is not necessarily going to add many stars to your crown, though you may be seeing stars after you've read all those essays. The research seems to indicate that, provided a reasonable amount of writing activity is going on, the way in which you assign and respond to the writing is much more important.

But what is a reasonable amount of writing? The answer will vary widely depending on your student load. Nevertheless, if you are asking for no writing at all, you are not contributing to the maintenance of students' skills, and you are not using one of the most valuable teaching tools. Students should write for your class several times during the semester, even if your load is heavy. I can suggest some ways to make that possible. You can find more suggestions in *How to Handle the Paper Load*.[2] Here are some methods teachers have used:

1. *Shorten the term paper, or replace it with one or several shorter exercises.* Many writing skills can be taught as well in four pages as in twenty.

2. *Employ various levels of response.* We all would, if we could, give every paper a careful analysis, but students can benefit from a less thorough response. Have them write single-page summaries, personal essays, or musings. Mark the papers "OK," or comment on one thing that works well and offer one suggestion for improvement. If students are keeping journals or doing reading summaries, take ten minutes during a class period to walk around and spot-check the journals, which the students should have open on their desks, and offer suggestions as you go. If they are handing in daily or weekly cases or lab reports, do detailed evalua-

tions only on certain "surprise" days; at other times merely check that students have handed in their assignments.

3. *Have others evaluate papers.* Students can give useful advice to one another. You can ask that each student have one classmate read his or her paper and offer suggestions. Then the writer revises, thus eliminating some of the problems you would have had to discuss. The name of the reader should appear on the final version, which is given to you. After the student receives your critique, he or she again shares the paper with the reader, who thus learns something about adequate evaluation—a valuable skill for many professionals. A student tutor, a select group of your best students, or one of your majors who is working for independent study credit can carry out the same role with more skill. The student tutor or aide may read every paper before you do and make some of the comments you would otherwise have to. Alternatively, a student aide can grade some of the papers each time, bringing problematic cases to you. Another method is to have students in small groups help one another (and make your job easier). Suggestions for making groups work well begin on page 41.

4. *Set priorities.* If you can't comment on every aspect of a paper, choose one or two. Or select a couple of aspects on which you will concentrate that semester: in every paper you might look for focus, both in the essay as a whole and in each paragraph. You comment only about that aspect of writing; students who have mastered it take little of your time. Or you could add economy or precise diction as an aspect to discuss with those students who have achieved clear focus. Or let one class be your priority: "This semester I'm going to work especially hard on writing in my Russian history class." Or choose a particular group of students: the seniors, or your majors, or those receiving C's.

5. *Select less time-consuming methods of response.* I think that the best way to guide students' writing is through individual conferences, and later on I will point out that the time difference between the conference and the written comment is less than it may seem. Nevertheless, in some circumstances you may have to select whatever is for you the least time-consuming method, balancing the possible loss of teaching effectiveness against your own time constraints. If you handle each paper individually, you may find that tapes or written comments are the quickest mode of response. You can also turn to methods that ask students to learn from your critiques of representative papers. You might give papers a grade with no comment and then single out five or six representative papers for detailed critiques, which you may present orally in class or in written form, handing out copies to each student or placing them on library reserve. Another method is to delineate six or a dozen of the most common problems that appear in your students' writing and give each type an initial. Then mark the papers with only the initials. Students receive code

sheets that explain the initials. Or better yet, take papers that illustrate two or three common problems and analyze them in detail in class, so that students with similar marks on their papers will understand what you mean.

In the best of all possible worlds you would choose none of these methods over the process of coaching each student through several drafts of every paper assigned. When time pressures force some compromise, however, it is better to take these measures than to have students do less and less writing.

What Kind of Writing?

I've already said that you may, under pressure of time, want to abandon the twenty-page term paper in favor of shorter pieces of various types. Beyond saving time, these moves may improve both the writing and the learning in your course.

If you have automatically been assigning only term papers and essay tests, examine again the functions that writing can serve in your course. Naturally you'll make your own list, but here are some possibilities:

1. To help students clarify or organize ideas.
2. To teach the forms of writing that students will use as professionals in your discipline.
3. To increase fluidity and to keep students in the habit of writing. Like the teenager who goes out after supper a few nights a week to shoot basketballs into the garage hoop, students don't have to aim at a serious or polished performance; they just have to stay in practice.
4. To show you how well students have mastered information or methodologies, so that you can improve your own instructional techniques.
5. To force students to read, or to read more attentively, or to finish a reading assignment by a certain date.
6. To exercise general writing skills such as organization, paragraph building, smooth wording, and correct usage.
7. To emphasize the most important concepts in the course.
8. To help you understand your students' feelings, questions, and confusions within their learning process.
9. To help you identify those students who require remedial work with a tutor, at a skills center, or with you or your assistant.
10. To provide a basis for estimating students' mastery of the course and for assigning grades.

11. To push the student to find more information or to think more deeply about the subject.
12. To get students involved in the course material as thinkers and writers, instead of just as listeners and readers.

In pursuing these various objectives you can employ a wide variety of writing assignments. In addition to the term paper, consider the book review, the summary of written sources, the persuasive essay, the case study, the journal, the grant or job proposal, the position paper, the definition, the annotated bibliography, the personal narrative, the description, the memo, the explanation of a process, the magazine or newspaper article, the report of an experience or task, the précis or abstract, the outline, the letter.

In choosing among these assignments, you will want to consider a variety of audiences that your students should write for. I discuss this in greater depth in Chapter 4, "Giving the Assignment," but for now the point is that students may with equal legitimacy write for themselves, their peers, their teacher, or any other well-defined audience, actual or hypothetical.

You will also want to consider the level of polish you require. At times your own and your students' goals may be well served by requiring only the thesis sentence, only the plan or outline, or only the rough draft. On the other hand, you can have students polish any genre: you can ask them to polish a journal entry, for example, until it's as carefully crafted as a term paper. (If you expect refinement in the more informal genres, however, you'll have to resist your students' tendency to equate journals and some other forms with unpolished writing.)

After all this cogitation, you may still come back to the same basic writing mode for your course, but you may also emerge with a greater variety. Sometimes such diversity fosters greater student interest and commitment to writing—an important result, and one worth working for. Most teachers find that when students are keenly interested in their writing, when they sense it as "real" communication, they produce work that is better in everything from organization to punctuation.

Within your own discipline, and depending on the purposes of your course, you will select your own mix of genres and audiences. You may find helpful this list of writing assignments that teachers in various disciplines have used successfully:

- Write a one-page inquiry or extended reflection, in which you let your mind play with questions that arise out of reading or class discussion. Share these with your teacher or peers.
- Write a letter to the editor of a local newspaper or to a government official.

- Write a history of the community, publish it as a booklet, and sell it at a community festival.
- Write an analysis of some aspect of the children's book collection of the local library (one student analyzed male and female sex stereotypes). Present the study, together with the list of recommended purchases or actions, to the library.
- Write a tourists' guide for a town or a historical site.
- Keep a journal of your responses to your reading, to class discussions, to peer writing, or to events in your experience that relate to the class. Share your comments with your teacher or peers.
- Prepare an exhibit or leaflet that presents information on a local health problem, a social issue, a fund drive, or an ethnic custom. Display or distribute the work in a local bank, library, or school.
- Prepare a laboratory manual for students in another science class.
- Begin a discussion with other class members, visitors to class, or people at a town council meeting or at the laundromat. Then prepare a written argument that establishes your position and clarifies your logic. Share the written argument with the original debaters, with peers in the class, or with the teacher.

You can think of other situations and other projects. The important principle is that writing is more intriguing and more compelling for students when it is more than merely an exercise, when it does more than tell a teacher what the teacher already knows, merely to prove that the students know it. If all the writing students do for your class falls into that category, try some other modes. Let students experience writing as a supple, flexible means of communicating with other human beings about all types of experience. Ask them to wrestle with writing in all its diverse uses. Ask them to write often. Ask them to write in situations where communication is as meaningful and genuine as possible.

What about Writing in Class?

Writing done in class should be treated as a first draft. Some students may be better than others at producing first drafts, and you may be interested in developing the ability to think and write better under the pressure of time. If so, suggest strategies for students to use during the writing itself or different ways of preparing for the essay before class. Here are some examples of what you might say in response to an essay exam.

Your first paragraph wastes time circling. Next time try to get more quickly to the point.
The imprecision of your words is a barrier to the reader's under-

standing. Next time try to choose your words more carefully, even if it means taking a bit more time on each paragraph and writing less.

You seem to have been caught off guard by this question, so your writing style is circular, clumsy, wordy, and unsure. Next time try to guess my questions ahead of time and prepare some sample answers. Then when you come to class, you can take parts of those sample answers, already cocked in your mind, and simply shoot them into place. You can amend others to fit the situation.

In other words, you are interested not in docking the student for every comma fault, or in editing every stylistic problem in the paper, but rather in giving the learner some general advice to follow in the next in-class writing assignment. You are not grading on content only (always a mistake if you wish students to understand the indissoluble union between knowledge and expression), but neither are you inappropriately editing a piece of writing that the writer has had no opportunity to revise or polish. You try to offer the student a helpful response appropriate to a first draft that will not be revised.

Sometimes an in-class essay may in fact serve as the first draft of a paper to be revised and resubmitted. If so, you'll want to offer comments that will help the student revise that particular paper. This may mean more specific attention to grammar and style and more detailed comments about organization.

Some general suggestions to the entire class may help to head off student mistakes. You can use the accompanying outline, "How to Take an Essay Exam," which John Miller, William Julian, and I developed at Central College in Iowa, where teachers in many disciplines have used it for a number of years; they simply hand out copies to their students. You may duplicate this form and use it with your own classes.

How to Take an Essay Examination

Essay exams are not a matter of quantity but of quality. The race goes not to the swiftest writer but to the one who best organizes and presents what he or she knows. The problem facing the student who must take an essay test is simple: how can that quality be achieved?

I. General principles
  A. Organize around a clear focus.
    You must have some point of view to help you organize and select the facts you wish to include. Choose a focus that is limited enough to cover in the time allowed and that allows you to include all the material the teacher will expect to find. Write a thesis sentence that

clearly states your focus or main point and that indicates the main sections of your answer. For most types of essay, the thesis sentence should state a conclusion, not merely announce the sections. For example, sentence A below merely announces the sections of the paper. It is certainly better than no thesis sentence at all, but in most cases it is not as helpful to your reader as a thesis that embodies your conclusion, as in B.

Q. Discuss the concept of love in D. H. Lawrence's novel *Women in Love.*

Thesis sentence A: This essay will discuss bisexual, homosexual, and familial love in Lawrence's *Women in Love.*

Thesis sentence B: An examination of bisexual, homosexual, and familial love in *Women in Love* reveals the hatred and the isolation that are present even in the closest love relationships.

B. Outline your answer.

Do not begin writing your answer without first making an outline. Write down the three or four main points you want to make. They should all help to develop, explain, or prove your thesis sentence.

C. Come right to the point.

Don't waste time with a general introduction or any sort of beating around the bush. It is usually a good idea to state the main point (thesis) of your answer at the beginning.

D. Stick to your subject.

Everything you say should relate directly to the subject you have announced in your thesis sentence. Do not try to tell everything you know. Essay tests measure the excellence of your ability to select, organize, and analyze the details you have mastered.

E. Be thorough within your limits.

Make your answer complete. If a question asks about a subject discussed in class or in your reading, the teacher probably expects you to deal with all the main points made there. In addition, after you have written your outline, ask yourself, "Have I left out anything important to the defense of my thesis sentence?"

F. Support generalities with specific and relevant evidence.

Evidence is crucial. The teacher is testing your detailed knowledge of a body of material, not just your ability to make or repeat generalizations. Show that you know the specific information. Do not merely state *what you* believe; explain *why* you believe it.

II. Some common essay topics

A. "Discuss X" or "Describe X" or "Analyze X."

The challenge in such questions lies in the student's ability to impose organization on a broad subject. First you must decide: How shall I limit X? How shall I divide X into sensible, manageable segments? Let us say the direction is "Discuss political elites." The very phrasing seems to entice you to blurt out everything and anything you happen to recall about elites and their societies. Resist temptation. Take time to write an outline and make efforts to limit your approach to an angle of the problem that will most favorably display your knowledge and understanding.

Sometimes you can better deal with a discuss-or-analyze topic if you turn it into one or more questions. Answers to these questions will give you suggestions for a thesis sentence and an outline. For example:

1. *Direction:* The Reformation was caused by economic factors. Discuss.

   Ask yourself: Was the Reformation caused solely by economic factors? Which noneconomic factors should I mention?

2. *Direction:* Analyze the theme of social class in nineteenth-century novels.

   Ask yourself: What do the authors of nineteenth-century novels think about social class? What do the novels' characters think? What social classes are illustrated in the novels?

B. Compare and/or contrast.

   If you are instructed to compare and/or contrast, you are still confronted with the basic problem of selecting a focus, organizing your facts, and indicating to the instructor what your approach will be. Don't automatically give every fact you know about X and then every fact about Y. Instead, outline the major similarities and/or differences. Under each similarity or difference discuss both X and Y, making specific and concrete comparisons.

C. Identify or define.

   Follow two rules: (1) put each item into a major category, and (2) separate it from all other items in this category.

D. Agree or disagree.

   Usually it is possible to write an A exam whether you agree or disagree; the instructor is interested in whether you can marshal evidence to support your position. Often it helps to keep in mind the major arguments on the other side and try to refute them in your essay.

III. Study hints

A. In looking over your notes, try to see relationships between parts, comparisions, and contrasts. Try to guess what might be some typical questions and outline answers to them.

B. Then study the outlines as well as your class notes.

IV. The exam

   A. Read the directions thoroughly. In particular, see if a question has more than one part, and answer all parts.

   B. Outline your answer before you begin writing. The outlines you prepared in studying should help a great deal here.

   C. Bring a watch and budget your time.

   D. If you run out of time, outline main points and examples, and write "out of time" to tell your professor what happened.

   E. Proofread your answer, if possible, to catch careless errors.

   F. Write precisely what you mean. Always choose the most specific and accurate word.

   G. Make every word do a job. Don't eliminate necessary examples and evidence, but do present them without wasted words.

Chapter Two

Coaching the Student Writer

Encouraging Productive Writing Behavior

At the age of ten my son once mixed, baked, and elaborately decorated a birthday cake, using a pastry tube to fashion painstaking roses, prim borders, and perfect lettering. Not until we had admired, lighted, sung, blown, wished, sliced, and tasted did we realize that the cake was so heavy we could hardly swallow it. If only I had monitored his progress in the early stages, I could have saved him all the work of polishing a fundamentally unsound product and taught him something about the care with which good cooks measure ingredients.

Students sometimes have only a fuzzy idea of how good writers produce their work. For example, one misconception is that divine inspiration plays a major role in the writing process. Only reluctantly do students come to believe that most good writers arduously generate and develop their ideas and that behind a fine essay probably lie several incubation periods and scores of revisions. If you are to help students write better, you must teach them how to behave when they are trying to produce effective pieces of writing.

In fact, some recent research shows that while little or no improvement in students' writing results from increasing the amount of writing assigned, the number of teacher markings, or the study of traditional or new grammar, there is demonstrable improvement when the teacher coaches students in the *process* of writing instead of merely judging the papers they turn in (Haynes, p. 87).

Coaching may seem too time-consuming, or too contrary to your own teaching style, but in the light of evidence of its importance, it seems worthwhile to do whatever is possible. This book, throughout, will suggest ways in which you might do some coaching despite constraints of time and style.

Take a moment to think about what good writing behavior is. Immediately you'll ask, "What sort of writing?" Your behavior is different for a memo, a committee report, or an article for a professional journal, and people in your field who are not teachers may engage in other types

16

of writing as well. Furthermore, good writers differ in their writing be-havior. For example, Janet Emig's study of the composing practices of six-teen professional and academic writers revealed that, for expository writing, some professionals made detailed outlines, some made rough outlines, and some made no written outlines at all. Student writers exhib-it the same variety of methods. In Emig's investigation of 109 themes written by 25 eleventh-grade English honors students, only 8.3% of the essays were preceded by a formal written outline and only 36.7% by some sort of written plan. The hardest pill for us pedagogues to swallow is that Emig found no difference in quality between the work of those who made outlines and that of writers who didn't.[1]

Another revelation about outlining: professional writers, Emig found, do not restrict outlining to the planning stages but may use it to-ward the end of the writing process as a way of checking organizational tightness or as a guideline to reworking the piece, perhaps after it has lain fallow (*Composing Processes*, p. 26).

All this leads to the conclusion that your attempt to help students develop more effective writing behavior should not consist merely of see-ing to it that every student makes an outline at a certain stage of the writ-ing process, though you will want to stress outlining as one good way to plan writing, and you may want to force the uninitiated to try it, just as I force my young son to try my spinach soufflé.

Well, then, what *is* effective writing behavior, and how can teachers help students develop it? First, choose a type of writing similar to the writing that students do in your class. Begin by making a list of the steps that you or other successful practitioners in your field follow in this type of writing. (Your list will be more accurate if you keep it as a diary, while you are actually writing a paper.) Include information about what moti-vates you to begin, how you plan your writing, how and when you begin to put ideas down on paper, and what function is served for you by rules such as "every paragraph should have a topic sentence" or "scientific pa-pers of this sort should begin with an introduction, followed by a review of the literature, followed by. . . ." Also, tell how you achieve good focus and organization, at what points you set aside a piece of writing for a while, how long these incubation periods last, what suggestions you seek from colleagues or friends, how many revisions you make, how much time you need for revising, how you achieve accuracy in punctuation and grammar, and how you decide when the piece is finished. Your record is a clue to some of the procedures that distinguish the behavior of successful writers from that of unsuccessful writers.

We have much to learn about the sorts of writing behavior that work best for different people in various situations. Nevertheless, based on what we do know, we can determine a general pattern of effective writing behavior that may more or less closely resemble your own best processes or those of articulate colleagues.

Ideally the writing process begins when one becomes aware of the need to synthesize, clarify, or record facts or ideas, either for oneself or for another audience. A writer may use a number of techniques to get the writing started: mulling silently; talking to the wall or to friends; dictating on tape; making notes from memory or observation; jotting down ideas in random fashion, just to get them on paper; reading either to find ideas or to verify and support ideas; writing notes and summaries based on reading; making lists of points; outlining; or systematically answering some questions such as the journalist's five W's. Recent research indicates that one fruitful activity good writers share is an active and extensive attempt to determine who their audience will be, what they want to do with that audience, and what stance or tone they should assume. In other words, they view the writing challenge more broadly than poor writers do.

Researchers are gathering this and other information about writers' behavior by a new method called "protocol analysis," in which writers tape-record their thoughts as they write. The tapes, called "protocols," are then combed for what they reveal about the writers' mental processes. Refinements of this and other research methods are likely to reveal a great deal.

What we know at this point is that some combination of these "cranking-up" methods—plus some subconscious germination, about which little is known—enables the person to produce a first draft. In the process of writing and revising this first copy, the author may very well discover new ideas. Writing, typing, or dictating this draft, the writer may stop, hesitate, look back over the work, say thoughts aloud, or skip ahead, leaving a section for later. In revising the first draft the writer may stumble on a structure or may sharpen or even radically alter the focus; in other words, the writing may serve as a means of clarification or discovery. Thus changes in the drafts may produce almost a whole new piece, based on something that appeared only tangentially in the first attempts. Some authors cut and paste, switching sections for a more effective progression of ideas. A writer may bring new material from the sidelines into the limelight or reduce stars to second billing, either by giving them less space or by positioning them in dimmer parts of the paper or the paragraph.

Ideally, consideration for the needs of the intended audience shapes the planning and writing from the beginning, but as the revision process goes on, concern for the needs of the reader takes a different form: the writer makes transitions explicit, provides definitions and explanations, corrects spelling and punctuation, and casts ideas into forms that will be clear to readers.

Along the way, good writers often seek help from "test" readers. They present their colleagues, spouses, or lovers with a draft and ask for their reactions and suggestions. A writer may also ask someone to correct spelling, punctuation, and grammar.

Throughout the process there are times of discouragement when, in Virginia Woolf's poignant image, "[the] mind, turned by anxiety, or other cause, from its scrutiny of blank paper, is like a lost child—wandering the house, sitting on the bottom steps to cry."[2] Writers discover their own best ways to get out of these sloughs—they may jog, sleep, push doggedly on, talk ideas through with a friend, turn to another task, or fix a hero sandwich.

Having conducted your own analysis of your writing behavior and that of others, and having read the model just presented, you might list the steps you think most students follow when they do similar writing for your class. Researchers have found that poorer students often produce only two drafts, both written the night before the paper is due. The first draft is not a means of discovering meaning or achieving focus but, rather, a sentence-by-sentence dogged production of words, generated by a basic idea and following a standard organizational pattern. The second draft is often merely a prettied-up version of the first: the student types the work neatly and removes mechanical errors for the benefit of the teacher, who is viewed as a hunter for errors. Though we know that good writers often change their focus, or discover it, while revising their drafts, these students do not go back and recast a paper in the light of their writing discoveries.[3]

Clearly the behavior of good professional writers differs markedly from that of many student writers, but better student writers come closer to following ideal procedures. One study found that more successful students spent more time in the planning stages, as well as in the writing process, and did significantly more revising.[4]

So there are two important groups of studies: those that show the inadequacies of student writing behavior and those that indicate that helping students with the writing process actually pays off.

Different teachers, exercising their ingenuity within their own disciplines and depending on their class loads, will find different ways to help students develop effective writing practices. It is important, however, to avoid imposing a rigid method on students—such as requiring outlines at a certain point in the writing process. Instead, teachers should try to make students conscious of their writing behavior and help them find their own best writing techniques. This list of questions and the suggestions that follow are intended as guides:

- How can I help students feel the involvement and interest that will make the writing process seem important to them?
- How can I push students to start early enough to allow time for effective planning, incubation, and revision?
- How can I help students learn to prod their minds to generate good ideas and good supporting material?
- How can I teach students effective ways to search for information

and to take useful notes with the least possible waste of time?

- How can I show students the various methods used to organize writing in my field, and how can I help them find the planning behavior that is best for them?
- How can I encourage students to revise extensively, as good writers usually do? How can I help students understand that revision is more than merely editing for mechanical and grammatical mistakes?
- How can I help students seek constructive suggestions during the writing process? How can I teach them the difference between the legitimate use of helpers and the illegitimate use? How can I provide a way for them to acknowledge their helpers?

Teachers in different disciplines, with different teaching styles, will answer these questions in different ways. The suggestions that follow merely indicate some answers that teachers have found to the questions just posed:

1. *If your assignment allows students to choose their own topics, suggest ways to develop a list of possible topics.*

2. *In giving the assignment, describe not only what the final product should look like but how students can generate ideas, plan their papers, and organize their thoughts.*

3. *Present in class several models of planning behavior* used by former students or by professionals. Show students outlines, free writing, and rough drafts done by you or other professionals. The chapter "The Student Rewrites" in Don Murray's *A Writer Teaches Writing* contains some good examples of professional revising.[5]

4. *Set up checkpoints* at which you or student tutors meet with the students individually to discuss progress. This takes time; if you are to introduce this kind of guidance for writing, you may want to cut down the number of assignments during the semester or assign shorter papers. The results of such individual conferences, however, are so satisfying that the work is worth doing, even if you can do it with only one class or for only some students. A conference of five to ten minutes during which you go over a student's thesis sentence can prevent a great deal of grief later on, can teach valuable lessons, and can result in a superior paper. If, in addition, you can later find ten or twenty minutes to go over a rough draft (perhaps of the first two pages) or to check an outline or other written plan, you will be engaged in the best kind of coaching. For advice on how to conduct such a conference, see pages 27–29.

5. *Ask for written progress reports.* At the very least, you can use these to impose a timetable so that students have to do at least some early planning. Set deadlines for students to hand in copies of their thesis sentences and outlines and rough drafts. They can keep the originals and continue to work on their papers. You do what you can with their plans; if you

don't have time to evaluate them, just mark them as handed in and keep them. At least you will have forced your students to plan ahead. If you can spare the time to select a few outlines or rough drafts and discuss them in class, all the better. The best method is to respond to each one with a suggestion for improvement.

6. *Have students share their progress reports.* Divide the class into small groups to discuss one another's thesis sentences, outlines, or rough drafts. Circulate among the groups to keep them on the track and to encourage constructive criticism. You may want to give students a written list of questions they can ask about one another's writing (see page 42).

7. *Pair students off in a buddy system.* Each buddy keeps in touch with the writing process of the other, recording progress and making suggestions. As the final papers come in, each student also turns in a report on the writing processes followed by the buddy. You can merely make sure that these are handed in, or if time permits you can read or scan them, respond to or summarize them in a discussion with the class, analyze a few in class, put them in some spot where all students can read them, or have a committee of students read them all and summarize them in a twenty-minute report to the class.

8. *Ask a successful upper-class student to come to your class* and describe how he or she handled your assignments successfully.

9. *Use a few of your best students,* an independent-study student, or a student assistant (perhaps one of your majors) as the checkpoint for students. You may either require that all students see this person or simply make the help available. I have arranged for a paid student assistant or a major working for independent-study credit to be available at stated hours in a certain conference room as consultant for my students as they planned and wrote their papers.

10. *Require each student to get at least one other student's signature* on the paper. The signer is one who has read and criticized the assignment. Even if you do not require the use of readers, you should ask students who use them to include acknowledgments in their papers.

The Place of Grades in Coaching

Be flexible in your dual role as coach and judge. You can achieve at least a workable combination of the two.

Many student papers handed in as final versions can usefully be regarded as first drafts, which could be mightily improved by revision based on the teacher's further coaching. But unfortunately, instead of a structure in which the instructor treats a paper as unfinished and then gives suggestions for further revision, most teachers create a structure in which students have no chance to revise, once they have handed in their papers, and receive no reward for doing so. Thus the instructor's careful comments on a paper seem to the students like treatment prescribed for a patient already dead. So after they see the all-important, unchangeable grade, they chuck their papers, each with its lucid and painstaking teacher comments, into the nearest wastebasket or into their notebooks, which often serve as wastebaskets. If the teacher rewards revision, however, the students are much more likely to make every effort to comprehend their instructor's suggestions and to put them into practice.

To create a structure in which revision is encouraged and rewarded, try allowing or even requiring students to revise their papers after discussing their work with you. This may mean setting deadlines early enough to allow for revision afterward. I have sometimes accepted revisions at any time, up to the last day of the semester. But since such a policy may lead to an unbearable flood of "oh my gosh isn't there something I can do in these last two days to raise my grade" attempts, usually I allow a two-week revision period for each assignment. After that deadline, I accept no revisions. Sometimes, if the revision needs another revision, I'll allow another two weeks.

In a conference or a written response to a paper that is going to be revised, you may want to indicate a tentative grade to give the student an estimate of the paper's level of excellence. But in recent years I have moved away from that practice, except when the student nervously presses for it. Instead, I regard papers as "finished" and "unfinished," to reinforce the concept that an unfinished product is not yet at a stage to be graded and to separate my coaching stance from my later judging stance. I find that most students work easily with the concepts of "finished" and "unfinished," once they get used to them, and that requests for grade estimates usually come only near the end of the paper's progress, at which time I can usually say with some confidence, "You're working at a B or an A level now, depending on how polished the final draft is." Or I might say, "The paper still isn't well organized, and unless you can achieve tight structure, it can't get above a D."

Here is a dilemma you may sometimes face. Say that in one conference you offer some suggestions. The student then goes off, follows those suggestions, and comes back, expecting that now the paper will meet with your full approval, which means that it will recieve an A. But you may have chosen at the first conference to mention only some of the paper's problems—the ones needing first priority. Or you may have marked some things as examples of what the student should amend throughout the entire paper. Or you may not have seen some problems that you later realize do need change. Or the handwriting on the drafts you saw earlier may have disguised faults that show up much more clearly in a later, typed version. A related situation is one in which the student, at an early conference, presses you for the grade he or she *will get* if all your suggestions are followed.

To protect myself against these difficulties, I refuse to predict grades at all, and when pressed to grade a draft, I will either refuse or, if I think the student needs the information, state a range: "The paper is somewhere between a C and a B at this point." Further, at each conference I say something like this:

> Now as you revise this, you will see other things that may need changing, or you will see other instances of some of the things I've marked on the paper, or you will find other problems that I may not have picked up at this reading. You are responsible for using your own critical sense to analyze this paper and to improve it as you revise. The next time I see it, I will react as a new reader, telling you what strikes me at that time as successful or unsuccessful. At each reading I try to give the paper a sensitive evaluation, but I don't claim that at any single reading I say everything I will eventually say about the paper.

Grading Writing

Eventually, coaching ends and you award a final grade. Here is a set of general guidelines used by many teachers who value writing in their classes. These guidelines apply to papers written outside of class:

A: The paper is well organized, even at the paragraph level. Sentences are smooth and carefully crafted. There are virtually no errors in punctuation or spelling, grammar or usage. Words are chosen with precision. Informal language or dialect is used only when appropriate. The paper avoids triteness and generalizations; the language is fresh and vivid. The paper is tight, not wordy.

B: The work is well organized, but the paragraph structure may sometimes be disjointed. The paper may have a few awkward passages and some errors in punctuation, spelling, grammar, and usage. The language may at times be too general; it may lack the freshness or precision of the A paper. But none of these errors is glaring or highly distracting.

C: The paper is basically well organized, though individual paragraphs may be disunified or misplaced. Generally, however, the paper shows that the writer has followed a logical plan. The writing is competent but wordy, general, imprecise, or trite. Sentences may at times be awkwardly constructed, but their meaning is clear. Grammar, punctuation, and spelling are not highly distracting, but there may be some errors.

D: The paper is poorly organized, though there is a recognizable thesis. Some sentences or passages may be so confused that their meaning does not clearly emerge. Words may be imprecise, incorrect, trite, or vague. In general, however, the paper is understandable.

F: The paper lacks a clear thesis, the language is so muddled as to be unclear in several spots, or the errors in punctuation, spelling, grammar, and usage are highly distracting.

Many teachers ask about the practice of giving two grades—one for "content" and one for "writing." A double grade may at times be appropriate, but I would never use those two labels. Instead, I would say that one grade was for "content and expression" and the other for "mechanics"—grammar, punctuation, spelling, and usage. The handling of mechanics is sometimes clearly distinguishable from other writing skills and may be radically out of keeping with the quality of the paper as a whole. The other aspects of good writing—clear organization, coherent paragraph structure, precise diction, crafted sentences—are so inseparable from content that I have never been able to give separate grades. Rather, I emphasize to my students that knowing and telling are so inextricably linked that in my class, as well as in the world outside, they will not be judged knowledgeable unless they can express their knowledge well. Some teachers take this stand with grammar and punctuation as well and simply never give double grades.

Chapter Three

Communicating with Students about Their Writing

Pen, Tape, or Conference?

Most home workshops include several kinds of saws. When you have wood to cut, you don't just grab the nearest one; you look them all over and choose the one best suited to the job. Likewise, when you want to give students advice about their writing, you shouldn't just seize the red pen because it happens to be the closest tool on your desk or because so many teachers use it. Instead, thoughtful teachers should consider how they can best communicate their responses to students' writing.

Written comments have the advantage of requiring only a teacher and a colored pen. That basic combination functions on a subway, on a bed, in front of the tv, or at the kitchen table. It may be noon or midnight. The teacher can wear any variety of clothing or facial expression and can attack the stack of papers in any way—read them all quickly before evaluating any; compare them with one another; ponder some, zip through others. Another advantage is that, once inscribed, the written comment is an ineradicable record of the teacher's suggestions; both instructor and student can refer to it at any time. But the red-ink method has several disadvantages. The teacher cannot be sure that comments are phrased so that students can understand them. And red ink makes for chilly communication. It does not allow for dialogue. Finally, writing an evaluation is more time-consuming and cumbersome than offering the same suggestions orally.

If you want to check the student's comprehension, if you want to relate more personally to the student, if you want to join with the student in exploring a paper's problems, if you want to profit from your ability to say more words in five minutes than you can write, then try some other system of communicating with students about their writing—tapes, for example, or individual conferences.

I've talked with teachers who have made the tape system work at the junior high, high school, and college levels. A cassette player seems to be part of the standard equipment most students have lying around their rooms nowadays. Some teachers use the school's language lab; others arrange a place where students can use a school-owned cassette player. Then, as the teacher returns a paper to the student, a cassette tape goes with it. On the tape, the teacher talks to the student about the strengths and weaknesses of the paper. The recording is more personal, you can say more, and the student is more likely to understand you than if you wrote out your comments. One great difficulty arises, of course: though many students think they can't go for a five-minute ride in their cars or take out the trash unless they have their favorite singer to entertain them on the cassette, they may never get around to slipping in the tape that will bring your voice to their ears. Either you can try to make tapes that outdo their stars in rhythm or ribaldry, or you can schedule a time for all students to listen to the tapes you have made for them. A system in which revision is rewarded also helps motivate students to listen to your suggestions for improvement. An article by Doris Weddington gives more information about using tapes.[1]

Most personal of all and, I believe, most effective, is the individual conference. There you give the student the time you would otherwise spend writing comments on the paper; you read the paper in the student's presence and share in person your pleasure at success and your suggestions for improvement. Together you plan further work.

The conference may last anywhere from five or ten minutes to half an hour; it may be scheduled or impromptu; it may be required or optional. Don Murray, in *A Writer Teaches Writing*, describes how he handled conferences in a high school setting, with a large number of students who had little free time. In a college setting, I simply pass around in class a sheet with blank appointment slots and let students fill them in. If necessary, I use a class hour to meet with students who can come only during that time. I then post the appointment schedule on my office door, so switchers and latecomers can sign up in the remaining blank spaces. You can be as relaxed as you wish about students keeping their appointments. Because I handle large numbers of students in conferences, I am not relaxed. I insist that students keep their scheduled conference and arrive on time. If they must miss, they are to tell me as soon as possible. For forgetters and oversleepers I do not give makeup conferences; in case of injuries or disasters, of course, I gladly do so. In class, and in writing, I announce my policy and explain that the conferences are a special gift of time from me to them. I expect them to respect my time. This method results in a "show" rate for conferences of ninety to one hundred percent, even with freshmen.

The conference method has many advantages: by watching expressions or engaging in dialogue you can tell whether the student understands what you say; you get past the coldness of red ink and into the warmth of person meeting person; you can scotch the old "she just drops 'em on the stairs" myth by letting the student watch you read and react to the paper; you encourage students to take responsibility for conducting and planning their own work. The conference method does lack certain conveniences: you can't implement it anyplace from the subway to the pub, anytime from midnight to noon. The conference does encourage both you and the student to pay close attention, however, and to function at top efficiency. If the acolyte is raptly watching the priestly functions, how can the priest daydream, dash off some muddled pronouncement, or munch peanuts?

One main principle and some guidelines can help the instructor make the best use of a student conference. The main principle is that teachers should not use the conference merely to say what they would otherwise write; the personal conference opens other possibilities, which should be exploited.

One guideline follows from this: the teacher should seize the opportunity to engage the student in a fuller and more personal discussion of the paper than would be possible by means of written comments. When a child brings you a drawing, you do not begin by succinctly pointing out its faults; you begin by responding to what it is meant to be: "Ah! a tree! Is that the same tree you climbed yesterday in the park?" A student's paper, like a child's drawing, is a gift, a self-revelation, an act of communication; the conference provides a rich opportunity to respond to it at that level. When you do so, you help the student perceive writing as a real communication, not as a dead and final *thing* that is either correct or incorrect.

A second guideline is this: the teacher should let the student share the reading and evaluating process. Suppose that the student sits facing you and hands you the paper. You then read it silently, perhaps making your own notes, which the student sees but is not close enough to read. Then, having finished reading, you finally lift your head and deliver your analysis. You have thus made the conference little more than an oral version of the traditional written evaluation. Furthermore, such a process inevitably makes the student sweat through anxious minutes during which your facial expressions and your unreadable marginal notes provoke a painful sense of exclusion. So the student sits there opposite you, chair tilted back in an unconscious attempt to disappear into the wall. Some students nervously begin talking to you, explaining some of their points or self-consciously offering their own guesses about their faults, as if by saying, "I just couldn't get that paragraph right," they can somehow meet and deflect the impending thrust of criticism. Some remain silent, chewing their fingernails or cracking their knuckles, letting their trapped eyes wander across your rows of books, which are at that moment merely the furniture of the inscrutable world from which you will emerge finally to pass upon the paper a judgment based on your own inscrutable principles.

Instead of leaving the sinners to stand barefoot in the cold like King Henry before the pope, take them to the hearth and let them participate in what you're doing. Even if you function best reading the paper silently before responding, let the student sit beside you and look on. Or read the paper aloud. Perhaps the best way to exploit the conference is to voice your opinions as you read the paper, even the first time through. Of course, your comments on the student's mastery of information or methodology will mingle with your suggestions about writing, but my examples here will deal mainly with the comments you might make about writing skills. You could, for example, scan the first paragraph and the last, glance through the middle, and say immediately, "All these paragraphs are short and choppy-looking, and your first and last paragraphs don't link together very well. That makes me wonder whether maybe you tried to cover too many different ideas in this paper. Let me read it word for word and see if that's what is happening." Then read. As you work, tell the student what you think each paragraph is about, or point out evidence that your first guess was correct, or when a passage shows some lilt of phrase, express your pleasure and say why you like what you've read. On display in Chicago's Natural History Museum is a transparent plastic model of a woman; one can watch the heart beat, the lungs inflate, the intestines contract. If you can be the transparent reader, you will grant the student the highly valuable privilege of watching someone respond to the paper sentence by sentence and paragraph by paragraph.

The sight of gastric contractions, of course, is not a sufficient vision for the teacher to vouchsafe. A third guideline: after reading the paper carefully and sharing your impressions, make what in a written evaluation would be a final comment: analyze, summarize, and indicate priorities. Students will not easily remember all you say, so it is often helpful to have them take notes or to tape your comments. Try to group and label strengths and weaknesses, and give the student specific directions for attacking problems.

In recommending this procedure, I should stress that you shouldn't be afraid to do the initial reading of a paper right in the conference, even though this practice can be hard to get used to. When I first began holding such conferences, I was afraid to let my students see me making an evaluation; I was used to forming the evaluation in privacy and then descending like Moses to present to the student the tablets engraved in red ink. I thought, what if I make a mistake? What if I form one opinion during the first reading and then, after rereading, change it? Unwilling to be transparent to my students, I collected all the papers, read them at home in the wee hours, made notes for the conference, and then, when a student came in, I had my evaluation ready. Consequently it sounded canned, and it failed to make use of all the possibilities inherent in the conference system. Furthermore, it took an amount of time that only fire-eyed beginners can give, when they're fresh out of grad school and brim-ful of zeal and energy. After that early fervor wears off, one must either abandon the conference method or learn to do the initial reading of the paper right there in front of the student. So I did. And I discovered that being "real" to students is highly effective. If I made an evaluation and then changed it, well, that's what sometimes happens when a real human being sits down to read somebody else's writing. If I could not immediately put my finger on what was "off" about a certain paper, I just asked the student to wait a moment while I wrestled with it. If I really was stumped or if I suspected a problem (like plagiarism) that I needed time to ponder, I asked the student to leave the paper with me and come back the next day.

Finally, there is another sort of conference you should consider: you can conduct it in such a way that you become not so much an evaluator as a consultant. Don Murray describes this method in a provocative article in *College English.*[2] The student's role is to discuss with the teacher successes and problems in the current work and plans for the next stages. The teacher primarily listens, encourages, responds, and gives advice when asked, but the student controls the conference. Such an approach, if consonant with your own teaching philosophy and style, seems to me highly promising and likely to yield results not easily attainable in other ways. It must surely heighten students' ability to analyze their own work, to plan their own writing progress, and to take responsibility for their own learning. The article exudes Murray's own particular spirit as a teacher and writer and provides worthwhile reading for teachers in every discipline.

Some dilemmas that occur in conferences—students asking you for grade estimates and predictions, for example, or misunderstanding your role as reader and coach—are discussed on pages 21–23.

Being a Transparent Reader

Whether you respond to a student in writing, on tape, or in conference, one guideline is highly important: be a transparent reader. Though I have suggested in the foregoing paragraphs some ways in which you can use the conference to let the writer see a reader's reactions, other methods of responding can also benefit from the transparent-reader idea. In using this approach, always remember that writing is not "wrong" in the same way that "two plus two equals five" is wrong. Instead, writing can more accurately be said to fail when it does not effectively communicate to its intended reader. Such failure may result from one of the many decisions a writer makes about content, proof, documentation, word choice, paragraph structure, and thematic organization. Similarly, in matters like comma placement and subject-verb agreement, the writer follows certain conventions to make the paper more easily comprehensible to the reader.

You may use the transparent-reader approach in your comments about content, methodology, and other matters relevant to your discipline, as well as your remarks about writing skills. To remind the student of the audience-centered nature of writing, an instructor might say or write, "I lost the train of your thought here," rather than "This paragraph is not coherent." The second response is not wrong; it just misses an opportunity to remind students that what we call "coherence" is not a mysterious, revealed principle but a way of ordering thoughts so that readers can easily grasp them. Such a statement also helps students understand that "coherence" may differ from essay to essay and that in all cases the test of whether or not a paragraph is coherent is how easily the reader can follow the thought progression. If students think you are picky about commas and periods and quotation marks, your best defense is to point out that as a reader you are distracted and confused by sentences not punctuated according to the conventions that normally govern writing of this sort. "Readers," you can tell your students, "are tough customers. It's dangerous to ask them to work unnecessarily hard just to take in your message. They might figure it isn't worth the effort."

The transparent-reader approach allows you to respond at several levels. You choose the level that suits your student's ability or your own expertise. At the most basic level, you simply state your own responses as a reader: "I had to read this sentence three times to understand it," or "At this point I realized you were repeating ideas I'd read before," or "I felt bored here." If there is a hypothetical audience, you can mention what you think that audience's reaction might be, or you may want to set up a situation in which you ask the student's peers to read the paper and respond to it as transparently as they can. At this level, the audience does not analyze or suggest solutions but merely records the delights and frustrations experienced in reading. The responsibility of determining how to get a better audience reaction is then left to the writer. The beauty of such an approach is that it keeps you from falling into the trap of rewriting the student's paper in your own words. It forces the student to ask, say, "How can I make this paragraph seem logical to her?" and to find an independent solution. Another advantage is that any attentive reader can use this technique. You need only develop a consciousness of your own responses and the ability to state those responses to students. You don't have to be a trained rhetorician, you don't have to know what "coherence" means, and you don't have to tell the student how to fix the problem. You just react. And remember to communicate your positive and pleasurable reactions as well as your negative ones. "This paragraph was clear to me even on the first reading," or "I appreciate your fine note of irony here."

If you think the student is capable of finding solutions to the writing problems that provoke your negative reactions and of repeating the successes that spur you to praise, you may wish to respond only on the first level. As you develop skill in analyzing writing, however, you will want to offer analyses to students who need them. Thus, on this second level, instead of merely saying "I got lost here," you might say, "I got lost here because you did not indicate clearly enough the relation between these two statements," or "This paragraph avoids monotony because you have varied the length and construction of your sentences," or "I had to read this sentence twice because there are two possible ways to interpret it."

Remain at the second level if you think the student can find solutions to the problems. Sometimes, though, it may be wise to move to a third level and suggest some alternatives. For example, you might say, "I got lost here. Try inserting a word or phrase to clarify the relationship between these two ideas, or perhaps turn the sentence around so that the idea I have underlined comes first." Such a comment still leaves the writer with some choices, but it offers guidance about how to amend a transition problem. In another instance you might say, "My reading was held up because there are two ways to understand this sentence. Insert a comma, or try recasting the sentence with 'choices' as the subject."

Suiting Response to Purpose

In some situations you will comment on papers that will not be revised. Then your goal is to give the student some advice to remember and use in future writing. You will want to concentrate on general labels or general counsel, using the papers as illustrations so that the students understand what you mean. This may involve commenting on many aspects of a paper's writing and content or on only one or two points you think students can grasp and use at that particular time.

If you are responding to a paper that will be revised, you may decide, especially with more advanced students, to mark everything you see. When there are a great many writing problems, however, or when there is one difficult problem, marking everything may not be useful. (My tennis teacher, fortunately, doesn't mention, at each lesson, all the failings he sees in my tennis game.)

Sometimes the paper will need major structural changes, so the prose will be radically altered anyway. In that case, it may be wise to treat that prose as you would in a paper that will not be revised—that is, offer the student diagnostic summaries, with the particular prose as your example. You might say, for instance, that the paper contains errors in punctuating quotations and that, before writing the final draft, the student should consult a handbook and straighten those out. You may, in addition, rumble warnings about apostrophes, spelling, and capitalization of proper nouns, but you need not mark every transgression of those rules. It is possible to warn even more generally: "I see many distracting problems in spelling, grammar, and punctuation that you'll need to clear up before a reader can move easily through your paper." Then see what problems the student can clear up independently, and concentrate next time on the errors that remain because the student didn't know how to fix them.

A different approach is to ask the student to correct some of the major mechanical flaws before you pay much attention to areas such as organization, paragraph unity, or wordiness. If you put mechanics first, you'll want also to respond to the paper's content in some way, so as to acknowledge the writer's thought and message. It is almost always a mistake to devote all your attention to errors, giving the student the impression that you view the paper not as a communication but as a collection of mistakes.

Whichever approach you take in a given situation, consider the total effect your comments will have, their usefulness to the student, and the message they convey both about what writing is and about your own concerns when you read student writing. We sometimes get so fixed on the paper as a thing to be marked that we forget that our primary aim is not to correct the essay but to help the student learn to write well.

Setting Goals and Rewarding Achievement

Beyond indicating priorities, the teacher who is working with a student on a series of papers or revisions over the course of a semester can set specific goals, thus creating an environment in which the student knows that the first step toward Jerusalem is to make it to the oak tree. That milestone reached, the teacher will be pleased, the student can take heart, and together they can mark out the next objective.

It is even possible to grade on the basis of this kind of incremental improvement. For example, you could say to a student, "If you rewrite this paper so that it has no sentence fragments and no run-on sentences, I will give the paper a C, even though you and I will know that you're still having problems with apostrophes, spelling, and transitions." Or you might say, "In the next paper, if you have arranged your subtopics according to a logical plan, I will give the paper a B, even though you are still having problems with grammar and usage." Once the student has mastered the areas in question, it will no longer be possible to get that B or C just by maintaining that mastery; the student must add another competency just to achieve the same grade. In this way, you reward the student for making progress and save the student who has many problems from the frustration of investing much effort in mastering a particular problem and still getting a D or an F on the paper. Of course, the disadvantage is that either the student or the employers and admissions officers who read the student's transcript may be misled about the actual quality of the writing. Thus each teacher must decide whether incremental grading will work in a particular context.

Whether or not you base grades on a student's incremental progress, you can certainly set priorities and give each student only as much advice as he or she can handle. You can generously praise one who masters the skill you have chosen to emphasize, even though other writing problems are still at large in the paper.

Using Praise

One of the easiest habits for a teacher to fall into is that of silently noting the well-written sections of a paper but commenting aloud or in writing only on the faults. Not only does this give the evaluation an unduly negative cast but it also throws away an excellent instructional method—telling students what they have done right. A student often hits on good writing only half consciously, like the blindfolded birthday child who heads toward the right part of the donkey but honestly doesn't know the tail's going in the proper place unless the audience squeals. The teacher ought to describe a paper's successes, so that the student can repeat them more consciously the next time.

Being Thorough and Specific

Positive or negative, a teacher's evaluation is not much good unless the student understands it thoroughly enough to be able to repeat the success or remedy the failure. When, as a child, I received a coded message from my pal Julie, I raced to my room to get our special decoding key and sat down promptly to translate. Such alacrity, however, is not likely to appear among students who receive from their teacher a paper whose margins contain codes like "Coh," "DM," "Trans" and "Frag." If you use such hieroglyphs, you should make certain that the student is strongly motivated to look up their meanings. The code key should be as available and comprehensible as you can make it. I have found it useful to prepare one-page printed explanations and exercises dealing with the most common problems, so that the student whose marginal comment grumbles "trans" receives, in the same fistful of pages with the returning essay, a printed explanation of the way in which one uses transitions to provide connective tissue in writing. It is best, though, to write complete explanations on the student's paper such as these:

> I like this paragraph because there is not a useless word in it. Everything is tight.
>
> You need a transition (a linking word or phrase) to clarify the relationship between these two ideas.

It is better to choose one or two successes or problems on a paper and comment on them in detail than to mark six or seven so briefly that the student understands none of them.

Specificity goes hand in hand with completeness. I once had a teacher who would write, next to a paragraph of my essay, the single comment, "awk." It sounded like Henny Penny, and I could picture my teacher fluttering her wings and squawking in outrage as she read my poor paragraph. But though it evokes a specific image of the teacher, the word "awkward" is not a specific indication of what is wrong with the paragraph or how the writing can be improved. Awkwardness can result from a number of problems: a misplaced modifier, an unidiomatic use of language, a vague conjunction. Sometimes "awk" can tell a relatively sophisticated writer all he or she needs to know to make the language smooth, but usually getting back a paper with some amorphous label like "good" or "awkward" or "poorly organized," with no more specific critique and no suggestions for remedy, is like having a mechanic tell you, "The engine doesn't sound right somehow," or a physician say, "Something is wrong with your stomach." Much of the rest of this handbook is concerned with demonstrating how teachers can evaluate successes and failures with greater specificity.

Naming and Summarizing

Naming and summarizing are important services that the teacher performs to help students see forests instead of trees. A three-page paper that comes back with twenty different marks on it can seem hopeless to the student unless the teacher points out, for example, that all the problems fall into three main categories or that most of the problems involve a failure to provide logical links between ideas. Then, too, when you name a fault or a strength, you give the student a way to identify it, remember it, and link it to suggestions from other teachers and readers. For example, I might tell a student, "This passage is too wordy; see whether you can condense it by combining some of the sentences and striking out useless or repetitious words." The student then says to me, with a slightly startled grin, "Oh, that's what Mrs. Parker told me about my writing last year"—as though it were a miracle that any two teachers would have anything like the same response to the same student's writing. I always find such "coincidences" rewarding. I feel that Mrs. Parker and I have made a bit of progress toward giving this student the idea that following certain common, identifiable guidelines can produce writing that will strike most readers as effective.

If You Don't Have Time

The old system that consists of announcing an assignment and not getting involved again until the final versions come in, of marking everything you see in a paper because your mind is more fixed on correcting mistakes than on teaching writing skills, and of handing back papers you'll never see again—this old system is so inefficient at improving students' writing that it is worthwhile to try the alternative of coaching the student during the writing process. If your time is limited, cut the length of required papers or reduce their number and carefully coach students through the writing and revisions of fewer and/or shorter pieces. Let peers or student assistants do some of the earlier coaching. Just as a football team has a defensive coach, you might ask some of your more skilled students to act as mechanics coaches or organization coaches for the rest of the class. Or you can organize groups of four or five students who will coach and respond to one another's writing.

If you must, offer coaching and conferences to only some students: one class each semester, or half the class for each assignment, or just five students a year. If your rowboat reaches the sinking *Titanic,* you can take on five victims, even though you can't save everyone.

The rewards for whatever ingenuity you can muster, whatever steps you can take, will be great. Switching from a traditional approach to a coaching position has, in my own experience and that of many other teachers, increased student satisfaction and appreciation. That students also write better is not only our overwhelming impression but an opinion supported by solid evidence.

Although it is undeniably time-consuming to coach the writing process—to read two or even several versions of a single paper and give thoughtful responses either in writing or, better yet, in individual conferences—these methods can to some extent replace such other practices as marking everything on every paper or having students merely write more, with no change in your approach. Coaching, then, can mean using the same amount of time more wisely or devoting extra time that will produce a heavy payoff in improved student writing.

Sample Teacher Responses to Student Writing

To illustrate specifically how you can respond to student writing, here are some critiques that faculty from various disciplines wrote in response to the student paper printed below. The assignment, in a biology class, was to write a one-page summary of an article about hawks.

Student Summary

Article summarized: Ron L. Snyder, "Some Prey Preference Factors
for a Red-Tailed Hawk." Auk, July 1975, pp. 547-52.

(1) The purpose of this study was to examine the role of
activity in prey selection. (2) The first of three experiments
reported herein examined the role of prey activity when a Red-
Tailed Hawk (Buteo jamaicensis) was offered a choice between two
live prey animals. (3) The second experiment examined changes
in prey activity preferences when the hawk was offered two
comparatively large prey animals. (4) In the third experiment the
hawk was offered two prey of different weights to determine if this
would affect the selection against more active prey.
(5) In the first experiment the hawk preferred the more active
of the two prey animals when no other differences were apparant
between them.
(6) The second experiment varied in its results. (7) If one of
the large prey was relatively inactive, the hawk went for it.
(8) Over many trials, however, the preference for the less active
animal was often replaced by a high-activity preference if the hawk
was successful in subduing the larger animals.
(9) Experiment three showed a clear preference for heavier, less
active prey. (10) Comparing the data in experiment one, showing a
strong preference for the more active prey, with the third where the
larger prey was less active and still preferred, may have
demonstrated a tendency in the hawk to choose the apparantly more
profitable prey item in terms of relative biomass.

Below are several teacher responses, all based on the assumption
that this paper would be revised. In addition to the overall comments
printed below, teachers made marginal notes about matters like the misspelled word in sentence (5) and the stilted use of "herein" in sentence
(2).

First Teacher's Written Response

I would like to see a more complete explanation of the problem
these experiments seek to address. What is at stake? What
possible combinations could or could not have resulted? In following through you need to take another look at some of your
sentences (see notations) for clarity. [Notations were at sentences (8) and (10).]

This teacher's comment calls for "a more complete explanation." By
itself, such a statement may lead to a longer paper that is no more satis-

factory. "Clearer" would have been a better word choice than "more complete." After some intervening words that contribute little, the teacher wisely follows with questions that should help the student. The second of the two questions ("What possible combinations could or could not have resulted?") is not as clearly stated as it could be, but nevertheless these questions are the strongest part of the teacher's response, because they mirror the reader's confusion, they suggest remedy in specific terms, and they focus on the central problem of the paper, which is that information about the three experiments is unclear, incomplete, and poorly organized.

The teacher's final comment is a good way to summarize some marginal notes on sentence style. She rightly pulls together those problems under one label—clarity. Though other sentences are unclear because of the basic organizational problems noted in the first part of the comment, sentences (8) and (10) are unclear because of their syntax. Thus the student would, as the teacher indicates, correct the clarity problem in sentences (8) and (10) as a follow-through for the clarity problems noted earlier.

Second Teacher's Written Response

It appears that there are 3 main factors that you want to discuss (size, activity, weight) and then want to compare. Am I correct?

If so, write one paragraph for each (T = 4 paragraphs) or 1 paragraph in which all 3 factors are discussed.

At present the content of each paragraph is not appropriate.

Can you explain this article using your own words, not the book's?

The first part of the comment tells the student what the reader was able to gather from the report and mirrors the reader's partial confusion—a good first-level teaching technique, simply recording one's own responses as a reader.

The second part of the comment suggests organizational patterns for the paper—a third-level response. One might go on to urge the student, as the first teacher did, to make the decision about organization on the basis of a clearer vision of the significance of the experiments ("What was at stake?").

The teacher's final injunction, suggesting that the student might be better off with a more independent formulation, represents the instructor's guess that the awkwardness of the paper results in part from the use of some half-digested sentences from the original article. This kind of guessing at the process behind a certain writing problem is effective and intelligent.

Third Teacher's Written Response

I had trouble figuring out the prey activity of the hawk. Perhaps if you put each experiment and result together this would help.

Though short, this response is effective. It reflects the reader's confusion ("I had trouble . . . ") and suggests a remedy ("Perhaps if you put . . . "). What is left out is a message to the student that necessary information is given to the reader too late or not at all. It is possible, however, that in reorganizing the paper the student will reconsider the whole question of what information to give about each experiment and where to include it. If you have time to write only a sentence or two, this comment illustrates an effective use of your energies.

Fourth Teacher's Written Response

Your information appears to me to be accurately presented from the source you cite. Your abstract is successful to a point. I like your *preview* sentence.

A few suggestions:
1. Begin with an orienting sentence or two before you state your purpose.
2. Watch your spelling, misused words, redundant words, etc.
   a. apparent, p. 2.
   b. herein, p. 1.
3. Amplify each experiment a bit more.
4. Grammar—if one of the . . . were, p. 3.

Last sentence needs rewriting to act as a residual or summary. Avoid closing without summary.

This comment does something no other does: it finds something to praise. The commendation of the first ("preview") sentence is merited, though I'm a little worried that the remark about accuracy may disguise for the student how seriously muddled the explanations of the experiments are. The first suggestion is puzzling. I'm not sure that the student will know what an "orienting sentence" is, especially since he's just been praised for his first sentence, whose purpose in fact is to orient the reader. Neither am I sure what the teacher means by "state your purpose." The purpose of the experiment, not the student's purpose, is what already appropriately occupies the first sentence.

This instructor rightly points to sentence (10) as problematic but does not make clear what the problem is. The student's last sentence serves appropriately as a summary of the experiments and an indication of their significance, but the syntax (sentence structure) is poor: there are too many words between the subject ("comparing") and the verb ("may have demonstrated").

The instructor's third suggestion asks for amplification of each experiment. This is a third-level comment without any earlier indication of the reader's inability to understand. The comment would be stronger if the teacher had said what amplification is needed—further information to avoid reader confusion about the weight and activity of the prey in the various experiments.

Fifth Teacher's Written Response

Jack, you do well to begin with a clear statement of the purpose. Next you seem to outline first the *choices* offered in each experiment and then the *results* of each. But the whole section was not clear as I read it. Suggestions:

1. Stick rigidly to a plan that gives *choices* for each experiment, then *results* for each, as now,

   or

   treat all info. on exp. 1 together, then all on exp. 2, then exp. 3. Choose whichever you think would be clearer to the reader.
2. For each exp., give all essential information. Ask yourself, What does the reader need to know, and when? For example, one of my questions was, In exp. 1 and 2, were both live prey equally active?
3. Your final sentence rightly presents the results and their significance, but it is clumsy because too many words separate subject from verb.

This comment I consider ideal: it reflects the reader's experience; it uses praise as a teaching tool; it operates on all three levels, as the instructor deems appropriate. In suggestion 1, for example, the teacher goes to level 3, offering specific remedies, but suggests two possibilities and reminds the writer that the choice should be based on reader needs. In suggestion 3, the teacher stops at level 2, identifying the sentence's problem but leaving the writer to find the remedy.

Typical Oral Conference (Same Paper)

TEACHER: *How do you feel about the paper?*

STUDENT: Well, I think I understood the experiments, but I don't know if it's, if they're written very clearly.

TEACHER: *OK, let me read and see whether it seems clear to me.* [*Pulls near so that both can see the paper.*] *"The purpose of this study was to examine the role of activity in prey selection." Now that's clear, for sure. I know exactly what the experiments were for.* [*Student chuckles. Teacher reads first paragraph.*] *Now I'm lost. I don't understand the differences between the three experiments.* [*Teacher reads paragraph over again, aloud.*] *I think what I'm missing is—or, what I don't know at this point is, um, whether the two animals were the same size in experiment 1. And, uh, in experiment 2, you don't tell me whether one of the animals was more active. They are both large, but do they differ in activity?*

STUDENT: Well, I say that later on, in here [points to paragraphs 2 and 3].

TEACHER: *OK, let me read on* [*reads paragraphs 2, 3, and 4*]. *OK, now let me see. Paragraph 2 makes the first experiment clear to me, but in paragraph 3 I'm still not understanding what happened in experiment 2.* [*Reads it again aloud.*] *I think maybe that "if" clause on the end comes too late. Maybe I need that information earlier in the sentence. Or maybe I need some of this information still earlier, when you first discuss experiment 2.*

STUDENT: Yeah, I see. OK.

TEACHER: *In fact, why do you break up the discussion of each experiment into two parts?*

STUDENT: Well, I don't know, but the first part sort of sets it up, you know, and the second part tells the results.

TEACHER: *So first you tell how all three were set up and then you tell the results of each one?*

STUDENT: Yeah, I guess.

TEACHER: [*Reads first three paragraphs again silently.*] *OK, now I see what you're doing. But still, I was confused when I read it. How do you think you can fix the confusion?*

STUDENT: Well, I have to give you more information up here at the top.

TEACHER: *How about giving me all the information on experiment 1, then all on experiment 2, and then on experiment 3?*

STUDENT: You mean each experiment, I talk about it just in one place, like in turns, all three?

TEACHER: *Um-hum. I think you could also follow your old plan, but you'd need to give more information in the earlier section. Why don't you just fiddle with it both ways, maybe have some other people read it, and see if you can get it so every reader understands and nobody feels confused on the way through.*

STUDENT: OK, yeah, that's fine.

TEACHER: *Your last sentence is a summary of the results, and that's good, but the sentence is clumsy. Can you fool with it to make it smoother?*

STUDENT: Let's see. [Reads last sentence aloud.] Yeah, I think I can get it better.

TEACHER: *Try. And if you can't I'll try to tell you more specifically how you could fix it. OK. Do you think that you can go back now and rewrite it? Do you think you know what to do?*

STUDENT: Yeah, I do. This is good.

The teacher, during the conference, tries to do several things, some of which wouldn't be possible in written comments: to ask questions, to get information about the student's recognition of problems, and to ascertain the student's ability to remedy difficulties. For example, the teacher merely says the last sentence is "clumsy"—a word that one would hesitate to use in a written comment, lest the student not know what to do with such a vague prescription. Yet here, in the conference, there is a way to determine whether the student at least *thinks* he can remedy the problem on the basis of that much guidance.

Student Writing Groups

Many teachers get good results by using writing groups of three to seven students, because students actually give good help to one another and also because they learn to analyze a colleague's paper—a skill that will serve them well in many professional situations. In addition, students often write and learn more effectively when they verbalize their ideas first in a group. An excellent guide to using groups is Mary Kay Healy's *Using Student Writing Response Groups in the Classroom* (Berkeley, Calif.: Bay Area Writing Project, 1980).

You can take a number of steps to ensure that the group works productively. First, use the group for initial brainstorming and for clarifying ideas. Have students explain to one another what they intend to do, or have them plan together how they might develop a topic, solve a research problem, or structure a paper. Later they can meet to go over one another's outlines and rough drafts. You'll have to do three things to make this procedure work. First, make clear to them that they are not in competition with one another for a limited number of top grades; they need to know that there is no penalty for them in helping a classmate. Second, meet briefly with each group to see that students stay on the topic, work hard, and learn from you how to do a serious and detailed critique of a fellow student's outline or rough draft. Third, guide them in criticizing their peers' work. One way to do this is to have them read the last section of Peter Elbow's *Writing without Teachers,*[3] which gives advice to group members about how to respond to one another's writing. Another way is to give each group guidelines for its effective functioning and a written outline of questions students should be answering about one another's papers. Here is a sample of such a sheet:

A Guide for Group Discussion of Drafts

1. Before handing out copies of the draft, the author should read aloud the first sentence of the paper. The group should then tell the author what that sentence leads them to think is the main point of the paper and what material will make up the body of the paper.
2. Then the author should hand out copies of the draft to all group members.
3. The author should read the paper aloud, twice.
4. There should be two or three minutes of silence to allow group members to digest the paper and gather their thoughts.
5. Group members should then, in turn, voice their reactions:
   a. State the main point of the paper in a single sentence. Who do you think is the audience for the paper? What is the paper's purpose?
   b. List the major subtopics in the paper. If the paper is long, list the subtopics in each major section.
   c. Were there any points at which you were confused about the subject or focus of the paper or its sections?
   d. Consider each section of the paper in turn. Is each developed with enough detail, evidence, and information?
   e. Do the points follow one another in an appropriate sequence?
   f. Is there other material that the author should include?
   g. Are the opening and concluding paragraphs accurate guides to the paper's theme and focus?
   h. Considering the paper paragraph by paragraph, what seems most vivid, clear, and memorable? Where is the language clumsy?
6. The writer should follow these guidelines:
   a. Do not argue with the readers, and do not explain what you meant. You are gathering data about audience response. So, simply gather it. If a particular response does not seem useful, you are free to ignore it when you revise your paper. But for you to spend the group's time arguing and explaining is wasteful and can cause the group to focus on understanding what you meant rather than on responding to what you wrote.
   b. It is usually best for you to remain silent, remembering carefully or writing down what readers say. In addition, you may want to:
      (1) Ask a reader to clarify or expand a statement, so that you understand it thoroughly.
      (2) Ask readers to respond to an idea you have for improvement of some aspect of the paper they're unhappy with.
      (3) Repeat to the group what you think they're saying, just to make sure communication is complete.

Chapter Four

Giving the Assignment

Sending people out to walk a trail without warning them that it has a pitfall is something Brer Fox would do to Brer Bear. Unfortunately teachers also do it to their students. Given the assumptions about writing common to our culture, given the training in writing dispensed in most of our schools, and given the propensity of human minds to follow the same worn paths to destruction, certain mistakes are so common in student papers that experienced teachers need only glance over the pages to sense with sinking heart the familiar profile of disaster and to know that there are probably ten similarly maimed essays in the stack. If you know what the pitfalls are, it makes sense to warn and guide the beginning voyager. This chapter discusses ways in which instructors can effectively plan and explain assignments so as to encourage success and avoid common mistakes.

Defining the Audience

Like your grandmother's hand-knit sweaters, good writing is fashioned with a specific person or audience in mind. You can help your students by defining the audience for whom they will write. A chemistry professor, for example, wants her students to learn how to write instructions for laboratory procedures. She asks them to describe on paper how to transfer a precipitate from a beaker to a filter. So far the teacher has spelled out her purpose in giving the assignment and the subject on which the students are to write, but she has not designated the audience to whom the explanation should be addressed, and unless she does, her students face a difficult task. They know that their teacher, who will read their papers, does not herself need to be told how to transfer a precipitate. But what *does* she need or want to know? To whom is the process to be explained? Which procedures should be spelled out and which taken for granted? What is the proper tone? How much technical language can be used? The problems are amply illustrated by the papers students actually wrote for this assignment. One writer begins, "Set up the filtration apparatus," assuming the reader already knows how to do that. Another paper spends the whole first page explaining how to set up the filtration apparatus. The real disasters are the papers that have no clear sense of audience. They explain some simple procedures and take others for granted; they at one time instruct an ignoramus and at another time coach a somewhat knowledgeable peer. By neglecting to define the characteristics of the audience, an instructor encourages students to think of writing as the production of an artifact rather than as a means of communication intended to serve the needs of a specific audience. To prepare students to do a better job a teacher might take time to ponder the kinds of audiences for student writing.

The Real Audience

The audience for some assignments is composed of real persons other than the teacher—those who will actually read the paper—for example, classmates, tourists, the editors of the school newspaper. You can help the student prepare the most effective message for the intended readers, but the readers themselves will prove the writer's effectiveness—by indicating that they understand the writer's ideas or expressing praise, by buying and using the tour guide, or by publishing the letter to the editor. For some audiences the writer may have to broadcast the seed with no way to measure the harvest. But even then an audience that will read the student's written message is known to exist. With such an audience the teacher's role is to emphasize the importance of writing with that audience in mind, meeting its expectations, deflecting its prejudices, and answering the questions it is likely to have. The teacher acts as coach, helping the writer prepare an address for the intended readers.

The Hypothetical Audience

If no real audience is present you can establish a hypothetical one. You might, for example, ask students to write reports for the governor of the state or proposals for a company's managing board. If you do establish a hypothetical audience, you will want to define it thoroughly so that students can shape their writing to suit their imaginary readers' tastes and needs.

The Teacher as Audience

In school writing, frequently—perhaps too frequently—the audience is assumed to be the teacher. I've suggested some ways to vary the audience, but it is clear that much writing is still going to be done for the teacher alone. When this is the case, it is common to assume that nothing more needs to be said about audience; we carefully explain subject matter, but we may say nothing about ourselves as readers. Yet if you think back over the familiar ways in which student papers written for your eyes go wrong, you will probably recall, as I do, that many papers are poor because students assume our knowledge of things that they should have explained or because they spell out details that we would have taken for granted or because they adopt a tone we find too familiar or too stuffy or too affected. These errors all reflect misjudgments about what the audience—the teacher—needs or likes. We could help our students greatly by being more specific about ourselves as audience.

Think for a moment about yourself as audience and about the dilemmas students face when asked to write papers for which you are the assumed reader. When you read most student writing, you are not totally you; there are likely to be hypothetical audiences mixed in with the "you" students write for. Let's say, for example, that you ask for an informative report about the nesting habits of red-tailed hawks. Now if the real you knows all there is to know about that subject, you're certainly not going to read this informative report to get informed. You may in fact be asking the student to write as though informing someone not knowledgeable about the subject. So there *is* a hypothetical audience, and you are the judge who decides how well the student has addressed this imaginary reader. If this is the case, define for the student who the pretended audience is, what the audience knows about hawks, how familiar it is with biological terms, and how it will want to use the information the report provides. Describe what you, as judge, will be looking for.

On the other hand, if you do not know all there is to know about hawks, the student may have explored the subject in more depth than you ever have. If so, perhaps the essay will function primarily to transfer information from an inexperienced student who has thoroughly explored an area to a reader who is more highly trained but who nevertheless has something to learn from the report and will enjoy this accession of knowledge. In these circumstances the student can freely use technical terms and can merely refer to, without explaining in depth, information the teacher already possesses. The student's tone will be that of pupil to teacher but also that of one colleague to another, sharing information about a subject of joint interest.

A third possibility is that the student will share with the teacher the learning and musing process. The teacher will learn not about red-tailed hawks but about the student. Such an essay will be more personal and reflective in tone. It is likely to record not only the information the writer gathered about the nesting of red-tailed hawks but also the process of developing the topic, the importance attached to this intellectual task, or the questions that remain about the subject or the research procedure.

Finally, the paper might be written primarily so that the teacher can judge whether the student has read the material about hawks, mastered the information, or learned the procedures for investigating nesting behavior. In the same way a person might repeat the directions you've just given for driving to your house at the seashore. The student writes so that the teacher can tell for sure that the student sees the connections, knows the information, or can apply the principles. The student tries to illustrate competence; the teacher simply plays the role of judge.

The hawk topic opens other possibilities, too. You could think of several right now. A group of British researchers delineated four categories of student writing addressed to the teacher:

Child (or adolescent) to trusted adult
Pupil to teacher—general (teacher-learner dialogue)
Pupil to teacher—particular relationship (based on a shared interest
    in a curriculum subject)
Pupil to examiner.[1]

You may not totally comprehend either these categories or mine; in fact, you may be mentally fashioning a set of terms you like better. But the point is, it is wrong to assume that when students know that you will be the reader you need say nothing more about the audience for their papers. You can make their assignments more fair and their journeys more successful if you carefully define for them the role you will play as reader and the expectations you will hold.

Helping Students Define and Focus the Topic

Giving pupils an opportunity to choose their topics or offering them a chance to develop individual responses to broad questions has many advantages as a teaching technique. Thus you can use essay questions such as "Discuss the economic, social, religious, and political results of the Crusades" or, my favorite, "The world is going to hell. Discuss." Another way to give options is to tell students they can write their term papers on any topic related to the subject matter of the course. For inexperienced writers, such freedom holds some dangers, but you can help by warning them against trying to cover too much and guiding them in limiting and defining topics. You should make it clear to students that you expect them, within the broad area you have delineated, to carve out a manageable territory for themselves or to survey the land from a single watchtower or to find a single vehicle in which to explore it. Otherwise many writers will try to cover the whole plain, and their work will lack both specificity and focus.

For example, a history teacher, during the study of modern Japan, asked students to read a novel that reflects that culture and then to "hand in a book report." He did not define the audience or the purpose, and he did not enlarge on the need for students to treat a limited aspect of the book. This is one of the papers he received:

Student Book Report on Junichiro Tanizaki's Diary of an Old Man

```
    The novel, Diary of a Mad Old Man, by Junichiro Tanizaki,
is a portrait of an old man who does not have much longer to live.
Tanizaki utilizes the diary form very effectively, telling a story
that could have taken place anywhere.  In the story, Tanizaki mixes
not only humor, but also a certain amount of sadness.
    Utsugi Tokusuke, who relates the story, is an old man in his
mid-seventies.  Tokusuke's body is beginning to fail; he has suffered
a heart attack which has caused problems in his arms and feet.
Despite his physical impairments, his mind is still capable of
functioning normally.
```

[The paragraph continues with more plot summary.

Then come three long paragraphs of continued plot summary, each centered on one of the novel's main characters.

Next appear three short paragraphs: one on death in the novel, one on sexual attitudes in the novel, and one on Japanese medical practices as reflected in the novel.

The concluding paragraph reads:]

```
    In the novel Tanizaki has given a rather subtle picture of
Tokyo and of a modern Japanese family.  The combinations of new with
old and western with Japanese makes the book insightful as well as
interesting.  However, the novel retains a universal flavor that is
difficult to miss in reading.
```

The paper is a grab bag. The student has not decided whether his audience knows the plot of the book, and he has not sufficiently narrowed his topic. The first and last paragraphs reflect the paper's lack of focus; they are conglomerations of statements about the novel, none of which gives a proper clue to the paper's main theme. If the teacher, at the time of the assignment, had given more specific guidance, the student might have written a stronger paper. For example, you might define the audience for this assignment in either of these two ways:

> You are writing this book report for someone who has read the novel and knows the plot but who needs help interpreting a particular aspect.

> You are writing this book report for a fellow student who has not read the book and who wants to know whether it is worth reading to get insights into some aspects of modern Japanese culture.

In addition to defining the audience, you could help the student narrow the topic by saying not merely that students should "hand in a book report" but that the book report should have a specific focus. Then you should give some examples:

In three pages you can't possibly put down everything there is to say about this novel. So don't try! Nor should you write down a series of random observations about the book in an attempt to cover as much as possible and thereby convince me that you've read the book. Instead, you should pick one aspect of modern Japanese society and explain to me in depth how the novel reflects it. Assume that I have read the book but that I want to hear your interpretation of and insights into that one aspect. You might choose death in modern Japan or family relationships or old age or Western technology or religion or medical practices or any other area that interests you.

If you want a somewhat broader treatment you could say, or better yet write, to the students:

In the book report you should summarize the novelist's view of life in modern Japan. You will need to organize your summary around three or four main ideas. Don't summarize the plot, don't tell how interesting the book is, and don't include anything except your main topics, plus examples or explanations that support each main idea.

To make the point even clearer, you might hand out or put on the screen an unfocused book report like the one in the example. Then you can point out to the class how much mere plot summary there is, how the plot summary fails to direct itself toward any particular point, how the writer mentions many different topics in a series of skinny paragraphs, and how in the opening and closing paragraphs he tosses in still other topics that are completely unrelated to anything else developed in the paper—topics like the use of the diary form, the mixture of humor and sadness, or the "universal flavor" of the novel.

Once you have given the assignment, with appropriate instructions and warnings about focus, you can use one of several methods to coach students as they arrive at their specific topic choices. These techniques are discussed in Chapter 5, "Helping Students Achieve Clear Focus."

Defining Success and Suggesting Procedures

Most teachers, when they put their minds to it, can come up with a list of two or three of the most crucial writing competencies or the qualities that characterize successful papers of the sort they assign. They can also suggest, if they take the time to ponder the matter, some strategies by which students can effectively plan and develop the assignments. Such analytic attention sometimes leads an instructor to change an assignment, rephrase it, or give different guidance to students as they work on it. At times such analysis also causes the teacher to change the sequence of assignments in a course or to develop writing tasks that are more consonant either with the students' abilities or with the goals of the course. Thus it is worth taking the time to define as carefully as possible the competencies and methods necessary for success in a given writing task, even if at first it seems difficult to put into words what is really happening in good papers.

Concentrate on one assignment at a time. Though certain characteristics are common to most effective writing, different assignments call for different skills, or certain skills may be more crucial for success in one kind of paper than in others. Everyone enjoys some of the same virtues in apples, but while size and juiciness are of primary importance to a hungry person, shape and color are the highest values for a still-life painter. Similarly, the success of a paper that explains to teenagers the effects of certain dietary deficiencies may depend primarily on the writer's ability to describe, in the most graphic and convincing way, the deleterious effects of a diet of Coke and potato chips. A paper on the same subject written for an audience of science professionals may need most of all to be precise about word choice and sentence structure so that the researchers can clearly understand all the information and use it for their own further investigations.

One way to analyze a given writing assignment is to complete it yourself, trying to be as self-conscious as possible about the skills and methods you have to use to make the paper effective. Give attention also to information-gathering techniques, problem-solving methods, and planning strategies that you find useful in doing that particular assignment.

Another method is to analyze some papers that students have written in the past to complete your assignment or one similar to it. A group of specialists evaluating a nationwide writing sample developed a sophisticated version of such a method. The professional procedure, called Primary Trait Scoring, is probably too time-consuming and complicated for classroom teachers to use in its original form, but it is useful to know how it is done, because teachers can use the same basic approach in a simplified form.[2]

The purpose of Primary Trait Scoring is to isolate the traits essential to effective completion of a given writing task. The first step is to read a group of papers written for a particular assignment to discover the central characteristics of successful papers; in other words, you learn precisely what students had to do to produce good papers for this assignment. You can then use that information to refine the assignment next time you make it and to give more helpful guidance to students.

To illustrate this kind of analysis, let's take the example of a college class in marketing. The instructor gave the forty-five students a case history of Toni Rocco's attempt to ensure the success of his new restaurant. The instructor wanted the students to analyze Toni's marketing policies, identify his mistakes, and suggest alternative procedures. The students were to write their essays during a fifty-minute class period.

Obviously it was crucial that students be sufficiently skilled in analysis of marketing techniques to decide which of Toni's actions were unwise. An analysis of the forty-five student papers written for this assignment shows, however, that some students who came to valid conclusions about Toni's marketing errors were nevertheless unable to write successful papers. So it is clear that the students had to have, in addition to the required knowledge, the ability to arrive quickly at a summary statement or statements about Toni's mistakes and to use that summary as a key to organizing the essay. Quotations from several papers will illustrate. This student's first paragraph immediately presented a basic interpretation of Toni's errors:

Though it appeared in reading this case that Rocco had some definite plans before opening his restaurant, his plans were strictly product oriented, rather than market oriented.

The student goes on to describe each of Toni's mistakes in terms of his overemphasis on product. Another student, after presenting some background information about Toni's Restaurant—background information that revealed the student's confusion about how much the audience could be expected to know about Toni—finally gets to that saving summary. She says that Toni "did not find a target market nor did he adequately provide a satisfactory marketing mix, especially in the area of promotion." The paper goes on to discuss Toni's mistakes under those two headings.

In contrast to these two rather successful papers, the following student's essay—although it contains the same insights as the other two—fails because it is not organized around those insights. As a result, the essay is a random list of Toni's mistakes; it does not cohere as an essay:

Poorly timed radio commercials change possibly to morning and early afternoon. He should have advertised more initially instead of later.
He was product oriented, thinking that if he offered a good place to eat people would come to him. Reputation comes after having been in business for awhile.
He didn't really have a target market. Didn't think about catering to his Italian neighbors, nor of extending his services beyond full-course dinner. When he located his restaurant he was thinking of the heavy traffic area, not about whether he actually could serve them as customers. He didn't research enough before opening

a restaurant, what his market is. He didn't use facts such as the
income, nationality, or location for deciding what his market is.
He might have considered serving breakfast and lunch, by varying
the size as well as kind of meals offered.

[The final paragraph suggests offering family-style meals and guesses that initially Toni was hiring more help than he needed. There is no sense of summary or conclusion.]

This student's paper is typical of a number of the less successful essays in the class; several were similarly disjointed. Instruction in the class had obviously been effective, however: this student and most others did express some sound ideas about what Toni did wrong and how he could have done better. The crucial element in writing successfully about Toni's experience was the student's ability to establish some overall view of Toni's mistakes to use as an organizing center for the paper. Some students may have been capable of achieving such an organization but incapable of doing so before the fifty minutes ran out. This student's paper may be one such effort. The highly elliptical and tentative first paragraph is like a windup. As the student begins to find her stride, the language gets smoother. Given the chance to rework this rough draft, she might have built her essay around two or three of her more significant insights—such as her statement that Toni did not sufficiently research his market and her assertion that he was too product-oriented. Whether the instructor should have offered a longer writing period, in the light of the fair number of papers that suffered from time constraints, is a question for debate. Part of the usefulness of this sort of analysis of student performance is that it does sometimes lead to changing the structure of the assignment. Even without changing the time limit, however, the instructor might well have been able to help some of his students if, working from his own knowledge of what would be crucial to his students' success in the writing they were about to undertake, he had warned and guided them before they began to write. He might have said:

> This exercise will test your ability to pick out the mistakes Toni made and suggest how he could have done better. Just listing mistakes in random order, however, will not make a successful essay, because your ideas will seem to the reader to be too jumbled and too hard to remember or follow. So you will need to find a way to organize Toni's mistakes into subgroups and to arrange them in an effective order. You might decide, for example, that Toni's main errors were all due to some single misguided notion or some significant omission. That should be your opening statement, and then you can treat the details as aspects of that one main problem. Alternatively,

you might decide that Toni made three primary mistakes, or four. Begin by stating them, and then go on to develop each in turn. A final way in which some students have organized this assignment successfully is to go through the four P's of marketing (place, promotion, product, price) and discuss Toni's mistakes or successes in each of the areas. The main point is that it is not enough for you to see what Toni should have done; to communicate your insights effectively to a reader who does not know what Toni's mistakes were, you have to organize your thoughts so that the reader can easily understand and remember them.

Some people begin this sort of organizing in their heads. If you're the head type, it might help to ask yourself this question: "What was Toni's main problem, or what were the primary types of mistakes he made?" Once you've mentally worked out an answer to the question, you can begin to write. Other people plan better on paper. If you're that type, you might begin by listing Toni's mistakes in random order as fast as you think of them. Don't take time to write this out in sentences. Then look over your list and try to group some mistakes together or decide which ones are aspects of the same larger problem. Then write out your ideas following that organization. Still other people have to write out ideas in sentences and then go back to cluster, order, and arrange. If you're this type, you are at a disadvantage in a timed assignment like this one, but if, after you have written for a while, you find yourself running out of time and sense that your ideas are still in random order, perhaps you can take the last few minutes to jot down an outline of how you would organize the next draft of your paper, so that I can see that you have an idea of what good organization is and that you were making progress toward it in this essay when you ran out of time.

An explanation such as this identifies for students the primary traits of successful papers; it warns of the pitfalls that can trap inexperienced writers working on this particular assignment, and it suggests several techniques for achieving effective communication. Note that standards should be expressed not as absolute rules but as ways of meeting the needs of the reader. For example, ideas should be grouped and organized so that the reader can easily understand and remember them.

Let's take a somewhat different assignment—this time from the field of biology—and analyze the particular skills students will need for success. Here an instructor asked a class to read articles from professional scientific journals—any articles that caught their interest. Then each student was to summarize the article in a single page and give a personal response. Here are three representative papers. We have already considered some typical teachers' comments on the one on hawks(see pages 35–41).

Student Summary and Reaction to Biology Article

Raymond J. Hock, The Physiology of High Altitude," Scientific American, 22 (1970), 52-62.

This article was very interesting. It told about the effects of high altitude has on a person. It mentioned how the breathing rate increases, heart rate increases, red blood cell production increases.

Something the article mentioned which is of great interest to me is the affect high altitude has on exercise. It pointed out how at 18,000 feet, the ability to bring in oxygen is only 50%.

The article went into the subject of how people who are living in high altitudes develop certain characteristics. One such thing is an increase in chest size.

There were studies done on rats and deer mouse. The deer mouse had increased size with increased altitude. This was true only up to a certain point. They also studied such things as adjustment to hypoxic environment, exercise, and metabolism. It was found in the study of mice, the higher altitude mice were less efficient in their use of oxygen during exercise. This was compared to the low altitude mice. There were actually little treadmills made to test the mice on during exercise.

The article had graphs to demonstrate different rates in metabolism, endurance, cell count, etc.

Student Summary and Reaction to Biology Article

Ron L. Snyder, "Some Prey Preference Factors for a Red-Tailed Hawk," Auk, July 1975, pp. 547-52.

The purpose of this study was to examine the role of activity in prey selection. The first of three experiements reported herein examined the role of prey activity when a Red-Tailed Hawk (Buteo jamaicensis) was offered a choice between two live prey animals. The second experiment examined changes in prey activity preferences when the hawk was offered two comparatively large prey animals. In the third experiment the hawk was offered two prey of different weights to determine if this would affect the selection against more active prey.

In the first experiment the hawk preferred the more active of the two prey animals when no other differences were apparant between them.

The second experiment varied in its results. If one of the large prey was relatively inactive, the hawk went for it. Over many trials, however, the preference for the less active animal was often replaced by a high-activity preference if the hawk was successful in subduing the larger animals.

Experiment three showed a clear preference for heavier, less active prey. Comparing the data in experiment one, showing a strong preference for the more active prey, with the third where the larger prey was less active and still preferred, may have demonstrated a tendency in the hawk to choose the apparently more profitable prey item in terms of relative biomass.

Student Summary and Reaction to Biology Article

W. A. Calder, "The Timing of Maternal Behavior of the Broad-tailed Hummingbird Preceding Nest Failure," Wilson Bulletin, 85:283-290.

The article dealt with an experiment done concerning the temporal behavior of female broad-tailed hummingbirds for the period preceding natural abandonment of the nests.

There were two classes of nesting failure to be considered: early and late failures. The early failures were due to infertile eggs and the death of a check. Attentiveness persisted four days beyond normal incubation period and at least one day after the chick was dead. In the latter nest, abandonment was preceded by a lengthening of the recess periods.

Of the late failures, three hens abandoned suddenly, while the other two exhibited a series of lengthened recesses. One of the latter two became hypothermic for a portion of the two nights preceding abandonment. The lengthened recesses are thought to be related to the declining food supply. Two chicks remained in both of those and one of the suddenly abandoned nests.

Overall, I thought the article was quite interesting. I found especially interesting the persistance of those hens with early nesting failures. It's as if the hen didn't want to believe her eggs were infertile or her chick had died, just as humans don't like to believe their babies are dead when it happens. I also never realized hens would abandon nests with live chicks in them. It makes me wonder about their reasons for their abandonment, especially in light of the persistance of some of the other hens.

The first trait of the summaries that successfully fulfilled the assignment is a clear explanation of the steps of an experiment. The altitude paper and the hawk paper are confusing; the hummingbird paper is less so, but perhaps only because that article involved an observation less complicated to explain. Even so, the writer is not as clear as she could have been. A key to success seems to be an early statement that tells the reader the purpose and the broad outline of the experiment, so that the rest of the steps are placed in a context.

Another quality of the good papers is attention to the structure of sentences, so that they accurately indicate relations between ideas. The altitude paper, in the next-to-last paragraph, for example, uses three sentences where one well-constructed sentence would have done a much better job: "Mice at high altitudes were less efficient than mice at low altitudes in their use of oxygen during exercise on treadmills." Some students may not possess the sophistication to construct such a sentence, but in giving instructions about this sort of paper, you can warn them to give particular attention to sentence structure.

A third quality of the good papers is an orderly presentation of the information and the student's reaction. The altitude study makes a major mistake in what it includes in the last paragraph. The hummingbird article, though much better organized, does not successfully order the material in the two middle paragraphs: for example, the information on lengthened recesses in paragraph 3 is cut in two by the sentence about hypothermia.

A final quality of excellence is some originality in the student's response to the article. The altitude study has a clue (the writer is most interested in the effect of altitude on exercise), but the summary does not focus on exercise in the way that paragraph 2 would lead the reader to expect. The hawk paper pretends that no response was asked for. The hummingbird paper does the best job, despite the writer's reliance on the word "interesting" (also found in the altitude paper and in I'd like you to guess how many others in this batch). In the hummingbird summary, the writer's genuine involvement shows through, and the reader is treated to a bit of musing that is most effective.

An instructor who has determined what students must do to produce successful responses to this assignment can shape instructions to provide maximum help, warning, and guidance. The teacher might say something like this:

> Your audience for these summaries is made up of members of your own class. You should explain as much as a classmate would need to know, in language familiar to your peers or in biological terms that you define for your readers. Many of you will find that it is hard to explain clearly the experiment described in the article. You can help yourself by first stating its purpose or main outline. Then see whether you can divide the experiment into stages. As you write, pay close attention to the construction of your sentences and try to choose words that express exactly what you mean. You might want to let a friend or roommate read the explanation, after you've tried a draft or two, and put a mark wherever he or she is unclear about the experiment you are describing.

A second aspect you should consider is the focus of your paper and its organization. You may want to summarize the article first and then give your response; if so, make sure that the summary leads toward your particular response. If, earlier in the paper, you provide information about your own interests, work this material smoothly into the flow of your paper.

You may wonder how to express your response. Avoid trite, general phrases such as "This article was very interesting." If it was interesting, say why. You might also discuss any questions you have about the topic or ways in which the article surprised you, confirmed your own ideas, or jogged your curiosity.

I hope that, with these examples as illustrations, you will be able to determine how students can succeed in completing your own assignment and that you can use that insight to determine what to say to them as you send them to their work.

Putting It in Writing

If the teacher writes out the topic choices, instructions about audience and purpose, warnings about focus, and hints about process and strategies for developing the paper, there is likely to be significant payoff for both the students and the teacher: the students will have less chance for confusion, misinterpretation, and you-didn't-say-that's; the teacher, while putting the assignment in writing, will have to be precise, organized, and definitive, and the resulting statement will provide the best possible basis for coaching students throughout the work on their papers.

Chapter Five

Helping Students Achieve Clear Focus

Helping Students Plan

Asking for a Written Prospectus

In addition to giving instructions and warnings when you make the assignment, as discussed on pages 46–48, you can use another technique to help students achieve clear focus: have them prepare a planning tool such as a prospectus, hypothesis, or thesis sentence (perhaps with an accompanying outline or a list of subtopics) that you or an assistant or a group of classmates will check.

Here, for example, is a prospectus form developed by Mildred Steele of Central College in Iowa:

Prospectus for a Research Paper

This is due on_____   Your name_____
The completed paper is due____   (Please fill out both copies of
                                   this sheet. Keep one, and turn in
                                   the other.)

My topic for my research paper is:_____

Some questions I hope my paper can answer are (at least 4 or 5):
1.
2.
3.
4.
5.

At least five sources that I think I will use (give author, title, etc.; include at least one that has been published within the past 1½ years):
1.
2.

3.

4.

5.

I will bring in my rough draft to be checked at least twice during the time I am writing it, once before ＿＿＿＿＿＿＿ and once before ＿＿＿＿＿＿＿.

I have written a research paper before: ☐many times; ☐seldom; ☐never.

The above topic is tentative, but please keep in touch with me if you make a major change in it. Otherwise I will assume that you are progressing in your background reading, note taking, and writing.

Be sure that you base your paper on source material and that you give full credit not only for direct quotations but also for ideas and statistics from others. Choose your quotations with care, and introduce them to your reader in your own words, commenting on their significance. Look up your topic in books, magazines, pamphlets—you might also interview an expert in the field, taking careful notes of what she or he says. Make sure that some of your sources are recent even if you base much of your work on an older source. Many new developments take place each year. Consult your copy of *Writing Research Papers* by Lester for suggestions, particularly for footnote and bibliography form. If you have never written a research paper before, or if you would like to brush up on research methods, ask me for a self-help booklet; in 50 minutes at the library you can give yourself an overview. Give your research paper the time and attention it deserves. You may add something to the world's knowledge.

© *M. R. Steele 1978*

Any format that asks students to state the topic they will cover, the thesis they will develop, or the questions they will answer can be a useful prospectus. You can also use the prospectus assignment sheet, as Steele does, to set deadlines that enforce early starts and to give additional advice and warnings about the writing task ahead. You can return the prospectuses with written suggestions, you can use them as the basis for a student-teacher conference, or you can ask students to share them with classmates and to respond, suggest, and support one another's efforts.

Coaching the Process of Planning

One of your most difficult tasks will be to convince students that sitting down to write a perfect hypothesis, prospectus, or thesis sentence is not the first thing most writers do and that producing a thesis sentence for your eyes cannot be left until the night before it's due. To counteract such practices you may want to set up an early checkpoint, when students talk with you, with a tutor, or with a classmate about their thoughts, their attempts to write, their reading notes, their lists, or whatever other planning strategies they are following.

I have had success, too, when I have had students hand in, along with their thesis sentences, the journals of the writing process that I have asked them to keep, so that I can see what they did to arrive at their plans. Even if I can spare only a minute to glance over a journal, keeping it has forced the student to be more conscious of planning techniques and to engage in enough of them to make a presentable journal.

To help you give more specific guidance about the types of planning available to the writer on the road to a clear focus, here is a list. Urge your students to develop some combination of these methods that proves effective for them.

1. *Talking.* A good way for students to clarify a thesis is to talk through an idea with friends, with a small discussion group that meets during the class hour or outside class, with you, or with a tutor. Sometimes you may want to schedule such talking; at other times you may simply want to encourage your students to arrange it on their own. A helpful source for them is the last half of Peter Elbow's book, *Writing without Teachers* (cited in Ch. 3), which gives suggestions to students about making teacherless discussion groups work for them as writers. Talking can sometimes be a solitary activity: many writers talk out their ideas to a wall or to the sky.

2. *Free writing or taping.* It is often helpful to a writer to blurt out ideas about a general topic. One can do this on tape and then listen to the tape or read a transcription of it, or one can sit down with pen or typewriter and just write for a specific period, say forty-five minutes. The key to this exercise is to keep writing, suspend editorial judgment, forget spelling and punctuation, forget even the attempt to find the right word, and just let the ideas spill out as freely as possible. Naturally, most of what emerges will be rough, irrelevant, mushy, vague, sloppy, and inept. Within such a spurt of ideas, however, the writer tries to find the "center of gravity," the idea that is trying to come through. The writer asks, What am I really saying? One way to handle the spurt of free writing is to circle the three best ideas or underline the most interesting or the most worthwhile sentence. Sometimes that sentence or phrase is the long-sought thesis, or at least the basis for it. Sometimes the student may want to write freely again around one of the ideas that emerged in the original pages or tape. The advantage of free writing is that it gets ideas flowing and sometimes unlocks for the writer a wealth of images, ideas, or insights that might never have emerged in a more constricted planning form such as the list or the outline. Again, Elbow's book—the first half this time—is a good guide to free-writing techniques.

3. *Listing and outlining.* For some writers, or in some writing situations, listing and outlining are highly valuable planning tools, either alone or in conjunction with free writing. A thesis sentence often starts as a list of random thoughts about a subject, gathered from pondering, reading, talking, or observing. Many students need to be encouraged to list ideas more fully and stay longer at the listing stage in order to generate a greater wealth of possible focuses for the paper. With a list in hand, the student begins to play with it, asking, Which ideas might make a good thesis for the paper? Which concepts can I combine? Which items are irrelevant to the topic? Which ideas are subsidiary to other points? Suggest that the student write ideas, evidence, reading notes, or questions on cards; arrange the cards in piles; then ask which of the piles can form the basis for a paper, or what central statement will cover several or all of the piles, or what the student would now say, after two hours of sorting the cards, if someone walked into the room and asked, "What do you want to say about all that material?"

4. *Forming a thesis sentence.* One form of written plan is the thesis sentence. If you require students to hand in thesis sentences, you will probably want to offer some guidelines such as these:

The thesis sentence is not necessarily the first sentence in the paper. The student asked to submit a thesis sentence sometimes pictures it beginning the paper and produces a sentence that is arresting as an introduction but not adequate as a focal point for the paper. Emphasize that the thesis sentence is a planning tool and may not appear per se in the paper. Its function is to guide the writer's work.

The thesis sentence should be a complete sentence. A single word or a phrase or a question is not wrong; it is simply an earlier, incomplete stage. The student must try to write a complete sentence that precisely summarizes what the paper will say.

The thesis sentence should have a workhorse verb. Urge students not to begin thesis sentences with comments like "this paper will discuss." Rather, the subject of the sentence should be the subject of the paper, and the verb should reflect what the writer will say about that subject. Urge also that writers avoid predicates like "is very interesting" or "is controversial" (unless the existence of controversy is the true point of the paper) or "has many results." Such phrases often occur in the working stages, but the writer should search for verbs that more precisely summarize the points of interest, the content of the controversy, or the particular results.

Other planning devices are the hypothesis, the conclusion, and the statement of a problem. Some of these will be more appropriate than others to your particular discipline or to the individual assignment you are giving. In some disciplines, of course, teaching students to form hypotheses is a task in which instructors constantly engage. It is worthwhile to devise ways to connect your instruction on hypothesis formation with the writing you are asking students to do. The key is to steer students away from the notion that the first thing they write for a scientific paper is the first word of page 1. Instead, encourage them first to produce a written hypothesis to use as a planning tool. Next, they might write an outline or draft of the "results" and/or the "discussion" section to serve as a guide to their research. This method of integrating writing and research is described in more detail in *The Science of Scientific Writing,* a student text written by an interdisciplinary group of faculty at the University of California at Davis.[1]

5. *Using Problem-Solving Techniques.* Students may choose a subject they want to write about and then have trouble coming to a thesis statement. At such times, it might be helpful to have them try the techniques of problem formulation used in management. One rhetorician, Richard Larson, has tried to show how teachers can use these problem-formation techniques to help students form thesis statements for their writing.[2] In the next chapter I return to Larson's concept, for once the problem is formulated, he shows how students can use the management strategies of problem solving to develop the content of their papers. Below is an indication of how the question "What is the problem?" can lead the student toward a specific focus.

SITUATION: The student wants to write about abortion but does not know how to formulate a thesis sentence or find a focus.

TEACHER SUGGESTION: *"Try to formulate a problem, either as a question or as a statement."*

RESULT: Student formulates several statements of the problem, any of which could serve as the basis for a paper:

Problem: We need to avoid murder while at the same time preventing the abuse and neglect of unwanted babies.

Problem: Should we pass a constitutional amendment prohibiting abortion?

Problem: At what point is a fetus a human being whom society must protect from being killed?

It strikes me that what Larson did in combining problem-solving techniques with the writing process and what the Davis faculty did in integrating hypothesis formation with scientific writing can be done in other disciplines with other methodologies. You may want to try using the thought processes or the investigative techniques of your particular discipline to help students through the writing process.

6. *Writing a draft of the paper.* Sometimes a thesis and outline do not emerge in their final form until the student has written at least one draft of the paper. For example, it may take the comforting presence of ten

written pages on the first point of the outline to give a writer the courage to realize that the first point is really the thesis of the whole paper.

Avoiding Unproductive Planning

Recent research indicates that four unproductive habits hinder students' writing in the early stages. You may wish to offer this research to your students; it is formulated for a student audience in Linda Flower's *Problem-Solving Strategies for Writing.*[3] Based on taped records of the behavior of students as they completed a writing task, Flower notes that the following weak strategies impede progress:

1. *A trial-and-error approach to producing sentences.* The writer keeps trying, over and over, to write a sentence that will sound good or to phrase an idea in its perfect form. In the early stages of writing, this technique can result in the writer's being obsessed with finding the right word or phrase instead of permitting the flow of ideas. Writers will thus spend precious time in early drafts playing over and over with alternative ways to open a single sentence (In today's world; For today's student; In today's high-pressure society) or circling back to previously rejected ideas and phrases.

2. *Perfect-draft strategy.* The writer begins with the first word of the paper and tries to produce a perfect final copy the first time through. The first paragraph alone may take hours as the student tries to attend at once to everything from focus to commas. In addition, the writer in this way is like the sculptor who casts a work in gold before working out the problems in clay. The writer should have a chance to learn from the process of trying out a draft of the paper before polishing the final form.

3. *Waiting for inspiration.* The writer waits until the whole piece is clearly in mind, or until words and sentences seem ready to flow easily onto the page, instead of using some writing as a technique to prepare, or prime, the flow.

4. *Words looking for an idea.* The writer begins a sentence structure, perhaps following inner cues about how the next idea *would be* expressed, before he or she has an idea that will fill the structure. The result is bombastic, empty prose.

Sending Students to Textbooks

The appropriate sections of composition texts can be helpful to students who need explanations of how to generate ideas and plan their writing. Such books are of several types: some begin with the techniques of writing sentences, then paragraphs, and then the entire paper. That's not the kind you want. Some are arranged by types of themes: the narrative theme, the descriptive theme, the comparative theme, and so on. That's not the kind you want, either. You want a text that takes the student through the steps of the writing process. The first sections of such a guide will generally discuss how to limit the topic, how to go through prewriting tasks, and how to compose an outline. Reading such chapters can be helpful, but encourage your students to adapt, evaluate, and select from what they read. Try to choose a text that acknowledges and describes a variety of prewriting and planning techniques and that reflects the latest research on the process of writing. Several good books will be published the next year or two, including, I hope, my own, whose present working title is *Writing in All Disciplines.* Meanwhile, the text for science students and Flower's book, both of which I've already mentioned, have recently been joined by *Writing in the Arts and Sciences* by Elaine Maimon and others.[4]

Responding to a Student's Planning Statement

Responding to a prospectus, thesis sentence, hypothesis, or statement of a problem is a technique that may take some practice on the part of the instructor, the tutor, or the writer's peers. It is useful to begin with a checklist: Is the formulation expressed as a complete sentence? Does it have a working verb? Are the words specific? Is it a subject that the student can develop from the available resources? When you or someone else works face to face with the student, the next step is often best handled as a series of questions addressed to the student, designed to stimulate further planning. Ask the writer, "What will convince your reader of the truth of your statement? What sort of evidence or development do you need to establish your points? What does your audience need from you? What do you want to happen to your reader as a result of having read your paper?" The student's answers to these queries will often result either in recognition of the weaknesses of the plan or in clues for its further development.

If you are not face to face with the student, you can give a useful response to a thesis or other planning statement by written comments. Alternatively, you might call together and work with a group of students whose planning statements show problems. Or arrange for each student who has problems to get help from two successful peers. The last two techniques will take less time than individual responses.

Whatever form your response takes, it is important not only to describe to the student where the planning *statement* needs change but also to learn what planning *behavior* the student has followed and to suggest helpful planning strategies.

Identifying and Remedying Unfocused Papers

When a paper first comes in, resist the temptation to read it straight through word by word, jumping on the first flaw you see. Instead, begin by scanning the paper for clues to its thesis and focus. One indication is paragraph length. If the paper consists of a number of very short paragraphs, chances are that the student has tried to cover too much territory and has not developed any of the ideas in sufficient depth. In fact, the paper may actually be nothing more than the first paragraphs of several potential papers.

Another way to determine quickly whether the paper has a sufficiently limited topic is to read the first and last paragraphs of the paper and ask yourself whether they have a common theme and emphasis. If they have little to do with each other, you may find that the student has switched subjects somewhere in the middle and has covered too much. You can sometimes find out where the student went wrong just by reading the first sentence of each paragraph.

If such a quick scan reveals that the writer indeed lacks focus or has tried to cover too much, and if your time is limited, you may perhaps choose not to spend time analyzing the faults in the paint job but to return the paper immediately for a reworking of the whole architectural plan. Begin by explaining that the essay is not a failure but a beginning; that many writers plan first in generalities and then narrow them down to more specific and limited topics. You might request that the student tell you, or write down in a single sentence, the main idea of this draft of the paper. The attempt to do so will both show what's wrong and help discover a clearer topic. If the area is still too broad, you might ask some of the unanswered questions, just to show the student how shallow the development is and how the paper too soon scurried on to another major point. Then ask the student to select just one of the topics in the paper or to conceive a single, more limited concept and then write another draft.

In the essay on women's liberation printed below, for example, a scan of paragraph length and a reading of the first and last paragraphs will, in a few seconds, reveal that the student has introduced several ideas outside the one he begins with—that women must accept the responsibilities and hardships that go with equality. The paper does not follow its originally stated thesis, nor does it develop any of its points in adequate depth.

Women's Liberation

I, like most male chauvinists, believe that equality for women is a valid fight, but I also feel that if women want to be liberated, they are going to have to be willing to go the distance. By this, women are going to be exactly equal as their male rivals. This includes, women in the armed forces, hard labor and many other jobs in which men have been more concerned with.

The advantages for women, as equals, except in the cases of equal pay for equal work, is very few. I really cannot see how women could possibly be benefited, by wanting to come out of their protective home, mother, housewife, shells, to work along side a man in some kind of hard backbreaking job. About the only logical advantage that a women would have would be where equal work gets equal pay. If women are qualified and can perform the same work that a man does, she should receive equal pay.

In contrast to the advantages, the disadvantages, I feel would hurt a liberated women than help. For full total equality, women would be subject to the draft and would have to serve alongside men in time of war. Any woman that would be for this, rather than a home life is crazy.

I think that women started the equality fight and have carried it much to far. They have carried the movement to a point where people are either joking or don't think the fighters are to serious about what they say.

It has been said that if women want to become exactly equal as men they will have to give up some of their luxuries. This includes, rights to child support, alimony in divorce settlements, abortion at the demand of the female, and centers for child care.

In the case of alimony, you can plainly see who is the one being discriminated against, yes the male. Alimony laws are unfair to men in the way it lets the women in a divorce settlement collect off her X husband even though the marriage breakup could have been the fault of the women. If equality laws are passed this will be one thing that most women will miss dearly.

As for child support, it could be looked upon as the joint responsibility of both parents for the welfare of their children.

In abortion cases, in some states it only requires only the consent of the female to have a medical abortion. This to would change along with other laws.

Some analysts feel that the Womens' Liberation movement is being carried on by white middle class educated females for whom it would benefit the most. The reason for this assumption is the lack of the movement to attract working, lower class, and black women. It can be said then that maybe these women do not want to become liberated. Most women are satisfied with this and have started organizations, such as the Pussycats to denounce the Liberation Movement. This organization is made up of women who do not want to become so-called equals with their men.

I feel that in the long run women are going to have to chose between a protective life, or one that they are asking for, one of total equality. They are going to have to give a little in order to receive a little. In contrast to other liberation movements in the

U.S. such as the gay people, blacks and other minorities, the
women's libers will probably have a tougher time trying to convince
society that their fight is a just and valid cause.

This paper need take only a minute or two of your time. In fact, it's not a paper at all, in the finished sense; it's a spurt of ideas and feelings out of which—with some encouragement, some guidance, and some questions from you—the student may be able to make a coherent, viable statement. When you have scanned it, you can immediately suggest that the student write another draft developing in more detail just one of the aspects touched on—that women must be willing to accept the responsibilities and hardships of being equal or that homemakers have little to gain from liberation or that women should receive equal pay for equal work or that women will have a tougher time than blacks or gays in convincing the American people that their cause is just. The teacher will also want to ask some questions that will lead to more reading and more careful support for whatever statement the student will make. The instructor may also give some warning concerning other problems in the paper: "Read your draft aloud to yourself so that you can hear the patterns—for example, 'in which women have been more concerned with' and 'would hurt women than help.' " But the teacher's essential philosophy is that the student first needs to master the principle of limiting and focusing the topic and supporting it sufficiently. When he has accomplished that, he can concentrate on other concerns, such as the acute problem with syntax or the spelling of "too."

Don't forget the value of praise as a teaching tool, even in a paper as badly flawed as this one. Paragraph one, though the language is clumsy, sets out a topic and suggests several appropriate subtopics. Although the paper frustrates the reader by not developing as this first paragraph leads one to expect, a seminal plan is present in the opening paragraph, and some of the paper's body begins to develop those points. Your most effective approach might be to emphasize what fits and encourage enlargement, instead of focusing on the chaos of the rest.

In the next student essay the paragraphs are of substantial length, so you don't have the short-paragraph clue to the paper's fuzzy focus. Again, however, it is possible to identify the focus problem quickly. Begin by reading the first two sentences and then the last sentence.

Dostoevsky's Notes from Underground

Notes from Underground has as its original title A Confession,
and it appears to be just that. Dostoevsky seems to be revelling
against the socialist ideology prevalent in Russia at the time.
He once went along with the idea that cruelty is produced by
social conditions, and that one can then alter social conditions and

Thesis?
)Thesis?

forever remove cruelty from the world. An event in Dostoevsky that typifies his early socialist thoughts occurred when one day he was on the way to the School of Engineering that he was attending at the time. He was looking out of the window of a bar when a coach stopped in front of the window and a man stepped out and came into the bar, drank some vodka and left in a rush, getting back up on the carriage and beating the driver cruelly on the neck. Bending over from the blows the driver beat the horses equally violently. Dostoevsky also went along with the idea that if one only allowed him to do it, man would react in his own best interests; this is necessary if socialism is to work.

Dostoevsky was subsequently sent to Siberia a few years later and stayed for ten years; this helped quite a bit in altering his ideas about man's nature. Fyodor devoted his entire first section in Notes from Underground to demonstrate the point that given a chance man would not react in his best interests but would rather do all he could to prove to himself that he has free choice. Avranhim Yanmolissky writes about Notes from Underground in his book Dostoevsky that "Human nature, his hero insists, is not so simple. Man is at the bottom an irrational creature. He not only loves creation but also destruction, not only well-being but also suffering; he loathes the mechanical, the predictable, the final. Reason is but part of the self; he knows what it has succeeded in learning, and some things it will never learn, all that's certain about history is that it has little to do with reason. What man wants is not to act rationally and to his own advantage but to act as he chooses." But what, then, of Plato??? In the Republic, at the end of Book I, we have the following passage between Socrates and Thrasymachos:

I'm lost., is this D's voice or yours?

> Soc: "The just man then is happy, and the unjust miserable."
> Thras: "Let it be so", he said.
> Soc: "But to be miserable is not profitable, to be happy, is."
> Thras: "Of course."
> Soc: "The, O Thrasymachos; blessed among men! Injustice is
> never more profitable than justice!"

Seems unconnected. Relate to what you've just quoted

If one values suffering as well as well-being then it is profitable to suffer sometimes. We can now see that injustice is sometimes profitable and justice unprofitable. Perhaps Dostoevsky felt this way partly because during that time in Russia the courts would let violent murderers go because they were victims of bad social conditions.

When? is a alist?

It is in this spirit that Fyodor speaks of such things as science which was believed to be, at that time in Russia, the miracle that was going to improve social conditions such that people can be happy all the time. The author, Chernyshevsky, speaks of the crystal palace that housed the London great exhibitions

When does D speak so, and how related to Notes?

of 1851, an exhibition of science and industry. Dostoevsky mentions this crystal tower as being an object of scorn, that man is not rational and needs an inattainable goal, and one should not accept the simplest logic (such as two times two is four) because logic builds on itself and will take over his thoughts in all areas. Man should be free to choose his own nature.

I'm confused
Relate to idea
that man is
or wants to
prove his
freedom

Notes from Underground presents a paradox to us because the underground man sometimes uses the fact that others have persecuted him as a reason for his own cruelty yet advocates the ability of the human to choose his own nature. The underground man recalls, when he was in school, his classmates bothering him; perhaps this is because it actually happened to Dostoevsky when he was in engineering school. In actuality the entire story is a paradox because he is trying to explain his reasons for behaving so cruelly to Liza and his very explanation sets up conventions, of the two times two variety, by which he behaves.

Confusing to me

Toward the end of the book he sees himself when describing to Liza a scene he had witnessed that morning. He had seen a dead prostitute being carried out, in a coffin, of a basement room and being dropped careflessly in the snow. The underground man is beginning to realize that merely to revel against a mechanistic universe and to cling to one's private whim is death because society no longer cares for you. His crowning cruelty is when he gives money to Liza for her kindness. With this act he shows himself to be totally divorced from life. I can now see why Dostoevsky then turned to Christianity for support, because it offers an inattainable goal during life (heaven) and it also lets you enter into society through love.

I'm confused.

How related?

How related?

The paper is a promising "muse" but not yet a clear communication to a reader. What is your main idea—Notes as refutation of D's early socialist ideas? The contradictions within Notes? If so, which is the central paradox you will treat? Or are you explaining D's turn to Christianity? Compose a single sentence expressing your main idea; then line up your subpoints to develop it.

To help you achieve clarity, try telling your idea or reading your draft to a friend who will stop you wherever she or he gets confused. My marginal notes have shown my confusion about this draft.

To achieve economy, take as an example your first 1½ ¶s. Eliminate information not necessary to your point. Condense the rest, avoiding repetitious or dead phrases. Use these techniques for your final drafts of the essay.

The first sentence proposes one idea—the novel as confession. The second suggests that the paper will treat the novel as a "revellion" (rebellion) against socialist ideology. The last sentence deals with Dostoevsky's turn to Christianity. The body of the paper centers on two topics: (1) *Notes* as a refutation of Dostoevsky's earlier socialism and (2) the contradictions of the protagonist in *Notes*. The paper is a "thinking out loud" piece in which these two questions dominate. The next steps must be to decide on one main point and then to order the body of the paper around that focus, meanwhile improving on the writer's present lack of clarity and his wordiness.

The way to begin is to impress on the student the extent and the nature of the reader's confusion, as I did in my marginal comments. Next, ask what is the main idea. Then ask the student to go through each paragraph, justifying it in terms of the main idea or else omitting it. Such a technique will probably lead to the elimination of the first sentence and perhaps also the material on Dostoevsky's Christianity. The student should revise or delete the material on socialism and on the paradoxes in *Notes,* depending on what the thesis is.

Now ask the student to plan a series of subtopics that will support the main focus of the paper. Finally, work with matters of economy (as I have done in my comment about the first $1\frac{1}{2}$ paragraphs) and with clarity of expression. The clarity problem may take care of itself once the focus is clear, or it may be amended when the student reads the paper to a friend who voices confusion, or it may require your guidance in matters of diction and syntax.

Focus in Research Papers

The bumpy road that leads to and from the long quotation in the previous paper is one example of a common focus problem: the faulty integration of quoted and paraphrased source material. Actually the problem has two aspects: (1) the student may be too dependent on quoted and paraphrased material, and/or (2) the student may fail to integrate quoted material smoothly and logically within the paper's own progression.

In discussing the first aspect, we often use the term "cut-and-paste jobs." The paper is little more than a spliced string of quotations or paraphrases lifted from the sources the student has used. To the student, we may say, "You use too much quoted material" or "More of the paper should be your own thoughts." But trying to add more original thoughts to a paper is like trying to add more chocolate chips after the cookies are baked.

A more helpful approach is to treat the overuse of sources as a problem of focus. You can tell students that they must not be captives of another author's focus but must instead establish their own, using what is relevant from the works of other authors to support their own points and their own direction. They must also meet the needs of their own audience and accomplish their own purpose, not some other author's.

In the early reading stages, I have found it helpful simply to require that students consult a certain minimum number of sources on a given issue. Reading more than one opinion, or even more than one presentation of straightforward facts, tends to free the student from the phrasing, tone, or point of view used by one author.

In the planning stages, the student must establish an original thesis that is limited, focused, and sharp. You should be right in there coaching at this point, because it is here that the foundation is laid either for a paper that is a shadow of some research source or for a paper that adopts a clear and original voice.

When the student decides on a focus, ask what sort of support, evidence, or information from written sources is necessary to develop that thesis effectively for the intended readers. A list of the required props sends students to the library like partying scavengers to the doors of neighbors, knowing it's a hairpin they need, not a match. Armed with agendas, they may alter or refocus their topics on the basis of further reading, but they are less likely to be tempted to imitate slavishly some Pied Piper's tune. Furthermore, reading with one's own goals and questions, say the reading experts, helps improve reading comprehension.

In the student paper below, the assignment was to read part of the anthropology text, select some particular point of interest, and write a short paper exploring and explaining that point. The assignment thus wisely encouraged focus, but the student will need help, in future drafts, to sharpen the focus of this essay.

The Early Years in Anthropology

One of the fundamental aggravations in anthropology is the paradox that this social science rarely employs use of the scientific method as a mechanism in its theoretical explanations. It can't. We cannot reduce explanations of human culture to simple syllogisms with pure deductive reasoning. Characteristic of anthropological field work is the unavoidable subjective viewpoint in theory building, an extraneous variable which Manners and Kaplan use to guage the relative 'immaturity' of anthropology as a science. "Much of what is called theory tends to be circular, tautological and ad hoc." (M & K in 'Notes') Manners and Kaplan point out a second paradox of theory development in noting that greater theoretical demands are made on the social sciences than the hard sciences.

The constant evaluation and reevaluation of theories is indicative of the lack of established laws in the social sciences in

explanations of human culture. Constant challenges to viewpoints
or methods keeps the discipline on its toes as anthropologists try
to explain the why's.

In attempting to explain the first why's in nineteenth century
anthropology, theory was employed. Theory necessarily implies some
sort of generalization, and comparativist anthropology attempted to
answer problems by analysis of the associated data which was
available.

There could be no theory in the perfect sense of the word
derived from pure relativistic anthropology. Manners and Kaplan
observe that the relativists leave us with the remainder to study
holistically, and to avoid being swayed by our own cultural
preconceptions. (M & K, Cult. Th, p. 6) In merely recognizing
the uniqueness of all cultures, relativists ignored cross-cultural
associations which are useful in analyzing the most important of all
the why's; they go no further than 'their own back yard' as though
afraid to venture speculation. Manners and Kaplan refer to the
destruction of many of the theories of the nineteenth century
armchair speculators by the continual pouring in of new facts as a
deterrent to forming or trusting generalizations.

The early theoretical generalizations were responsible for the
growth of anthropology as a discipline and encouraged the collection
of new data to attempt to resolve debated theories or to create new
ones in ethnological research. Clearly, comparativism was the real
basis for anthropological research. The evolutionists of the
nineteenth century "laid down the foundations for an organized
discipline where none had existed before," (M & K, p. 43) and
utilized the comparative method in analyzing stages of evolution in
human culture.

Spencer's rich background in embryology and morphology was the
basis for his selection of the biological organism for his analogy
in the development of cultures. He also referred to the human body
and its countless systems in describing the structure and functioning
of the interrelated parts to the whole.

Implicit to the growth of an organism is increase in size and
and number, with a corresponding increase in structure. Spencer
secondly recognizes differentiation of parts after the early stages
of integration, and that the vitality of both social and biological
organisms increase as fast as the functions within its structure
become specialized. (M & K, 27)

Spencer implies a direct unilineal descent in his essay on
cultural evolution. He treats his concept of a culture as if it has
no interaction with the rest of the world. While Spencer's
biological organisms may have been studied in vitro, human culture
can not be. There may be contacts between isolated cultures which

give society an imput of cultural technology or differentiation
before its (evolutionary) time was due.

Morgan, on the other hand defined several stages of evolution.
Spencer did not type them but offered that along the line of social
evolution, one point was more advanced than another. Morgan's
approach was similar to Spenser's due to its overriding unilineal
approach to evolution in culture. He sees changes in the Arts of
Subsistence as the forerunners to changes in culture. Morgan
distinguishes his periods of culture based on its materialistic
technology, and refuses to offer the notion that a culture could be
trapped between periods, that is having characteristics of two
periods. Clearly, Morgan and Spenser were easy prey for the
diffusionists in implying no contact between relatively simple and
advanced cultures. In describing his evolutionary stages, Morgan
does not explain the reasons for how the culture advanced to the
next period. Certainly, it wasn't pre-determined that a culture
would have to invent the bow and arrow to escape the title of
savage, and achieve the promotion to barbarian. Further, a
culture's technology is in accordance with its ecological framework,
and conditions may exempt it from Morgan's advancement through
technology. A fishing community may have a complex alphabet and
writing system with no need for the bow and arrow or smelting
technology.

Tylor, however, is the only evolutionist to querry how
diffusion may upset the evolutionary progression. (Tylor, 68)
He discusses 'survivals' to comparatively analyze cultural elements
which had their origin in archaic forms. Tylor also differs in
that he used cross-cultural comparisons of religious complexes
rather than materialistic or organic evolutionistic approaches. He
does not adhere to a unilineal progression in his four stages. In
referring to them as stages, he still does imply a natural
progression in complexity from animism to science. Tylor has an
interesting approach, but he places too much emphasis on religion,
while ignoring other aspects of culture. This restricts his
analysis entirely too much, and limits any kind of broad generalizations. All three theorists, and others of their time used the
comparative method to formulate their approaches to evolutionary
understanding of culture. While evolutionism is decidedly not the
best theoretical approach, it initiated a formidable quest for
theory in anthropology.

A reading of the first and last paragraphs of this essay reveals that
they have little relationship to each other. The first four sentences make
the reader expect that the paper will explain the methods of formulating
theory in anthropology—a field in which neither the scientific method

nor syllogistic reasoning is entirely satisfactory. Following this line, we would expect the discussions of Spencer, Morgan, and Tylor to focus on their early struggles to formulate viable theories despite the difficulties inherent in the discipline. The actual discussions of each anthropologist, however, do not fulfill these expectations. Instead, they are a hodgepodge, consisting either of unfocused summaries of the anthropologists' theories or of unsupported interpretations such as "he places too much emphasis on religion" or "evolutionism is decidedly not the best approach." In these descriptions of the anthropologists, the student does not seem to know clearly who the audience is, what the main point of the essay is, or which of the many available facts about Spencer, Morgan, and Tylor ought to be included and which omitted.

Interspersed in the discussion of the three theorists, or tacked on to the end of the essay, are several statements that could serve as thesis sentences but do not:

- Nineteenth century theories were destroyed by the inpouring of new facts, a process which deterred anthropologists from forming or trusting generalizations.
- Early theoretical generalizations were responsible for the growth of anthropology as a discipline.
- Comparativism was the real basis for anthropological research.
- Evolutionism is not the best theoretical approach but it initiated a quest for theory in anthropology.
- Anthropology progressed from relativism, which ignored cross-cultural associations, to Spencer and Morgan who followed a unilinear approach, to finally Tylor, who for the first time dealt with diffusion.

If I were responding to this student in writing, I would ask for a statement of audience and purpose. I would underline possible thesis sentences and urge the student to choose one of them, or some other statement, as the thesis of the essay. Then I would suggest some techniques for developing the thesis.

In an oral conference, I would ask who the audience is. Then, either as a stand-in for that audience or in my own role as reader, I would voice my confusion about what the real point of the essay is. I would ask for verbal clarification of the essay's thesis, and then would have the student make a list of the sorts of information needed to support and develop that thesis.

We can expect that, in the process of rewriting around a clear focus, the student will clarify the explanations of the anthropological theories and smooth out some awkward sentences. Consequently, I would not at this point focus on the stylistic problems, even though they are acute. I would probably voice a warning, however, about problems such as those in paragraph 8, and I might even take a few moments to focus on that paragraph as an example of the kind of revision that will have to be done for the final draft.

If such a paragraph appeared in the final draft, I would certainly urge revision of its confused verb tenses, its misplacement of phrases (for example "in his essay on cultural evolution" should precede "implies"), its confusion of pronoun reference in the second sentence, and its imprecise, jargonistic diction (the term "cultural technology or differentiation" didn't mean anything even to the teacher of the course).

In the next essay, the student has used two or three sources as the basis for an informative essay on the Chisso Company's poisoning of the environment around the Japanese city of Minamata. The sources, not the student, are in control.

The Strange Disease

Possible focus— the outward diffusion   *intro.*

The chemical company called Chisso poisoned the fishing waters of Minamata, poisoned the aquatic food chain, and eventually poisoned a great number of the inhabitants. Chisso poured industrial piosons through waste pipes until Minamata Bay was a sludge dump.

2

As the poisoning continued, fishing in the bay continued and the fishermen knew only that their catches were getting smaller. They ate much of the fish that they did not sell or gave it to neighbors. If a family member became ill, that person received more of the best fish available, for the Japanese believe "a sick body must have the best food we can provide."

Many of those dependent upon the fish and shellfish began to show symptoms of an unusual sickness. Many became severely ill. Some died. The sickness, its cause a mystery, became known as the "strange disease." It was also noted that cats showed the strange symptoms; went crazy and often flung themselves into the sea as "suicides."

3

The first clear case was reported in 1953. Looking back, it becomes obvious that earlier deaths and illnesses were connected with the "strange disease." One clue comes from the Japanese mother's tradition--disappearing now--of preserving her baby's umbilical cord in a box. Examination of the cords of children who had the disease would, years later, reveal traces of the cause.

Possible focus— wooing Chisso, then being destroyed by Chisso   *1*

Minamata was a restful farming and fishing area, sprawling out from its downtown center to clusters of small homes on the gentle hillsides and along the indentations and cirves of small natural harbors protected by seawalls.

Minamata was also a factory town, dominated by the Chisso corporation, once a mere carbide and fertilizer company, now a petrochemical company and a maker of plastics. Back in 1907, village leaders felt the winds of prosperity when they convinced the founder of the company to build in Minamata.

By 1925, Chisso was paying Minamata fishermen a very small indemnity for damage to their fishing areas. Chisso didn't mind. The theory was to continue to dump and to buy off the complainers with the smallest possible pay-off. It was cheaper to pay than to care.

The fishing began to deteriorate. In 1932, Chisso began the production of acetaldehyde (a substance used in making drugs, plastics and perfumes). The process for the production of acetaldehyde required the use of a mercury compound as a catalyst. In the 1930's Chisso also expanded into Korea. These days must have been Chisso's finest.

The early 1950's saw a strong upward turn in the production and sales of acetaldehyde. The company realized they would need a new factory and new techniques and they raced to make the most possible money from the old Minamata plant.

It was early in 1956 that the "strange disease" took on the proportions of an epidemic and finally became known as the "Minamata disease." In April of 1956, a five-year-old girl entered the pediatrics department of Chisso's Minamata hospital suffering symptoms of severe brain damage. She could not walk. She was in severe delirium.

Among neighbors, an uneasiness developed. Then appeared a fear that the disease was contagious. The fear soon turned neighbor against neighbor. People began to notice that the "suicidal" cats - in fact, almost all cats - had disappeared.

A number of causes were investigated, from alcoholism to syphillis. No cause was found.

On May 1, 1956, Dr. Hajime Hosokawa of the Chisso company Hospital discovered that fish diets were directly related to the outbreaks.

Some investigators began claiming that nearly sixty poisons were being dumped into the sea by Chisso. Chisso sidestepped the problems and denied that the factory or its employees could be held responsible. The theories went even as far as the belief that ammuniation sunk at the end of the war was the cause.

By July of 1959, a group of Kunamoto University reported that organic mercury was the cause. Many committees were formed. One met only four times, then mysteriously disappeared. It had been sponsored by the Japanese Chemical Association, of which Chisso was a member. Another committee reported bluntly that the cause was definitely mercury poisoning, and was disbanded the next day. Chisso was still in charge.

In October, 1959, a carefully concealed series of cat *Relate to*
experiments by Chisso's own Dr. Hosokawa proved Chisso's guilt *other Hos.*
to its management. He simply fed some acetaldehyde effluent   *¶*
directly to a cat. He was forbidden more of the effluent and was
taken off the experiments. Chisoo had Hosakawa's proof.

In 1959, members of the Fishermen's Union stormed the factory,
demanding further indemnity and a cleaning of the bay. After a
bitter fury produced many injuries, the fishermen gave up.

After 1959, the protest ceased, fishermen returned to fishing,
patients became quiet and still Chisso continued to make a profit.
Chisso did install a "Cyclator" designed to treat waste water, that
turned out to be a token gesture due to the fact that it was often
bypassed.

In spite of its many denials, Chisso finally found itself
forced into court in 1969 - after a trial lasting nearly four years,
the court concluded that Chisso had continued to poison the waters
until 1968, when Chisso stopped the mercury method of production
because the system had become outmoded.

The pollution had affacted as many as 10,000 people. Some may
not even be aware that they are victims, as the mercury silently
steals health from the victim.

Were the winds of prosperity really blowing on Minamata, or
were they more like the winds of misfortune and suffering?

The story you tell is full of convincing and vivid detail. Now what you need is to find a focus — a reason for telling the story — a dominant impression or idea you want to convey to your reader. Write that focus in a sentence.

Now tell the details in such a way that they support your main focus. You will want to avoid repetition (see my "2" and "3") and to avoid misplacement of material that belongs earlier or later (see my "1"). But you won't necessarily follow my sequence 1, 2, 3, Your sequence will be determined by your focus.

The repetitions may be an initial clue to this paper's problems. It becomes clear that the first four paragraphs are paraphrased from one
source and the following material from another with the result that paragraph 5 starts again at the beginning of the chronology. The confusion
about the date and role of Hosokawa's experiments may also spring from
the student's having taken two or three versions of the Minamata story
and pasted them together end to end. The seams show badly.

It is tempting to focus, in fact, on the seams. But if we merely urge the elimination of repetition and the blending of the various accounts, we do not solve the whole problem. The real dilemma is that the student does not know the audience, the purpose, or the focus for the essay. There are some isolated clues that might eventually be developed into a focus—for example, the first paragraph's emphasis on the environmental diffusion of the poison or the last paragraph's contrast between the village's initial wooing of the company and its eventual destruction by the company. Other aspects of the story could be the center of the account— for example, the eventual cessation of pollution, not because society was able to stop Chisso, but because the mercury process became unprofitable. In a talk with the student, or in a written comment, you should concentrate on achieving a focus, a reason for telling the story of Minamata, a primary impression the writer wants to leave with the reader. Then you can encourage the student not merely to hook together the various accounts but to tell the Minamata story so that it supports the focus and purpose of the essay.

I said earlier that two problems are subsumed under the heading "Focus in Research Papers." The first, as we have discussed, is that students are too dependent on source materials and do not establish individual purpose and focus. The second is that students sometimes do not know how to make a smooth weave as they bring in quotations or other source material. Probably the best way for them to get a sense of how to blend in source material is to have them read articles and books by writers who do this successfully. In addition, there are rhetoric texts and writing handbooks that treat the issue specifically, and you might encourage students to turn to such a manual. First, though, you can give them these helpful guidelines:

1. *Use direct quotations only if the exact words of the source are important.* Students will often include large blocks of quoted material simply because the language is smoother than anything they could write, or because they can't call up other words to express the message, or because they don't really understand the source precisely enough to paraphrase it. If this last is the case, you may have to explain the source or suggest that students not use materials that are written over their heads.

2. *Resource material should be relevant to the topic and should prove what the writer intends it to prove.* You often find that the student has brought in a quotation or source that is an anomaly. Yet the writer goes on as though the point had been successfully supported. Either the student has not understood the source or has not been able to master the mode of substantiation or the pattern of thinking needed to prove the point. One way to work with such a student is to remove the source material momentarily from consideration, ask for a statement of the point the student is trying to make, and then ask the student to explain the type of support or proof

that would establish or develop that point. If the student succeeds in this, then ask what point the offending quotation makes. If the student comprehends the source, he or she will recognize that the point of the source material does not suit the purpose at hand. If the student cannot perform this last step, there is probably a reading comprehension problem.

3. *The text must provide a proper context for the quotation or paraphrase.* Have the student consider which of the following functions the words around the quotation must perform for the intended audience:

    a. Give background information to help the reader place the source material in context.

    b. Summarize unquoted parts of the source.

    c. Evaluate the reliability of the source.

    d. State the main point that the source supports.

    e. Relate the main point of the source to other parts of the essay.

Focus in Journals

It is possible to have your students do some writing that is not meant to be "worked up"—in journals, for example. When this is the case, expectations should be made clear all around. Your response to the writing will change. You will want to respond personally to the ideas expressed, to prod further thinking, to push toward more creative musing on the next pages of the journal, or to encourage a greater volume of writing.

Sometimes, however, you will want crafted work not only in the formal papers students write in your class but also in the more informal genres. The journal or the personal reflection can be as carefully worked up as any other genre. (You will be struggling, however, against students' inclination to equate journal form with one-draft musing.) Let's take, for example, a rambling section from one student's journal, kept for a class in cross-cultural communication.

From a Student Journal

An area that really stands out in my mind is that of social status. If all men are to be equal, why do we even have this social status? Yet I have a better question: "Have you even seen a poor politician, doctor, or lawyer?" This status kick means nothing to me, as long as it continues to be based on an individual's income level. To change things for the better, I think people should be hired because of their qualitifications rather than status and money. Many of your young, brilliant, and capable people end up doing a gas station job or being a garbage man, simply because they lack enough financial resources to be for instance a lawyer. The example of garbage men and gas station attendants being low in status is also a big hoax.

If this paragraph is not going to be revised, you will want either to listen to the musing without comment or to express appreciation for the sharing of the writer's thoughts or to encourage perseverance in the keeping of the journal. In addition, you may want to respond as you would in an oral conversation, refuting or questioning the writer's ideas so that the student in turn responds; the journal then may become dialogue.

On the other hand, you may want to encourage the student to "write up" some ideas as a formal essay. If so, you are changing genres, and you should encourage the types of reading, support, and proof appropriate to formal academic papers. You will treat this journal entry as a preparation for an academic paper.

A third alternative is to ask the student to revise and polish the paragraph *as a journal entry*. The student then crafts the writing more carefully but does not change its genre; it remains personal, informal, and conversational. You will want to encourage the student to establish a focus first, since lack of focus is the primary trait that keeps this paragraph from communicating well. Then you will want to help the student develop appropriate ways to flesh out the main idea in a manner consonant with the genre. Finally, syntax, punctuation, and other aspects will need attention. Remember that in informal or personal genres a discursive or stream-of-consciousness organization may be appropriate.

A more carefully crafted version of the journal paragraph might well look like this:

```
    I don't believe that the social status of your job should play
the role it does in your life.  My aunt should introduce me to her
friends with the same pride in her voice, whether she can announce
"Dennis plans to go into law" or "Dennis plans to go into garbage
collection."  But then I ask myself, do I view my own friends
differently, even in subtle ways, depending on what they do or plan
to do?  Have my best high school friend Ronnie and I grown apart
because our paths are separate now or because I have subtly pulled
back from him, since I'm in college and he's slicing joints at our
local meat market back home?  If it is true that in our society we
cannot help being affected by social status, I wonder whether there
are societies in which social status is less influential, or even
nonexistent--where Aunt Jane really would be equally proud, and
where Ronnie and I, always invited to the same parties, would be
social equals?
```

The journal entry has not abandoned its contractions or its personal, musing tone. It has, however, focused on a single idea and developed it with vivid detail. Thoughts are carefully arranged, and the paragraph has a clear beginning and end.

Focus within a Genre Requiring Conventional Sequence

In some types of writing, such as lab reports, clinical reports, scientific articles, cases, legal briefs, and so on, there is an accepted order of parts. For example, the scientific report generally begins with an introduction that defines the question and its importance. Then there is a review of the literature, followed by a section on materials and methods, followed by results and, finally, discussion. It is entirely appropriate, when such conventional formats exist, for you to give students explicit instructions about the expected format. But a pitfall for them is thinking that the conventional sequence is the only focus they will need. Into the various required sections they throw whatever seems to them to have something to do with the title of that section. Thus the scientific report emerges with too much detail about one part of the methodology and not enough detail about another, or the introduction does not appropriately support the results and the discussion. The paper resembles one of those puzzles in which, by turning the parts, the child can create a creature with the face of Goofy, the body of Mickey, and the feet of Donald. All the bodily parts are there, but they are not organized around a coherent center. Thus, when teaching students to write in genres that have conventional sequences, make clear that the content of each section must work toward the central purpose and focus of the particular report. It often helps to ask students for written statements of their audience and purpose and for single-sentence summaries of the main ideas they want to communicate.

The same problem can arise when you suggest a sequence for a term paper or an essay test. A possible organizational pattern may be inherent in the questions you ask in your assignment, or you may try to give students a solid start by writing down some possible subtopics. If you give out anything that looks like a set of sections or subtopics, students may assume that the sequence itself is the only focus they need and may believe that, if they write something in each section, the paper will hold together. It is wise, in phrasing such questions—or in giving such directions on exams, essays, and term papers—to remind students that they need a clear focus to determine the content of their subsections, the order of material within the sections, and the emphasis that any single idea receives.

Irrelevance and Imbalance

Sometimes a focus problem shows up as the presence of irrelevant material in an otherwise well-focused paper. Ask such a student to identify the topic sentence and then justify each major point according to its relevance to that topic. Asked to explain ideas in this way, the student will often see the irrelevance.

A related problem is that sometimes students give truly pertinent material more space or more emphasis than its relative importance justifies. In this case, it is usually helpful to ask the student, "Why do you give more space to point X than to point Y?" or "Why do you give one fifth of your total essay to idea Z?" Once again, when asked to justify a writing decision, the student can often recognize bloated or underemphasized material.

A combination of these faults is illustrated in the first part of this student teacher's analysis of a high school art program (names of towns and individuals have been changed).

An Analysis of Prairietown's High School Art Department

Prairietown is basically an agricultural community. Most of the area is either directly concerned with agriculture or indirectly affected by the farm area. Most of the retail stores are designed to aid the agricultural area by providing supplies for the work done there.

Some of the residents work for industry. Two main industries are established in Prairietown, these being Drow Corporation and United Manufacturing Company. As well as residents working for these two industries, some are employed by smaller industries and also by two major industries in Queenstown: Best Window Company, and Vreelen Manufacturing Company.

[The paper goes on to describe the school, its art facilities, and its art program and then makes several suggestions for improvement, which are, in summary:

A. Place more emphasis on applied and environmental art, which will be practical for Prairietown students as adults.

B. Develop better rapport between the Prairietown citizens and the high school art department.

C. Arrange for more flexible, dispersed seating in the art room, and move more activities outside to avoid a feeling of stifled immobility.]

In your comments about the first two paragraphs of the paper, your main task is to question the student's reasons for including or excluding details about Prairietown, stressing the sketch of the town must be relevant to the main point: suggested changes in the school's art department. Thus your written, taped, or oral comment might go something like this:

Of all the thousands of things one could say about Prairietown, you can include only a few; therefore you should include or omit details on the basis of whether or not they help you make your most important point clear. Your main purpose in this paper is to suggest changes in the art department. What details about the community would help convince the reader that those changes are advisable? Try rewriting your first two paragraphs so that they prepare the ground for your final suggestions.

In conference you might go through some of the details, asking the student to explain why they are relevant. The two of you would probably come up with an analysis of the paper something like this:

> Paragraph 1: The information is relevant because it will help the reader understand why the art department should take a practical approach. It could be improved by making that relevance clearer and the details more vivid.
>
> Paragraph 2: The first sentence may be relevant to the topic, but the writer needs to clarify how it fits in. The rest of the paragraph, in which the writer lists the manufacturing companies and states that some of them are in a nearby town, is not pertinent, unless the fact that some students' parents work outside the town affects plans to build better rapport between parents and the art department. Although the later recommendation makes no mention of this possibility, the writer may wish to add it.

In fact, at this point in the conference, the examination of the irrelevance of the first paragraphs will begin to influence the entire paper. Pondering what to include, the student may remember that the window company gives free wood scraps to many townspeople who have wood-based hobbies. Including this information would lead to the sensible suggestion, later on, that the art department increase its concentration on wood crafts. In addition, the two towns are remarkable in that each has a strong quilting society. It is wise to ask how the art department could benefit from such a tradition. Thus jolted into reexamining the first paragraphs, the student may well come up with an improved set of recommendations at the paper's end.

First and Last Paragraphs

Mismatched entry and exit paragraphs may indicate, as explained earlier, that the paper covers too much ground. If the body does cohere around a single topic, however, those flyaway conglomerations at the essay's beginning and end merely show that the student needs help learning to swish readers efficiently and effectively in and out of the paper.

Opening Paragraphs

Here are some guidelines you can use in helping students write effective first paragraphs.

1. *Emphasize the principle of the "true clue."* A common problem is that the student may begin the paper, or a section of it, with misleading, overly generalized, or irrelevant material before actually saying what the paper or section will be about. One way to explain this sort of poor opening to students is to compare it to a dog that circles a spot several times before lying down on it. Point out the student's circles and find the spot at which the writer finally drops down on the true topic. That's where the paper should start. Teach your students to check their own papers for circles before handing them in.

Sometimes, instead of circling or giving miscues, students write a sentence or paragraph that emphasizes what should be subordinate and buries what should be primary. This opening paragraph is an example:

```
The nongraded school and the graded school are very much alike
because so far a definite destinction has not been made.  The ideal
nongraded school and the nongraded school in practice today are two
very different concepts.
```

[The essay continues with a critique of the ways in which actual nongraded schools fail to live up to the idea, and in fact turn out to be much like graded schools.]

The paper, businesslike, rightly begins with matter germane to its main topic; however, sentence structure and sentence order blur the focus. Ask the student whether the real topic of the paper is the comparison between actual nongraded schools and graded schools or the contrast between ideal nongraded schools and actual ones. Another way might be to ask what the real subject is: ideal nongraded schools, actual nongraded schools, or graded schools? What the student should discover is that the paragraph would be strengthened by switching its first two sentences to place proper emphasis on actual nongraded schools as the true subject of the paper. The revised paragraph might read something like this:

```
The nongraded school in practice today is very far from the
ideal.  In fact, actual nongraded schools are not much different
from ordinary graded schools.
```

One special type of first paragraph deserves a separate word—the paragraph that begins with a description of the process by which the writer settled on the subject:

```
When I first read this book I didn't understand it very well,
but after thinking about it I decided to write on....
```

```
For my project in general zoology this term I have been working
with mice, and have discovered that....
```

For some purposes and audiences this approach may be effective, but often it merely delays the establishment of proper focus. To remedy the problem, the student should be encouraged to begin with a sentence that makes a statement about the topic itself, not about the writer's trip toward it:

> Elaine Roberts' new novel is about how a young girl achieves courage.

> My research in zoology this term showed that mice are affected by overcrowding in three ways.

2. *Work for specificity.* Often you can encourage students to write good opening paragraphs by suggesting that they avoid the phrase "This paper will . . ." Thus the writer is forced to move from an opening like example A, below, to the much more specific and helpful example B:

A. This paper will discuss the influence of World War II upon world food production.

B. World War II resulted in more sophisticated technology for world food production, but it also contributed to international tensions that would impede distribution of the food produced.

3. *Encourage liveliness.* Students who feel insecure about writing or who believe that they must use forty-dollar words and formal sentences to sound learned will produce nothing but the type of formal topic sentence illustrated by example B above. You can suggest that, depending on their purpose and audience, they introduce their topic in more informal or vivid language.

C. World War II led to the use of bigger and better harvesting machines, but it also contributed to the international tensions that kept the harvested grain from reaching hungry mouths.

A topic need not, in fact, be introduced by a textbook topic sentence at all. It can be broached by a striking metaphor, an arresting statistic, or a vivid anecdote, provided such an opener gives the reader a true clue to the topic. Oft-quoted shibboleths to the contrary, a writer can even use the pronouns "I" and "you" if they seem natural and effective. For example, the paper on World War II and food could open like this:

D. In the years following World War II my mother's relatives in Germany were harvesting more grain, with bigger reapers, than ever before, but my father's relatives in neighboring Poland went to bed hungry every night.

Sometimes a student needs to formulate a textbook topic sentence first, as a guide to the paper's focus, but can later change to a more arresting introduction. For example, one student opened the first draft of a paper with this sentence:

```
The migration of Mexicans across the border into the U.S. is a
growing problem in America today.
```

The topic sentence was an accurate introduction to the paper, but it lacked spark. Later, the student revised his paper so that it opened like this:

```
If you think Mexicans are lazy, you should check with the U.S.
Immigration authorities.  Mexicans swim rivers, trek hundreds of
miles, cross swamps, evade hunters, cling to the bottoms of trucks,
have themselves camouflaged in loads of hay--all to get to the U.S.A.
```

Concluding Paragraphs

A concluding paragraph can do an adequate job merely by summarizing the main points of the paper or by stating the conclusion to be drawn from them. Such an ending is especially appropriate for a lengthy, complicated paper, where the reader may need a summary. Unfortunately, however, students frequently attach a long, formal tail to a short, informal dog.

On some occasions, the student's summary will be in proper proportion but will omit some important points. Or the emphasis of the summary may be different from that of the rest of the paper. Or a paper may simply end without any conclusion or with a paragraph that contains what Pooh Bear would call "A Collection of Interesting Thoughts."

Other faults of students' concluding paragraphs include banal, self-conscious statements such as "I found this topic most interesting and I hope the reader has also." Or sometimes the tone turns pious: "A study of the life of Abraham Lincoln leads us to a greater appreciation of the virtues of this great leader."

A remedy for all these problems might be to have the student verbalize just what the conclusion should accomplish for the particular audience. In view of the tone and style of the paper as a whole, could the conclusion be flip, utilitarian, brief, lengthy, anecdotal? In planning the conclusion, the student may find it helpful to write a utilitarian summary of the paper's main points, just to keep on the track. That summary can then be the beacon guiding the actual conclusion—an incident, quotation, question, or fillip that is more intricately carved, more surprising, or more offbeat.

Chapter Six

Helping Students Develop and Support Ideas

Once you have scanned the paper for topic limitation and focus, you are ready to check the development of its ideas. The first question to ask is, Do the subpoints sufficiently develop the topic? Second, are individual sections and paragraphs as full and as well-supported as they should be?

Development problems may sometimes be the cause of focus problems. When students do not know how to break down or develop an idea after they have stated it, they will drop it, go on to another, and continue to plop more separate rocks on the pile until it reaches the requisite size. The result might look suspiciously like the women's liberation paper discussed in the previous chapter.

Not knowing how to develop an idea may also lead students to write papers that state the same idea over and over at the same level of generality, or that keep introducing irrelevant material, or that are padded with verbiage. When you encounter such problems, you may find it useful to forgo marking the paper "wordy" or "too general" and instead find out whether the student knows how to flesh out an idea. You can help such students by showing them techniques by which they can fully and vividly develop their topics. It's back again to teaching the *process* of writing.

Eliciting a Time Commitment

The first question to ask is what techniques and what time frame the student used to develop the ideas in the paper. You may find that he or she simply sat down the night before the paper was due and wrote straight through, putting down "some ideas" about the subject as they came. Or there may have been an attempt at generating ideas, or planning the paper, that did not produce satisfactory results. If this is the case, then the writer needs to work on techniques for finding things to say about an idea—what rhetoricians call heuristics.

Such students first of all have to make a time commitment. Evidence shows that successful writers spend more time in the planning stages than do poorer writers (Stallard, 211, 217). So you should first encourage the students to spend time planning. Once they make that commitment they can use various techniques to generate and arrange subtopics and details.

Helping Students Generate Ideas

You may help students generate ideas for developing their topics by providing them with guides or by helping them compose their own. Such guides can take several forms—lists, questions, patterns of thought, and watchwords.

Lists

One type of list is the sequence of parts for a structured genre such as the lab report, the clinical report, or the legal brief. These forms are useful both in generating and in organizing ideas, and I discuss them in more detail in the next chapter. Students using such a list will sometimes need to employ some of the methods below to generate material within the parts of the traditional format.

One useful guide to developing ideas is a list of the classical "topoi," or ways of developing ideas, used by rhetoricians from Aristotle to the present. One version lists the means of developing ideas as description, narration, classification, comparison, contrast, analogy, cause-effect, partition, and enumeration. The writer can mentally review these possibilities, asking, "Can I develop my idea by analogy? By narration? By contrast?"

To see how such a list might work, let us imagine the student who has decided to write a paper against the use of marijuana. The paper is to be addressed to college students. The writer, pondering how to develop the paper, goes mentally down the list:

DESCRIPTION: Maybe I could describe society as it would be if everyone used marijuana. Or I can describe some people who have messed themselves up by smoking pot.

NARRATION: I could tell the story of marijuana use in the United States or in other countries, or the story of the drug's effects on a specific town, school, or person.

CLASSIFICATION: I could classify marijuana as a mind-altering drug and appeal to people's feelings against having their minds tampered with.

COMPARISON: I could compare marijuana with alcohol, as many people do to justify it, but my comparison could show how many of the horrors that result from alcohol use also happen with marijuana.

CONTRAST: I could contrast the characteristics of users and nonusers in my
school to show how marijuana causes students to drop out or lose
control of their lives. Or maybe I could contrast the life of one or
more persons before and after they began heavy marijuana use.

ANALOGY: I might draw an analogy between the story of Snow White and
the use of pot: in both cases a young person is "put to sleep" and
withdraws from the normal process of maturing, falling in love, and
taking a place in the adult world. Or maybe Peter Pan—the age-old
fear of assuming adult responsibilities and the desire to live in a fan-
tasy land of the senses.

CAUSE-EFFECT: I could analyze the causes, as far as they are known, for pot
use among Americans today. I could also describe the effects of
heavy use on social relationships, schoolwork, and other responsibilities and on a person's health (genetic damage, etc.).

PARTITION: I could divide marijuana users into groups or marijuana use
into its various aspects.

ENUMERATION: I could describe for the reader several persons I've known
who have been harmed by marijuana.

The above list is based on rhetorical modes; students can also mentally review other kinds of lists. Ponder the various perspectives on an issue that guide exploration in your discipline and see whether you can
formulate from them a useful idea-generating device for students. One
formulation makes use of the various ways in which an investigator can
view an object or a system. Drawing on these perspectives and on a seminal heuristic by Young, Becker, and Pike, one rhetorician has developed a
simple list of five aspects for students to consider as they develop ideas
about a topic.[1] For example, in planning a paper on seventeenth-century
American witchcraft, the writer can view it in any of these ways:

1. *As an isolated, static entity.* Who were the people involved? What happened? What features characterized the phenomenon?
2. *As one among many of a class.* How does it differ from, or resemble,
   witchcraft in other cultures or eras? How is it different from or similar to other contemporary social movements?
3. *As part of a larger system.* How does it fit seventeenth-century American culture?
4. *As a process rather than as a static entity.* How did it come into being?
   How has it changed? What are its modern forms?
5. *As a system rather than as an entity.* What were the various dynamics
   and influences operating in the witch trials?

You or your students can compose such a list of perspectives, based
either on patterns of thought in your discipline or on approaches relevant
to the assignment you've given.

Questions

In addition to the list of perspectives, there can be a list of questions. A well-known example is the journalist's five W's—who? what? where? when? why? These questions are helpful in many kinds of writing besides newspaper stories, and you might want to suggest that your students use the five W's, or some variation of them, as an idea starter.

It is possible to compose a list of pertinent questions for any assignment in any discipline, and you may want to hand one out or have your students, in small groups, compile one. Here, for example, is a list of questions to prod the thoughts of a person who is reviewing or analyzing fiction. I have adapted it from a similar list compiled from a number of sources and distributed by the library of Towson State University in Towson, Maryland.

How to Write a Book Review (Fiction)

The major purpose of a book review may be simply to create interest in the book, but for most academic assignments its purpose is to report on the nature and quality of the content.

It is important to know very clearly who is the audience for your book review and what is your purpose in writing for that audience. Some questions to ask yourself are: Who is my reader? How much, if anything, does the reader already know about the book, or the topic the book deals with? Since I cannot tell everything about the book, what are the key ideas I want to get across? Do I want my reader to be persuaded that the book has some major strengths or weaknesses? Do I want my reader to better understand some aspects of the book—its structure, its literary devices, its approach to the problem, its underlying assumptions?

Once your audience and purpose are clear, the list of questions below will help you analyze most works. A good review usually focuses on one of these questions or a coherent group of them.

I. Questions about characters
   A. Has the author indicated the personality of the main character by what he or she says (and thinks)? By what the character does? By what other characters say about him or her? By what the author says about him or her, speaking as either the storyteller or an observer of the action?
   B. Describe a major character (attitudes, behavior) at the beginning of the book. What happens to the character and why? How does the experience affect the character? What new attitudes and behavior does he or she show at the end? What has the author shown about his or her own values by showing this change of character?

C. What two major characters are contrasted? What roles do they play in the story?

D. What two major characters or groups are in conflict? Why? How does each respond? Does the outcome of the conflict seem true to your own sense of human experience, or is the outcome merely exciting and surprising?

E. Which characters seem believable and which seem unbelievable?

II. Questions about plot

A. Is the plot fresh or commonplace or stereotyped?

B. How does the author complicate the plot and add suspense? By adding surprising incidents? By withholding information? By depending on characters to create incidents? Give examples. What are the means by which the author works out and solves the complications of plot?

III. Questions about idea content

A. What is the view of life (the message or the moral experience)? How does the methodology illustrate or support this view? How convincing is the author? Is the message important, bad, helpful, dangerous, or what?

B. How does the idea affect the style and structure of the work?

C. What facts or ideas specially informed you? How are the facts or ideas presented? Why does the new knowledge impress you? Does it change any ideas you previously had? Is the knowledge useful?

IV. Questions for comparing the book with another

A. How are the two books similar?

B. Give details and examples of the similarities in plot, characters, and outcome.

C. Which of the two books seems more successful in handling the matters on which the two are similar?

VI. Questions for collections of short stories

A. What is similar in the contents of the stories? (Stories by the same author are likely to have similar characters or situations. Stories by different authors are usually collected by editors around a particular subject—for example, baseball stories.)

B. Discuss two or more stories that best demonstrate the similarity.

C. What does the similarity show about the author's view of people or life or about his or her way of entertaining readers?

Patterns of Thought

In addition to lists of rhetorical techniques or perspectives and lists of questions, the prescribed modes of thought in a discipline or situation can help produce ideas. Richard Larson, for example, suggests that writers, to generate material for a paper, go through the steps of problem solving used by management. The writer begins by stating the topic as a problem (see page 61), to find the focus of the paper, and then follows these steps:

1. Define the problem: formulate a sentence that exactly states the problem to be attacked.
2. Determine why the problem is indeed a problem.
3. Enumerate the goals that must be served by whatever action is taken.
4. Where possible, determine which goals have the highest priority.
5. Find the procedure that might attain the stated goals.
6. Predict the consequences of each possible action.
7. Weigh the consequences; which are likely to best achieve the stated goals?
8. Evaluate the choice that seems superior, and plan how to reduce its negative consequences. (Larson, pp. 628–35)

Just as management's problem-solving methods can help to generate matter and sequence for a paper, so too can the methods used in other disciplines. For example, *The Science of Scientific Writing,* cited in Chapter 5, teaches students to integrate the steps of the scientific method with the writing of scientific papers. One could also explore the steps used in developing a drawing, writing a piece of music, diagnosing illness, locating the cause of mechanical breakdown, or establishing legal guilt or innocence. Perhaps such procedures could serve in some situations as heuristics—idea starters. There is much to be done in integrating the methodology of various disciplines with the writing process, and you may be able to do some of it in your own discipline and your own classroom.

Watchwords

In addition to lists, questions, and patterns of thought, watchwords or mottoes can serve the student as periscopes to sight the wealth of ways to develop an idea. Some useful watchwords are:

1. *Trace your path.* You have arrived at a certain conclusion (the train was noisy; the plan won't work). You can't expect readers to join you on that mountaintop of certainty unless you lead them up the slope by the same path you took. How did you conclude that the train was noisy? You heard the clack of the wheels, the rattle of trays, the hubbub of conversation, the cries of the porters, the wailing of a baby. Let the reader hear them, too, in vivid detail.

   Or, how did you come to the conclusion that the plan won't work? Trace for the reader, step by step, the evidence you observed or read and the line of reasoning you followed.

2. *Show, don't tell.* Don't just tell me that Americans waste water, draw me a word picture so that I can see and experience it. Show me the teenager standing at the sink, letting the faucet run full force while he leisurely brushes his teeth. Compare the number of buckets the American family's daily water supply would fill with the number used daily by Iranians or Tanzanians.

Imagining the Total Writing Situation

Lists, questions, patterns of thought, and watchwords are useful techniques to help students proceed after they have found their topics. But these techniques are ideally part of a broader approach. Recent research illustrates a marked difference in the ways skillful and unskillful writers approach their work: the poorer ones, in the process of producing their finished pieces, are tied to their topics, considering the subject in very narrow terms, without thinking much about the needs of the audience, about what they as writers wish to do for that audience, about what tone they ought to take with the reader, or about what limitations and opportunities might be present in the total situation in which their composition would be read. The good writers, on the other hand, spend much more time and effort thinking through those aspects, representing the assignment to themselves as a complex speech act, defining the problems and challenges offered by the particular audience, purpose, and situation. The researchers conclude that "Writers discover what they want to do by insistently, energetically exploring the entire problem before them and building for themselves a unique image of the problem they want to solve." The implication for teachers is this: "If we can teach students to explore and define their own problems, even within the constraints of an assignment, we can help them to create inspiration instead of wait for it."[2] You may know better than I how, in your own discipline, to help students represent to themselves the needs of the audience and the demands of the total rhetorical situation. One method might be to have them write down, and hand in along with their assignments, their answers to some questions: Who are my readers? What are their characteristics, expectations, and needs? What do I want to do for them? What tone or point of view should I take? If answering these questions is part of the assignment, students may learn to ponder these elements as they plan their papers. Another way to bring these questions to students' attention is to discuss them in class or ask students to break briefly into groups to discuss them with one another. However you handle it, good evidence suggests that if you can get students to present to themselves the problems of the writing situation in complex and inclusive terms, they will produce better writing.

I have suggested some mental aids to developing ideas. The physical act of planning can be carried out in a number of ways, as discussed on pages 57–63.

Helping Students Develop Rich Paragraphs

Students have trouble not only in assembling subtopics and material for the paper as a whole but also in writing full and well-supported paragraphs for their papers. Often paragraphs are undernourished. Either they lack some important idea, fact, or definition or they simply need the healthy glow of detail, incident, illustration, example, or proof to make them spring vibrantly out at the reader.

For example, this paragraph appears in a paper about the results of overpopulation, and it is followed by a paragraph on the food shortages caused by overpopulation:

    Urban congestion is another evil of having more people than the
    land can sustain. Parks and cities made of tar paper and asphalt
    cannot let anything survive but parasites. All this in the name of
    progress and making room for more people.

The paragraph is underpopulated. Its purpose is to convince us that urban congestion is an unbearable blight, so inimical to human happiness that we must be willing to take action against the overpopulation that causes it. But the paragraph does not have enough vivid and convincing details to make the reader experience the result of overpopulation. The closest the student comes to success is the middle sentence, with its phrase "tar paper and asphalt." The wise teacher would commend this detail and ask for more. Tell the student to *show* the reader how awful urban congestion is, to make the reader feel, hear, see, smell, and experience urban crowding.

An example of the well-developed paragraph comes from a paper on the reasons for gang violence. The writer does not content himself with windy generalizations or vague and impoverished language. Instead, after opening each of the two paragraphs with general statements (you learn to face gangs; you begin to feel power), the writer offers the reader a rich mead of vivid, convincing detail:

Part of a Student Paper on Gang Violence

    In the part of Los Angeles where I come from, you learn at an
    early age to face gangs in ways that most people would consider a
    bad dream or a good horror movie. When you are seven or eight you

learn to deal with the four big guys who want to take your mother's
cigarette money as you walk to the store. To protect yourself
against these big boys, and also to become like them, you get to
running with your neighborhood friends.

When you and your friends are together you begin to feel power.
You think you are a man because you had sex with the neighborhood
whore. Nobody can tell you what to do; nobody can tell you they
know how you feel. You learn to take abuse but most important you
learn to abuse people. You are standing on a corner with guys and
girls your own age. . . . and there's nothing to do. You turn and
look and there's a young dude coming down the street going to the
store for his mother. You and the gang stop him and while his money
and other valuables are being taken, you stand back and say to
yourself, "I'm glad it's you this time, man, and not me."

Paragraphs can often be appropriately enriched if students know
how to draw on their own experiences and imaginations. The first student
could have mined what she knew about city living to create a much more
vivid picture of the effects of crowding; the second student memorably
and genuinely enriched his paper on the reasons for gang violence by describing his own experience.

A related problem is that students looking for ways to develop ideas
do not know how to use printed sources as hunting grounds. For example,
here is a selection of paragraphs from students who, all using exactly the
same sources, were asked to describe the responses of various groups to
the closing of juvenile reform schools in Massachusetts in the late 1960s.
One of the important negative reactions came from the staff members in
the old reform schools. One student explained the staff's hostility with
this vague and meager paragraph (the superscript numbers in this extract
and the following ones refer to end notes in the students' papers):

Staff also caused a problem for Dr. Miller, because they had
not been oriented to the rapid closure and the complete turnaround
in the mode of handling delinquents.

Another member of the class wrote a longer paragraph that, on the
surface, appears better developed:

Employees saw their functions change and then disappear. Ken
Guza, an administrative assistant at the Department of Youth
Services said that personnel saw their jobs in trouble and found
ways of fighting back.[39] "The more kids ran, the more the staff
could insist there was a need for institutionalization."[40]

The first sentence of this paragraph does not clearly indicate the relationship of the paragraph's content to the concept of negative reactions, which is the subject of this section of the paper. A better first sentence would be more general: "Another negative group was made up of employees who, because they saw their functions change and then disappear, became hostile." After the first sentence, this paragraph seems to develop the idea at some length, but actually it rather ineffectively piles up a series of still general and repetitious statements. The second sentence describes the staff's situation in terms about as general as those in the first sentence:

Sentence 2	*Sentence 1*
saw their functions change and then disappear.	saw their jobs in trouble.

So, although the second sentence seems to further the paragraph's development, it adds little to the reader's specific knowledge about the employees' situation. It does introduce a description of the employees' actions: they "found ways of fighting back." That statement, however, is also general, lacking any specific details. Such details might logically come in the third sentence, but instead the writer uses the third sentence to present a quotation that tells how the staff thought they would benefit from encouraging their charges to run away. But since we have not previously been told that encouraging inmates to run away was the way the staff fought back, we are left with a gap between sentences two and three. This second student, then, although his paragraph is longer than that of the first student, has not used the additional words to develop his idea as well as he might have. The first sentence is not general enough; the rest of the paragraph needs more detail.

A third student has come much closer to a good balance of the general and the specific, and to an effective development of the paragraph:

The older staff were also against his program. Many of them felt the new ways of treatment would cause them to lose their command over the children. The older staff were also unskilled in learning the new ways of treatment, which made them worry about losing their jobs.[52] When a plan to close down an institution was known, the staff encouraged the children to run away, fight, and have riots. The staff even went as far as putting up an escape route. By having the children keep running away, it was supposed to show how they need to be institutionalized.[53]

Though the last sentence is awkwardly phrased and ought perhaps to be integrated into an earlier part of the paragraph, the student has used the information from the research sources to flesh out the paragraph with specific details, all of which explain and develop a clear topic statement.

To help students realize the need for full development of paragraphs, try asking them questions that will spur further development, or try circling the generalities in their papers and asking students to back them up with specific details. For example, in the second paragraph above, you might circle the phrase "ways of fighting back" and write in the margin, "Give details to explain this generality" or "What ways did they use?" Or reflect the paragraph's lack of impact on you as reader: "I'm not keenly gripped by the staff's dilemma." Or suggest methods of development: "You need more details here. Try expanding with an example or an analogy."

One planning strategy useful in developing rich paragraphs is to review the list of rhetorical devices: comparison, contrast, analogy, and so on (see pages 87–88). Another good technique is free writing; suggest that the student blurt out on paper whatever comes to mind on the subject of that paragraph. The writer should not stop, at that point, to find just the right word, to phrase the sentence perfectly, or to spell everything correctly. The object is to generate a rich flow of ideas and images that the writer can then comb for ideas to strengthen the paragraph.

Chapter Seven

Helping Students Organize Ideas

Discourse may be well or poorly organized at any level: the eight subtopics in a twenty-page paper may be poorly arranged; so may the eight words in a sentence. Nevertheless, the organization of sentences is a somewhat different matter from the organization of subtopics and paragraphs. Therefore, this chapter deals with organization on the larger scale, and Chapter 8 treats it on the smaller scale.

In evaluating the organization of the paper as a whole, you should look for two basic flaws: first, the sequence of subtopics may not be effective; second, the sequence may not be sufficiently apparent to the reader.

Methods of Teaching Organization

Though we have much to learn about what "logical" or "effective" sequencing is and how writers achieve it and readers recognize it, nevertheless it pays to ponder the current theories. One approach says that the minds of readers tend to work in certain fixed patterns, such as comparison, enumeration of parts, cause and effect, and analogy. Such patterns may be inherent or learned; they may be universal, or they may be in part culturally determined. In any case, when discourse follows the patterns imprinted in our minds we consider it well organized. Thus, according to this theory, the process of achieving good organization is analogous to the process by which children, through hearing their native tongue, master the basic ways of organizing sentences and learn to form sentences they've never heard before that nevertheless seem logical to listeners. A five-year-old English speaker, for example, will not tug at your elbow and say, "I want a sandwich jelly," though in some languages the words would be organized in that order.

A second approach says that good organization consists in the writer's setting up expectations and then fulfilling them in ways that satisfy the reader. Each word, sentence, or paragraph, according to this theory, leads the reader to expect certain kinds of argument or information to appear next, and the unspoken exigencies of the writing situation engender still other expectations. When the writer meets these expectations, the reader feels that the writing is well organized.

These two theories suggest two pedagogical methods, not necessarily mutually exclusive, for helping students arrange subtopics logically and effectively. One strategy is to familiarize students with the patterns of thought common to all readers, or common to readers in a particular discipline, so that the students, like younger members of the jelly-sandwich set, can almost instinctively arrange new material in an order that will strike readers as right. You can have students find the patterns inductively by reading and outlining good examples and then writing, or discussing in class, the sort of organization common to all the examples. The idea that students learn by reading model pieces of writing is supported by studies that show that having students do more reading in a course improves their writing competence (Haynes, pp. 84–87).

A second pedagogical method is to have students analyze the expectations they are setting up with each sentence they write. In evaluating their papers, read the first sentence of the paper or of a section and tell the student how you expect the paper to proceed. Classmates or tutors can also offer this kind of help.

You can combine these pedagogical approaches as you instruct students about the sequence of parts in their papers. In some disciplines such instruction is explicit, since certain kinds of writing, such as lab reports, are organized in traditional ways. If this is true for your discipline or for your assignment, give clear, thorough instructions to your students. Some guidelines and some examples of such instructions follow. If you are not dealing with highly structured genres, you can skip this section and turn to page 106.

The following suggestions may help you formulate effective guides for your students as you prepare written or oral instructions on a lab report, a case study, or some other assignment:

1. Include statements about the audience and the purpose.
2. Discuss not only the arrangement of the parts but also the function of that sequence, in terms of usefulness to the reader and the expectations of the reader.
3. Provide good examples of the type of writing you are discussing.
4. Emphasize the need for a central focus and for coherence within each part.
5. Tell students clearly what situations might require them to alter the traditional sequence or to abandon it for a different plan.

Below are two sets of written instructions, composed for students by two classroom teachers. The first, a guide for writing physics lab reports, emphasizes the reader's needs and the rationale behind the recommended sequence. It also does a good job of warning students against some common errors or misconceptions, and it wisely suggests that, in preparing the report for submission, the writer seek suggestions from peers. The second handout, intended for students in a speech clinic, makes effective use of examples to illustrate the kind of writing the teacher is recommending.

Directions for Writing a Lab Report

(Developed by Xavier Spiegel for students in physics and engineering at Loyola College of Baltimore.)

Introduction

The "scientific method" is a phrase used to describe procedures followed by most successful experimentalists: stating the problem, searching the literature for relevant information, observing and collecting data, forming hypotheses, testing and modifying these hypotheses, and publishing results. We notice in this methodology that the beginning and the end of all experimental work involve the communication of experimental results. This serves to underscore the importance of communication in scientific experimentation. The communication of experimental results is accomplished by various means, such as the laboratory report, the technical report or paper, and the research paper.

The laboratory report, technical paper, and scientific article have one thing in common: they are written documents composed to communicate information and ideas. The laboratory report is generally written for an instructor or a fellow student. A technical paper is usually an in-house document of an organization and has limited circulation, whereas a scientific article is published for a larger audience in a scientific or professional journal. In the context of this course we will use the term "laboratory report" interchangeably with "technical paper" and "scientific article." Just as there are conventions for writing a letter, there are conventions for writing a laboratory report. We can draw comparisons between a letter and a laboratory report to explain the way in which the scientific community shares its experiences, develops new laws, and generally broadens our knowledge of nature.

The Laboratory Report in General

A letter has eight essential parts:

Address of author
Date
Greeting
Introduction

Body
Closing remarks
Complimentary closing
Signature

The purpose of each of these should be obvious, but to ensure that we agree, let us examine briefly the reason for such a structured document. The name and address of the author are given so that a reader who wishes to answer the letter can reply quickly and efficiently. The date is included to give the letter a reference in time—to date the information. The introduction tells the reader why the letter is being written, and the body of the letter transmits the information. The closing remarks generally draw conclusions, ask for advice, or reiterate important parts of the body; and the signature tells the reader who is writing the letter.

A laboratory report has fifteen essential parts:

Name of author
Date
Address
Abstract
Title
Object
Theory
Procedure
Apparatus
Data
Sample Calculation
Results
Conclusions
Discussion
References

The purpose of the date and the name and address of the author are the same as for the letter. In a lab report, they also serve as documentation for scientific credit for any new discovery or theory. The title and abstract are similar to the greeting in a letter.

The writer would like the report to reach the appropriate audience. The first step is to select a journal that publishes articles on the subject. But those who buy a particular journal seldom read all the articles, and the title of the report is meant to allow selection by those interested in the author's special area. The title, however, is not sufficient indication of the exact subject, and the abstract, which is a short summary of the report, further narrows the audience to those who are interested in this specialized approach or experiment.

The object of a laboratory report corresponds to the introduction of a letter. The procedure, apparatus, data, sample calculations, results, and conclusions correspond to the body. The discussion section corresponds to the closing remarks of a letter. The reference section documents information that the author supplies to the reader.

The Laboratory Report in Particular: The Object, Theory, Procedure, Apparatus, Data, Sample Calculations, Results, and Conclusions

The object-of-the-experiment section states, usually in only a sentence or two, exactly what the writer will do in the report.

The theory section explains the guiding principles or laws that govern the phenomenon being investigated. The author can assume that the reader is generally knowledgeable in the subject area and knows as much about the theory as the author did before starting to work on this experiment. This means that the writer should not bore the reader with the obvious. It also means that the author should try not to lose the reader by assuming too much or supplying only sketchy details. The theory section will generally include a mathematical derivation of the equations governing the phenomenon under investigation. Since these are seldom original and can usually be found in textbooks or other articles, they should be documented, as is often true of the whole theory section. The most popular reference system in use today in scientific journals relies on numbered superscripts. Equations should be clearly labeled (e.g., Eq. 1) so that they can be referred to later. Since the theory does not depend on either the procedure or the apparatus, it should be general and include any boundary conditions or limitations that apply.

The procedure section describes the particular measurements taken and the number of times each was taken. The writer should not lead the reader by the hand, as in a cookbook or instruction manual, but should give the general approach to the measurements. Often authors are tempted to write in the imperative, ordering the reader to take this measurement or that measurement and to be certain of this or that, but such a tone should be avoided. The author can assume that the reader is familiar with the general laboratory equipment and procedures. The reader will assume that the author would not perform the experiment without knowing the proper use and care of the equipment or without checking for faulty equipment. Procedure Sections generally vary between one paragraph and three, depending on the complexity of the experiment.

The apparatus section can be simply a list of the apparatus used, but it usually includes a line drawing or picture to illustrate the equipment better. Each drawing or picture should have a name and a title. A name (e.g., Fig. 1) helps the reader refer to it easily, and a title (Apparatus for Simple Pendulum Experiment) aids the reader who just skims the report looking at figures and pictures to get an idea of what it includes. The author should not include a drawing or picture of apparatus that is in general use. For example, most laboratories have various types of thermometers, so that a drawing of a thermometer would be unnecessary;

a statement of the thermometer's range and its smallest division, however, would be useful.

The data section of the report is a display of the measurements. This can be handled in various ways, but the most popular forms are tabular and graphic. A table should have a name and a title and should list the variables measured, the units of measurement, and the accuracy of the measuring device. A graph also has a name and title, and the abscissa and ordinate are clearly labeled as to variable, dimension, and scale divisions. Graphs should be drawn on graph paper in such a way that the data points and the error flags show clearly and the curve extends across two thirds of the paper. This is all that should appear on the graph; calculations, equations, and comments should be left to the text of the paper.

The sample calculation, although not always necessary, is meant to lead the reader to a thorough understanding of any complex or difficult calculation necessary for the complete understanding of the report. If a sample calculation is necessary the author should define the variables used and explain where the values for the variables were obtained and exactly how the calculation proceeds. A good guideline here is a basic text in the particular subject area concerned.

The results section can be a simple statement of the final result of the calculations or a few sentences summing up the scientific facts discovered.

The conclusions are the author's interpretation of the results and the experiment as a whole. They tell the reader what the particular results mean in terms of the object and theory presented earlier in the report.

The discussion section of the report presents the author's personal speculations or views on what further experimentation would be necessary to complete a new concept or theory. This is also the author's chance to determine the state of the art and the value of such an experiment or to suggest modifications that others might make in future experiments.

The references, as mentioned previously, support the information that the author used in the report. They are used in place of or in addition to footnotes. The author supplies this information to enlighten the reader about details not included in the report, to document confirming or controversial theory and data, and to inform the reader of any other materials that would help in understanding the report.

After Completing the First Draft of a Laboratory Report

Since *communication* is the goal of the laboratory report, it is often helpful to have a colleague read the report and judge whether it is indeed clear, concise, and comprehensible. It is best to choose someone who has the necessary background to grasp your experimental work and to evaluate the report but who has not been involved in writing the report and can thus discern whether the report does indeed say what the author intended to say. In addition, it is useful for the author to reread the report to check for common mistakes:

1. Are the correct person and tense used throughout the report?
2. Are spelling, punctuation, grammar, and syntax correct?
3. Are quotations properly footnoted, and is credit given for ideas taken from others and used with only minor modifications?
4. Are all graphs and figures labeled with descriptive titles and referred to in the text of the report?
5. Are graphs plotted correctly? Is the scale of reasonable size? Are the experimental points plotted with error flags? Is the curve *smooth*?
6. Are equations numbered, particularly those used or referred to in other sections of the report?
7. Are all symbols in the equations adequately defined?
8. Are numerical data and results presented with the appropriate number of significant digits and/or a statement of precision?

Writing a Diagnostic Evaluation

(developed by Linda Spencer, Speech and Hearing Center, Loyola College in Baltimore)

Diagnostic Evaluation

Name: Date of Evaluation:
Address: Date of Birth:
                                               Phone:
Parents' Names: Age:
Referral Source: Sex:

Reports Sent to:

Identification
Name, age, sex, parents, sibling order, school. For example:
> Jimmy is a four-year-old white male, the oldest of three children. Parents are separated, and Jimmy lives with his mother. He is enrolled at Happy Acres Nursery School and attends every morning.

History
Summarize all the data on the client's history that you have obtained from such sources as the case history, a physician's or psychologist's report, informants (parent, foster parent, counselor, or anyone else who accompanies the client), or the client, in the case of an adult.

Use separate paragraphs for each type of information, beginning with prenatal history and birth, including anything significant from the neonatal period, then motor development up to the present, then general health, and finally speech and language development. History extends up to the parents' or adult client's present concerns and description of the problem. (In previous report styles this contemporary information was entered under a section entitled "Chief Complaint.")

Behavioral Observations

Describe the child's or adult's behavior or appearance when you first met him or her, and then describe how he or she acted in the room, that is, the degree of cooperation (separated easily and attended well throughout an hour of testing; cried loudly and asked that his mother return to the room; answered all questions readily and in detail, suggesting eagerness to receive assistance with this problem). Also, describe play behavior and other indicants of cognitive level, such as knowledge of colors and body parts. Indicate how valid you feel your observations are.

Test Results

Receptive Skills: Separate into paragraphs each bit of test information, with hearing test results appearing in the first paragraph. Then devote a separate paragraph to each receptive test you administered (discrimination, reception). For example:

> Joey's responses to pure-tone screening indicated normal hearing bilaterally. The Northwestern Syntax Screening Test (NSST), receptive portion, was administered to assess Joey's understanding of English syntax and morphology. (Or, this test uses a picture-pointing response to assess a child's understanding of English syntax and morphology.) Joey responded correctly to _____ out of 40 possible items, placing his performance in the _____ percentile (don't abbreviate "percentile") for normal children age 4–10 to 4–11.

Incorrect responses were noted for the following syntactic elements: regular past tense, *who* versus *what,* etc.

Expressive Skills: Here enter, in this order, results of oral peripheral examination; articulation test results, including your own perception of intelligibility in conversation; expressive syntax test; voice quality; fluency and rate; an overall indication of expressive ability or characteristics. Regardless of the presenting problem, assess all areas of communication and describe your findings here. Some examples:

> An oral peripheral examination indicated normal structure and function.
>
> *Not:* The oral peripheral examination was normal (the child's mouth was normal, not the examination).
>
> *Or:* Although oral structures appeared normal, movement was slow, as indicated by the following oral diadochokinetic rates: /pʌ/—5 in 5 seconds; /tʌ/—4 in 5 seconds; /kʌ/—2 in 5 seconds. The three-syllable utterance /pʌtʌkʌ/was not produced in order, suggesting poor (or inadequate) oral sequencing skills. These voiceless stop plosives were produced with inadequate intraoral pressure, as well, suggesting reduced strength in the oral structures.

The Goldman-Fristoe Test of Articulation was administered to assess single-word articulation ability. The following phoneme errors were noted:

Initial	*Medial*	*Final*
n/g	d/g	-/g

An indication of distinctive feature errors is then in order. For example, articulation errors were characterized, in general, by the use of stops for fricatives and reduction of all phoneme blends that incorporated /s/, /1/, and /r/. Then say something like this: Despite the large number of phoneme errors noted on this test, intelligibility in conversation was fair, even when the topic was not known to the clinician.

If the presenting problem is fluency, present the fluency rate for each context in which you obtained speech samples. For example:

Context	*Fluency*
Counting	90%
Reciting	75%

Then, describe the dysfluency pattern, noting whole- or part-word repetitions, interjections, blocks on initial phonemes, etc., and secondary symptoms, such as foot tapping and eye blinking.

Psycholinguistic Skills: Interpret your ITPA results here, in terms of significant deviations from mean or median scale scores, noting apparent areas of strength and weakness.

Summary and Recommendations

The first paragraph is a summary of all pertinent information obtained during the evaluation. Start out like this: Joey is a three-year-old boy who is the oldest son of May and Ralph Smith. The family brought him to this center because of their concern with the unintelligibility of his speech. Test results and observations indicate that receptive language skills and expressive syntax are at age level. Articulation skills are poor, however, resulting in poor intelligibility. Joey is quite stimulable, though, for most error phonemes and attended well in the therapy setting.

Or, Joey's speech is characterized by multiple consonant substitutions and vowel distortions rendering conversational speech nearly unintelligible.

It is recommended that Joey receive articulation therapy for two half hours weekly. Prognosis for improvement is good, since Joey's other language skills are at age level, and he can produce several phonemes with stimulation at this time.

The single long-range therapy goal for this child is the attainment of age-appropriate phonological skills. Specific short-term therapy goals will be established after probe procedures have been completed.

Linda E. Spencer, Ph.D., or
Carolyn Martin, M.S., or
Libby Kumin, Ph.D.
Clinical Supervisor

Mary A. Jones, B.A.
Graduate Student Clinician

Some general notes:

1. Your first draft should be as complete as possible and in legible form.
2. Avoid colloquial phrases, such as "lots of," for "several"; "going to," for "will"; "sounds," for "phonemes," and so on.
3. The word "presently" means "in a short time." Don't use it to mean "now" or "at the present time."
4. Do not include in the Summary any information that did not appear in the body of the report.
5. Behavioral descriptions should appear in your report; often these are more important than test scores.
6. Check the spellings of words you are unfamiliar with.
7. Use the past tense in describing test results and behavior unless you are mentioning a behavior that is ongoing or typical. For example, you may say that Joey "goes to the store by himself" but switch to past tense to say that "he misarticulated a number of phonemes."
8. Avoid the use of such words as "could," "could not," or "not able to." These terms suggest that you have complete knowledge of the client's capabilities, when this rarely is the case. Instead, say what the client did or did not do, and indicate that this suggests or indicates a particular condition with which you may be familiar.
9. If you administer a test battery, such as the Detroit or the ITPA, that yields a variety of scores, enter this information in the form of a table on a separate page. For the ITPA, include subtest names, raw scores, age scores, scaled scores, and deviations from mean or median score. Enter only your interpretation of the test results in the body of the report.

Responding to the Disorganized Paper

In talking with a student about a paper that is not well organized, you can, by proposing change, encourage the student to describe the organizing principle: "What would happen in the paper if you switched point 5 with point 2?" Just pick any two points, regardless of whether the interchange would be an improvement. In response to your question, the student will say, "No, that wouldn't work (or yes, that would be a good idea) because . . .," and then will state the organizational plan that guides the paper and mandates that the sections come in x order, not y order. The student may not have clearly recognized the need for such a plan, so when you suggest exchanging points 5 and 2, the student needs to race desperately around some inner barnyard of ideas and offer up the first lame chicken that comes to mind. But even so, the writer has now stated an organizing principle, and you have a basis for driving home the necessity of arranging subtopics according to a conscious rationale. Now you are able to discuss other possible organizing principles for this particular paper, settle on the best one, and then use it to order the writer's subtopics.

Here is an example of how a teacher might work with a student on a paper whose subtopics are not arranged effectively (the superscripts refer to the students' footnotes).

Welfare Cheaters

The modern welfare system is certainly musunderstood by the majority of the middle class in this country. One frequently hears the following typical remarks: "People on welfare could work but are too lazy." "They should have to work." "A person on welfare lives more comfortably than I do." "We spend too much on welfare." "Persons on welfare have more kids just to get more welfare." "Most welfare goes to blacks."

I believe the above are typical remarks that the welfare system is credited with, and that they give an overall view of what is thought of the welfare system. The statistics of welfare are quite different however. Welfare recipients have monetary income ranging from below $1,702 per year for a single person to a ceiling of $5,722 for a family of sever or more.[1] The two largest categories of welfare recipients are the very old and the very young. The welfare expenditure in the United States is 6.5% of the gross national produce, which in comparison to European countries of which the average expenditure is 14% of the GNP, is lower than any two put together.[2] The people on welfare for metropolitan areas consisted of 27% blacks. Finally, only one out of five that could receive aid, do![3]

You will probably want to point out, first, that the statistics in paragraph 2 appear in a different order from the misconceptions in paragraph 1. To help the student see this, ask whether after reading paragraph 1, the reader would have any expectations about which statistics in paragraph 2 would come first and which would come last. The student should see that the reader expects the first statistic of paragraph 2 to refute the first misconception in paragraph 1. Now the writer is on her way to a rationale by which to rearrange all the facts in paragraph 2. In the process she may realize that she needs some other statistics or that she needs to verify her data more explicitly. She also has a problem with awkward phrasing, but it may be that in reworking to remedy other problems, she will subject her language to sufficient scrutiny to smooth it out; if not, you and she can handle the problem by using the techniques discussed in Chapter 8.

Sometimes a student has consciously chosen one ordering principle when another would be more effective. In contrast-comparison writing, for example, there are two basic types:

Plan 1: A1, A2, A3, B1, B2, B3
Plan 2: A1, B1, A2, B2, A3, B3

Knowing that the basic job is to compare two things, the writer should be aware of these two fundamental choices and should consider the advantages and disadvantages of each. In the paper on welfare, for example, we could justify abandoning Plan 1, in which all the A's—the misconceptions—are clustered in the first paragraph and all the B's—the refuting facts—are grouped together in the second paragraph. Plan 2 is most useful in this kind of paper, where the A's are not tightly linked in a sequence or logic of their own and where it is important to make immediate comparisons on a small scale. Here the advantage of Plan 2 is that one misconception of the middle class (A1) would be immediately followed by the fact that disproves it (B1). Thus the prejudice would not be allowed either to stand in the reader's mind or to become fuzzy in the memory; it would instead be immediately abolished by the quick presentation of a contradicting fact. Even if the student should finally decide to stay with Plan 1, her choice should be based on a consideration of the options. Contrast-comparison papers offer perhaps the tightest set of choices, but other types of writing, too, will exhibit common formulas. Persuasive arguments often follow this order:

- Introduce the issue: Tell what it is and why it is important. Present necessary information or definitions.
- Acknowledge, and respond to, the opposition's major points.
- Present several of the strongest arguments for your own point.
- Conclude.

Reading a student's essay or scanning the scratch outline you have made of it will sometimes reveal that the student has treated the same topic in two different places or that two subtopics are so similar as to be repetitious. We saw repetition in the single paragraph discussed on page 95. In this paper the echoes span a greater distance. A method of talking with students about organization in such cases is to circle the repeated ideas and ask the student to tell you the difference between one concept and the other. The writer, unable to pinpoint any significant difference, will realize that he or she has said essentially the same thing in two separate places and needs to reorganize the paper.

Careful reading of the next paper, written for a drama class, reveals that the student, after a misleading first paragraph, goes on to discuss four ways in which the white women in these very different black dramas are similar to one another: all are lonely, all (except Lula) are naive, all assume that they should control any situation between themselves and a black man, and all believe that the black man will want such a relationship to be sexual. The insights are astute. The writer, however, needs help in crystallizing the points of the essay, avoiding repetition, and providing the reader with transitions and with an introductory paragraph that reveals the paper's real subject. To provide a basis for improvement, you might mark each of the four subtopics as they occur, thus quickly revealing the repetition and scattering of ideas. In an oral conference, you could ask the student to identify the main points about the women and then to assign each sentence of the essay to one of those main points. The result would be a set of jottings similar to the ones already marked on the paper. Once the student has identified the topic of each sentence, it becomes easy to combine sentences dealing with the same topic, to write a single, coherent treatment of each of the four points in turn, and then to write a clear lead paragraph.

The White Woman in Some Representative Black Plays

(1) Only in Bullins' Gentleman Caller, a revolutionary play directed toward blacks, does the white woman fail to triumph over the black man. In Blues for Mr. Charlie and Dutchman, shockers intended for whites, the white woman succeeds as the vehicle of destruction for the black man.

(2) One common denominator for these representatives of the white bitch is loneliness. Lula has trapped herself in a never-ending murder scene and never makes contact with another person. *lonely* Madame has an ineffective husband who is always shaving in the bathroom. Jo married Lyle later than would be expected. She was the town librarian, the last white virgin in town. Even after marrying Lyle there are hints of her loneliness. Lyle leaves home *naive* alot to decrease the number of virgins in Blacktown. Naieve fits Madame and Jo. Neither seems aware of what blacks are like. Madame has some stereotyped ideas about what to expect while Jo seems to lack even that much. Jo questions Parnell about her husband and black women but she doesn't really recognize his tomcattin'. *control* At any rate both are certain that they should be in control of any situation dealing with a black. Madame is the hostess and guides, or so she thinks, the meeting with the gentleman caller. When Richard comes into the store, Jo assumes she should be in control and becomes dismayed when she realizes that Richard has the

naive situation in hand. Lula remains apart as being the aware one. She
is going to enlighten Clay and is far from being naieve. From the
control minute she sits down beside him, Lula begins her campaign to draw
Clay out of his middle class stupor.

control   (3) All three women are self-confident toward black men. They
are white women, therefore most admired and most beautiful. They
assume they should guide the relationship with black men. The
relationship is inevitably sexual. Lula gives Clay the come-on
sex when she starts up her banter with him, munching away on her apple.
Madame makes a play for the gentleman caller and assumes he's hot to
get in bed with her. She's surprised when he refuses to do anything.
At the store Jo becomes frightened when she sees Richard is not
afraid of her. Jo assumes he's after her, never figuring that
Richard might not even want her. The incident assumes even greater
sexual meaning at the trial when Jo dramatizes the supposed sexual
advances by Richard.

*You make four intelligent points, but can you see how scattered
they are? Treat each in turn, with clear transitions and first
sentences. Then write a first paragraph that introduces the
true subject. Your present introduction is misleading.*

The next section of this chapter discusses organization in longer,
more sophisticated student papers. If you don't care to read this section,
skip to page 120.

Achieving a careful sequence of ideas is one area in which more sophisticated students can often benefit from your careful critique. In some
situations you may spend a great deal of time with a student who has little idea about how to organize even the simplest writing; at other times,
however, you may want to be rigorous and thorough in helping one of
your better students, also. Unfortunately, in many colleges the really
good students go all the way through school without anyone's offering
them the kind of detailed critique of their writing that poor writers get all
the time. Often no one helps the competent writers to grow into excellent
writers. First, for example, let's look at a paper written for a political science class by a capable student majoring in journalism. The assignment
was to evaluate Allison and Szanton's book, *Remaking Foreign Policy.* Students faced the expected problems of establishing a sufficiently defined
focus, writing in the critique genre, and avoiding mere summary in favor
of a thoughtful confrontation of the material. The audience was the
teacher; the students' purpose was to share their critical analyses with an
interested mentor. In several ways the student whose paper appears below responded very well to the challenge of the assignment. He solved
the focus problem by concentrating on Allison and Szanton's recommen-

dations for changes in the CIA. To give himself a basis for comparison and analysis, he used two other works—one by Corson and the other by Marchetti and Mark—realizing that those works could be interestingly integrated into his discussion of Allison and Szanton's position. He comes up with a paper that is a creative cross between a critique of Allison and Szanton and a paper on reform of the CIA. As a reading of the paper will show you, however, the ideas are not well arranged; consequently, the paper is hard to follow. That, plus the paper's length, makes this paper somewhat heavy reading. I have chosen an example of this length, however, because it is a length we are often asked to handle, and I did not want to work only with shorter examples. The problems in sequence for sophisticated students often show up in their longer papers. It is worth helping them overcome such difficulties, so that they learn to organize longer pieces.

American Foreign Policy: A Critical Review

Intro:

Graham Allison and Peter Szanton, in their book, Remaking Foreign Policy, argue for drastic reforms in government intelligence. Some of the changes they propose have merit, but others, specifically his plan to split the Central Intelligence Agency, are shortsighted.

Allison would separate CIA operations from analytical intelligence and the Director of Central Intelligence would no longer head the entire community. Presently, he argues, the DCI "must attempt to command services with which his own compete." An "Assistant to the President for Intelligence" would oversee intelligence activities without bias. What Allison is seeking, through all of this, is a de-emphasis of covert activities, tighter supervision of intelligence and a more accurate flow of information to the President (Graham Allison and Peter Szanton, 1976, p. 210).

1a

Allison seems to be most upset with clandestine agents furthering their own interests. The most notable example came during the Vietnam War when President Johnson received biased and inaccurate information from the CIA concerning American chances for success (Allison and Szanton, p. 203).

3

2

The need for control is obvious. But splitting the CIA into two autonomous organizations isn't the answer. The proposal is not entirely without precedent. Following the breakup of the Office of Strategic Services after World War II there was a hectic period in which many facets of the "Smith plan" were used. The Smith plan, as William R. Corson observed in The Armies of Ignorance, "sets forth quite eloquently the discredited doctrine of separation of intelligence functions from their operational necessities" (William R. Corson, 1977, p. 249).

2a

Intelligence operations and analysis are very different, yet very inseparable as Harry Truman discovered in the time preceding the formation of the CIA.

> "...it was clear to Truman that the formula he had endorsed, which separated the functions of analytical intelligence and operations...was an unmitigated disaster" (Corson, p. 274)

Furthermore, Allison admits that the new agency, "without clandestine programs of its own or supervisory responsibility for the rest of the community" might become "a bureaucratic lightweight, readily elbowed aside" (Allison Szanton, p. 204). Said Dean Acheson, "no committee can govern and no man can administer without his own people, money and authority." (Corson, p. 267)

Allison also makes the argument that

2b

> "the disappearance of the CIA would relieve the nation of a name and organization that will otherwise remain a target of derision, suspicion, and perhaps attack (Allison and Szanton, p. 203).

The fact is, public support of the CIA and covert operations increased over the past few years (Public Opinion, Mar/May, 1979).

And what effects would such drastic changes have within the community? Certainly there would be resistance. Despite all of the uproar over the CIA, the presidents themselves have been in favor of

1c

extensive covert actions, either by direct authorization or by promising to look the other way, as Corson describes. President Kennedy did not end clandestine authorization with the Bay of Pigs operation. Corson reports that later, Richard Bissell, the Deputy Director for Plans for the CIA got "'chewed out in the Cabinet Room of the White House by the Brothers Kennedy for sitting on his ass and not doing anything about getting rid of Castro and the Castro regime'" (Corson, p. 391).

Write Victor Marchetti and John D. Marks in their controversial work, The CIA and the Cult of Intelligence,

> "The CIA has a momentum of its own....They do not want to give up their covert activities...They believe in these methods and they rather enjoy the game. Of course, with a presidential mandate they would have to stop, but the country has not had a chief executive since the agency's inception who has not believed in the fundamental need and rightness of CIA intervention in the internal affairs of other nations" (Victor Marchetti and John D. Mark, 1974, p. 372).

What the community really wants is to maintain the status quo. Said one observer of the Ford administration, "'the CIA and DOD will love George Bush and Don Rumsfeld...because neither will make any real waves'" (Corson, p. 446).

3

1

Still, Allison is correct in his claims that tighter control of intelligence is needed. The community generally will not disobey a direct order, but "if lacking precise instructions about what to do and not to do, can be expected to do what it thinks is called for by policy statements" (Corson, p. 475). It is at this point that, time and again, trouble starts.

The struggle for presidential control of intelligence which
Corson depicts in his opening chapter is very real.

> "It was only later that Truman and his successors came to
> understand that while they might propose policy...(others) could
> and did effectively dispose of these policy decisions in
> accordance with their own perceptions of America's national
> interest...Like Robert E. Lee, Truman and those who have
> followed him can only issue orders and hope" (Corson, p. 279).

The community doesn't directly disobey, Corson argues, but will
take liberties. "Because they must implement policy which may be
improperly drawn or determined, there is a temptation on their part
to throw some sand in the gears" (Corson, p. 432-433).

Testified former director William Colby, "'It is entirely
possible that some person can do something not authorized'" (Corson,
p. 441).

Of course, vague orders often are intentional as presidents
seek to maintain "plausible denial should activities be uncovered
(Corson, p. 475). What is needed, both Corson and Allison agree, is
a reduction (not elimination) of covert operations and closer
presidential and Congressional supervision.

There are no ironclad, foolproof measures to stop abuses of
power, says Corson, "but the force of law, especially authorities
and effective congressional oversight, would provide a realistic
deterrent in almost all conceivable situations" (Corson, p. 459).

Neither Corson nor Allison is prepared to abolish covert
operations, but both think they should be limited. Corson makes
several points, most notably that the operations alert the other
government, "thereby complicating the task of getting further
intelligence information" (Corson, p. 473). For the future, Corson
also emphasizes analysis.

> "In essence, secret intelligence information would have
> as its purpose and justification giving diplomacy a better
> chance to succeed instead of being used to set in motion
> covert actions which create more problems than they solve"
> (Corson, p. 474).

By giving the DCI more power he should presumably have more
control and should also be able to give a more accurate picture to
the president. As noted, Johnson had trouble getting good information on Vietnam although it might be pointed out that Johnson did
receive some CIA reports which were not so optimistic (Allison,
p. 196-197). Often, perhaps, presidents listen to what they want to
hear. Dissenting reports are always available. Writes Corson,

> "The president can if he chooses require the inclusion
> of dissent in preparation of written intelligence estimates,
> or invite the testimony of the proponents and dissenters when
> an estimate is being considered for acceptance as the basis for
> a policy decision at the highest levels" (Corson, p. 456).

A role for Congress would also keep the CIA in line without
severely hampering the president's decision-making powers.

"It would...make clear to the Congress the ambiguities
inherent in the intelligence estimating process concerning
the capabilities and intentions of potential and actual
opponents in impending crises. Second, it would provide a
sound basis for what has euphemistically been referred to in
the past as 'prior consultations with the Congress.' And
third, it could conceivably dampen Congress' carping criticisms
of presidential foreign policy decisions by giving the SSC a
much better appreciation of what is known and not known about
the consequences of a presidential decision" (Corson, p. 457)

Of course, Congressional involvement raises the question of
combining the requirements of democracy with the need for secrecy
(Corson, p. 447). Many would argue that letting Congress in on
secrets is as good as making them public. Yet as *[name of instructor]*
remarked, "Congress can keep its mouth shut when it
wants to."

Although current director William Stansfield is moving toward
the above-mentioned goals, many, including Senator Daniel P.
Moynihan, feel that Congressional involvement is poorly set-up.
Presently, eight committee look at parts of the intelligence scene
(Orr Kelly, 1979), pp. 27-32). A single committee such as Allison
proposes would have more effective authority, involve less
bureaucratic slow-ups, and get a better idea of what is going on
(Allison and Szanton, pp. 209-210).

Conclusion

    Thus, Allison is correct in his call for CIA control. Future
intelligence targets, writes, Corson, require

"sources who are capable of knowing the meaning and
significance of equations written on a blackboard and not
sources who only know how to blow up a bridge or are adept
at 'silent killing'" (Corson, p. 482).

But that control can be accomplished without all of the severe
measures Allison proposes. We don't need an intelligence agency so
crippled that it becomes just more bureaucratic fat, powerless to
act quickly. In other words, the "committee urge", which Corson
found in the Smith plan, must be avoided. It's

"a recurring phenomenon in government, especially among
career administrators who, when faced with the fact of inept
of indifferent leadership by elected and appointed officials,
favor an organizational or interorganizational response to
offset that leadership void...Rarely do these actions achieve
their intended purposes because regardless...There is no
substitute for direct and concerned leadership on the part of
elected and appointed officials" (Corson, pp. 267-268).

[The paper concludes with a bibliography.]

   Both the first and the last paragraphs state the student's thesis: some
of Allison and Szanton's recommendations for limiting the CIA have merit, but, as Corson's book illustrates, their plan to split the CIA will not
work. However, though the initial and concluding paragraphs maintain
focus and though the paper contains appropriate material for a strong es-

say, the reader is confused because points are not well sequenced. Below is an outline the student might logically have followed in analyzing the suggestions of someone with whom he partly agrees and partly disagrees or in describing a problem for which he is going to reject some solutions and embrace others:

Introduction: statement of the student's thesis, plus summary of Allison and Szanton's plan.

1. Student agrees with the authors that there are major abuses. Analyzes categories of abuse and reasons for abuse.
2. Student disagrees with the authors' plan to split the CIA and tells why it will not work.
3. Student agrees with Allison and Szanton, and with Corson, that tighter control is needed and suggests some specific measures.

Conclusion: summary.

It would probably be a mistake to give the student this outline. Instead, ask him to outline his paper or to list the main points of all its paragraphs. Then get him to identify his three main points and arrange his material accordingly.

Another way to approach this paper is to express your confusion and your awareness of repetition. For example, when you first begin to lose the train of thought, write "I don't follow; you are presenting ideas helter-skelter." Next to paragraph 3 you might write, "Here and again later at several points, you mention abuses. Why split up the discussion of that subject?" Questioned about the dispersion of one point, the student will have to reexamine his entire plan.

After reexamining the paper, he may come up with a plan somewhat different from the one I have suggested. In fact, he may try to justify something close to the plan he has. If so, you can then discuss the relative merits of various organizational schemes. You will also need to stress the need for connective material and for signposts that tell the reader what the writer is doing. In addition, emphasize the need for paragraph coherence. For example, paragraphs 5 through 8 are choppy and disorganized; the student should combine some of them and write better transitions and topic sentences.

The next example is a review of Robert Ardrey's *The Hunting Hypothesis,* written by a young man who later won a Danforth Fellowship. A teacher could make a significant contribution to the training of such a highly talented person by working with him here on the sequence of ideas, which is not quite as tight as it could be.

A View of the Hunting Hypothesis

(1) In many ways man is a unique creature. He kills his own kind and yet can exhibit an intense care for them. He has a complex social organization far above that of any other species in its versatility and complexity. Man has developed tool use to a high degree not found in any other animal. Robert Ardrey, in <u>The Hunting Hypothesis</u>, seeks to answer the question of why man is what he is. He would answer with the statement than man is man because of his evolutionary past as a hunter.

(2) During the Pliocene the great forests of Africa began to recede. Under extended periods of drought the lakes and streams began to dry up. Africa became predominantly savanah. In this period of time our ancestors were forced from a fruit-eating forest-dwelling life into the dry plains of Pliocene Africa. Ardrey states that they were poorly adapted for scavenging, they could not digest the grains of grasses, and thus they were forced rapidly into the hunting life. Gradually their feet adjusted, their stance became more erect, and they discovered the value of tools in the hunt. For millions of years our ancestors faced a selective pressure pushing them to become more effective hunters. Ardrey believes that the movement toward improved hunting was not merely a physical change, but is reflected in our mental heritage as well.

(3) In the early 1950's Dr. Raymond Dart was finding Australopithecus, a segment of the human evolutionary line, in South Africa. With the fossil remains Dart found evidence that Australopithecus had hunted armed. This means that three million years ago man subsisted as a hunter.

(4) The idea that man has a talent for hunting with a mind that leans in that direction contradicts many modern philosophies. Rouseau's peace-loving uncorrupted man becomes somewhat unlikely. The "Tabula Rasa", or blank sheet, which is the mind of an infant suddenly is given a built in propensity and talent for violence. The belief in the power of economic goals which is held by Marxist and Capitalist alike is weakened if man is by nature a hunter.

(5) Evidence has been found to support the hypothesis. In caves inhabited millions of years ago have been found bones and weapons used by the ancestors of men. Alternative theories such as man the scavenger and man the seed-eater are disputed by Ardrey. Early man, claims Ardrey, could not have been a successful scavenger. His feet were not adapted for the speed to reach a kill first, and his sense of smell was too poor for early detection of a kill. He was a creature too weak to drive off other scavengers or predators from a kill. Ardrey turns to biochemistry for some of his points. Man could not have been a seedeater, Ardrey claims, because man can

Seems awkwardly inserted between the fossil and biochemical support for A's hypothesis. Could you find a better spot for this idea?

not digest many seeds raw. "None of our vegetable staffs of life -
our wheat, our rice, our maize, our beans - can be eaten raw in any
quantity at all without remarkable digestive uproar," (Ardrey, 1977).
Cooking is required to make these foods digestible. Man did not
have fire until 40-50 thousand years ago. Furthermore, in the
analysis of coprolites, fossilized fecal material, there have been
no grains found, although evidence suggests that if present they
would be preserved.

(6) Our behavior also lends support to the hunting hypothesis.
Man tends to work well in groups of about ten. This is about the
size a good hunting pack would be. The coordination that groups of
humans exhibit and the fact that one member of the group functions
as a leader also lend themselves well to a hunting life. The
territoriality we exhibit, not so much individually but as organized
groups with a deadly efficiency, suggests the protection of a
hunting range by its owners. Ardrey points out that these traits
are not necessary to the degree they are found in man unless man has
a background of meat-eating and hunting. Our ability to cooperate
to the point of building a society such as we have is not necessary
to a vegetarian who must merely search for edible plants. It is
this ability to cooperate in moving toward a single tangible goal
which has given man the ability to create a culture based on goals.
A vegetarian or a scavenger exists on a much more regular set of
actions; the first hunting for grains, the second hunting for a kill
from which it can drive the owners.

(7) Ardrey also believes in the development of art as a
survival trait. "We would not have survived without art," he says.
According to Ardrey, art arose from magic. Magic for early man was
a way to ritualize hunting. The two together (art and magic)
provided both instruction and a ritual procedure for obtaining luck.
It was a way of maintaining enthusiasm for the hunt between actual
hunting expeditions. Art also becomes a sublimation of the hunting
urge in man.

(8) In modern times hunting for a living is generally
maladaptive. Ardrey believes that anything which sublimates hunting
is a valuable activity. The competition we face in virtually all
facets of life is foundthere because of our need for the hunt.
Without the chase and kill in some form or other man becomes bored.
Perhaps this urge to hunt is a part of the problem of a search for
meaning which the race of man continally wrestles with. Yet many
men have found meaning in the pursuit of a business career. In
business men are willing to spend inordinately large amounts of time
in the pursuit of business goals. These goals - the fight for a
contract or the financial destruction of a rival (driving him off of

one's own territory) — are easily explained as sublimations of
hunting. The delight which man takes in hunting for sport does not
make sense for a vegetarian. Ardrey points out that what is of
survival value is made pleasurable. Hunting has no real value to
a vegetarian.

(9) The writer does not have the background of information to
measure the truth of Robert Ardrey's rhetoric. It is convincingly
presented and the information I do have available does not
contradict it, in fact it supports his conclusions. If we accept
the hypothesis as valid there are some conclusions to be derived
from it in understanding ourselves and our roles in our techno-
logical society.

(10) A biological urge has been frustrated. There is little
room for the hunt in Tokyo. But the urge is still there, pushing
for something which is an impossibility. For some it can be
sublimated in business or sports, perhaps a somewhat passive
viewing of television violence will suffice. But our society
consists of a large range of individuals. For some the sublimation
is only partially successful, for others it is almost useless. And
for few will a substitute activity provide equal satisfaction. This
frustration will have the effect of increasing stress in man. In a
culture in which stress is already high because of other factors
this effect can hardly be doing much for our racial happiness and
sanity.

I felt lost here what is the connection?

(11) The freedom and right to own a gun <u>is one of the more</u>
<u>hotly debated issues of the present time</u>. The guns are dangerous.
It is only necessary to read the paper to find instances of a child
being killed or wounded by his father's gun in an accident. We do
not wish to lose the instrument symbolic of hunting. If that symbol
and possibility of hunting is there, if that self image as a hunter
can be had by a gun, then its' possesion makes the loss of real
hunting a little more tolerable.

Is this the idea you want to highlig[ht]

(12) The pursuit of an activity as horrible as war seems such a
pointless and painful action. But where else in our world can a
real hunt be had? One is pitting one's life on the outcome of the
hunt. The odds are not much different than they were millions of
years ago. Yet the danger is obviously there. There obviously are
many aspects of it which are hated. Few would admit to enjoying the
actual killing. But the idea of war, the training for it, and the
fascination with it in books and movies point to it as a substitute
for hunting.

(13) Many aspects of the hunting hypothesis seem rather
negative. However, in our talent for cooperation and our ability to
pursue a goal lies the hope for escaping some of our hunting
tendencies. The key point here is that these urges are only

tendencies. They can be escaped, and our minds which evolved for
the pursuit of the hunt have the capability to find that escape.

There are two points at which the sequence of ideas could be improved in this essay. One is in paragraphs 4 and 5, where material about
modern philosophies interrupts an otherwise smooth flow between the
information about fossil remains and the other evidence, much of it biochemical, with which Ardrey refutes theories about man as seed eater or
as scavenger. The second point is in paragraph 6. Repetition arises from
the organizational plan the writer has chosen:

I. Behavior that lends itself to the hunting life

  A. Working well in groups of ten

  B. Coordination among groups and leadership patterns in groups

  C. Territoriality

II. Behavior necessary only for meat-eating hunters

  A. Cooperation not necessary to plant searchers

  B. Cooperation toward a goal different from actions of vegetarians and
scavengers

My comments to the student ask him to justify the interruption and
the repetition. With a student at this level of ability, such questions
should be enough to start the search for better alternatives, without my
having to suggest specific solutions. I expect that paragraph 4, if it sur-
vives at all, will appear either just before or just after paragraph 9. The
student will probably reduce paragraph 6 to what is presently point II in
my outline. If workable, the questioning technique is sounder because it
prevents the student from blindly following the teacher's suggestions to
move a paragraph to spot X or to integrate the two halves of paragraph 6.
There is a third problem in paragraphs 10 through 13, which seem to
me not to hold together very well. The theme of frustration is nicely developed in paragraph 10, but then the reader needs some transitional material to indicate how the paragraphs on gun ownership fit in. To jog the
writer into revision at this junction, I might do two things: first, reflect
my difficulty in following his train of thought from paragraph 10 to paragraph 11 and, second, question the present first sentence of paragraph 11,
which provides no transition and no clue to the true focus of the paragraph. It is not the debate about guns we are primarily interested in; it is
the fact that many people cling to so dangerous an expression of their

hunting instinct. A sentence that makes a transition and also leads into the subject of paragraph 11 might read something like this: "If our stress is not sublimated in relatively harmless activities like sports and tv, it may emerge in more dangerous and deadly forms. For example, many Americans, in the face of hot debate, stoutly maintain their right to own and use guns. The guns are dangerous."

In addition to making these comments on organization, I would, in a full critique of this paper, probably also point out some mechanical problems and some aspects of diction, just to help a fine writer learn to polish his writing to even greater perfection. Praise, too, would form a significant part of my response—praise for the interesting first paragraph, for other felicities of phrasing, and for the points at which the essay effectively and accurately summarizes Ardrey's points.

Transitions

I have just suggested some approaches you can take if the paper does not follow a discernible outline because the student has not arrived at sufficiently developed and effectively ordered subtopics. Sometimes, however, the student does have a sensible organization in mind but cannot make it clear to the reader. So again, but for a different reason, the paper fails the acid test: can a reader perusing the paper reproduce, without the use of ESP, the writer's outline? When logical thought patterns are present but not clearly evident, the student needs to learn how to give clues to the organizational plan of the paper. Usually this is a matter of learning to supply accurate topic statements and smooth transitions.

You should emphasize that it is the writer's responsibility to provide you, as the reader, with enough clues so that you can reconstruct the outline as you read the paper. You can tell the student that when a paragraph first engages the reader's eye, it must rapidly announce what it is about and how it fits into what the reader has just read. The paragraph may start right off with a "square" topic sentence of the good old rhetoric-book variety, or it may use more subtle or more imaginative markers. But it must not let the reader wonder or wander. Like airplane pilots on foggy nights, readers need to receive enough bleeps so that they always know where they are.

Students sometimes need reminders about the ways a writer can indicate a shift from one point to another and can spell out the relation between two ideas. Here are some common transitions:

- *Single words:* because, but, therefore, however, next, nevertheless, since, moreover, etc.
- *Structural devices:* repetition of key words, parallel structure, use of pronouns.

- *Phrases or sentences:*

  The second major impact of radiation exposure is. . . .

  After having gained the person's trust in all these ways, the interviewer must now. . . .

  The same duality that appears in Freud's theories appears again, somewhat altered, in those of Adler.

  Can such a cycle of self-defeating actions be broken?

  Proponents of the bill, on the other hand, base their argument on Labor Department statistics.

The following paper illustrates the sort that results when a student has a logical outline in mind but fails to make that outline sufficiently clear.

Men's Roles

clarify relations between sentences

(1) Men suffer the effects of traditional gender roles more than women. || Behavioral patterns that are innate come into conflict with the assigned roles that culture attempts to instill in its youth. || Culture expects boys to mature faster than girls even though boys actually mature slower than girls. An act of opposite sex behavior carried out by a boy is frowned upon to a greater degree than if performed by a girl. Similar behavior of a boy and of a girl is often met with scorn for the boy and acceptance for the girl. The concept that only men must achieve and be aggressive is a prime cause of their suffering.

I'm lost. how does this relate to what I've just read?

(2) If it is true that the central nervous system differs between males and females, then it should cause differences in the behavior of male and female children. There should be differences in behavioral patterns even before the force of cultural environment takes hold on the two sexes.

(3) It is difficult to conduct a study of young infants under six months of age because of their lack of body control and inability to communicate effectively. (Therefore,) the study subjects must be at least six months old in order to perform a relevant study. *good transition*

(4) A study of infants which was conducted by J. Kagan and M. Lewis (1965) produced the following results of innate differences. *again provide transition*

6 months

Male	Female
1) "Greatest cardiac deceleration, (a measure of attention) to an intermittent tone."	"Greater cardiac deceleration to complex jazz music"

13 months

Male	Female
2) Preference for the low complexity stimuli	Preference for high complexity stimuli
3) Slower language development	Earlier language development

(5) Girls mature faster than boys even though society expects the opposite. It enables girls to conform to the cultural standards of behavior as well as avoid the stress that accompanies conflict with cultural standards. Since culture views infantile behavior as feminine, boys are pressured to abandon their innate behavior and to conform to the assigned masculine role. The high percentage of males with psychological problems reinforces the claim that men suffer more than women because boys are forced to change their behavioral patterns which creates physical and mental stress. Culture does not force girls out of their infantile behavior because culture views it as feminine. Therefore, girls seldom experience the stress of altering their role.

[handwritten margin notes: Transition - however? but? on the other hand]

(6) A tomboy is barely noticed by others, but a boy who is reserved and passive is branded as a sissy by his peers. I have a tomboy and a passive boy on my bus route. After transporting her home, she often climbs a tree on her yard in order to show off for the others on the bus. The students on the bus do not respond with any negative reactions. || The boy is often ridiculed as being a girl for insignificant acts such as not being able to open his window. This results from his age and physical capacity, but not from his personality or personal traits. He tends to be moving towards a state of insecurity while the tomboy seems to be unaffected. Culture is responsible for his insecurity because it forced a sex role that conflicts with his natural personality.

[handwritten margin note: Let me know you've begun your second point, and what that point is, before you get into Tomboys and sissies.]

(7) Culture is especially disruptive when it inhibits an act by one sex while encouraging similar acts by the other sex. A six year old boy on my bus was teased about not being a man because he was crying after bumping his head on a seat. A young girl on my bus was encouraged by her older sister to "let it out" when she was crying. Boys are always trying to prove their masculinity by feats of strength and fighting. Girls are scolded by their older siblings as not being "ladylike" when they engage in physical confrontations. Society teaches males to be "nobody's fool" while it implies that females are "emotional fools."

[handwritten margin note: Fine transition and topic sentence]

(8) I was insecure in my youth, because culture tried to force me to be aggressive and competitive. My personality has always leaned toward being reserved and cooperative. I felt insecure in regard to boys because I thought they were superior if they

[handwritten margin note: Repetition of this word from #1 helps reader see you're beginning your 4th point. Good]

displayed aggressive traits. My insecurity in regard to girls
stemmed from my concept that I would be inadequate for a girl since
I did not possess the aggressive trait that girls valued highly.
I suffered greatly from the feeling that I was below standards in
the eyes of girls. If society had been less rigid in defining what
a boy's role should be, then I would have fit into society more
confidently.

(9) Society has succeeded in deceiving the children on my bus
into believing that males should be active leaders who will control
and operate the country while their "love objects" remain at home to
cook, clean, and get pregnant. The males suffer the problem of
achieving their active leadership, but the girls, whose only goal
in life is to get married and have kids, find it easy to get
pregnant. Males who completely accept their assigned roles become
very aggressive, independent, and competitive in order to become a
"success." The importance of "success" causes severe stresses for
men that women who are at home do not experience. This competitive
stress reduces men's life expectancy, enjoyment of life, and ability
to relate to others.

(10) The male dominated society has brought males short-run
benefits with high long-run costs. Men will continue to suffer more
problems in life than women unless we open up all areas of our
culture to both sexes. If we increase opportunity for all, then
both sexes will have equal footing in society. The evolution of
society from one of barriers to one of opportunities will make all
of our lives more enjoyable and long lasting.

Your essay is well organized, but you have to give readers more connections and more clues to reveal that organization.

On first reading, this paper seems disjointed, but further scrutiny
reveals that the sequence is carefully arranged. The first sentence announces the topic, and the rest of the first paragraph outlines the four
main sections. The rest of the paper develops each of the four in turn.
Very logical, very well organized. But the writer has not provided connective tissue and clues about organization to enable you, the reader, to grasp
the plan of the paper as you read it. You feel as if you're led along blindfolded. The guide may be heading straight to the destination, but you still
feel lost and insecure.

In working with a student who has this weakness, you can approach
the issue like so many other aspects of writing, by talking about reader
expectations. My written comments show how you can do this if you are
writing your response to the student. In a conference, you might read
aloud the first and second sentences of the paper and voice your confu-

sion about how the second sentence is related to the first. Do the same for the rest of the first paragraph. Then move to the second paragraph and read its first sentence. Again voice your confusion: "How does this business about the central nervous system relate to the topics mentioned in the first paragraph?" Your goal in this questioning process is to help the student see that the essay is tossing the reader one isolated statement after another, with nothing that helps the reader understand how all this material fits together. Then ask the student to revise the paper, providing the clues and the transitions that readers need. Perhaps the writer will come back with something like the paper that follows. The new transitions and topic statements are in italic type, and I have left the essay's remaining flaws alone, in the interests of concentrating only on the addition of connective tissue. You will often find, though, that the student, in revising to correct one problem, makes other improvements along the way. If not you will want to deal with stylistic problems, handling of data and quotations, and so forth—either along with your comments about transitions or at some later time.

Revised Version of "Men's Roles"

(1) Men suffer the effects of traditional gender roles more than women. One reason men are so disadvantaged is that their innate behavioral patterns come into conflict with the assigned roles that culture attempts to instill in its youth. For example, culture expects boys to mature faster than girls even though boys actually mature slower than girls. A second reason for the difficulties of boys is that an act of opposite sex behavior carried out by a boy is frowned upon to a greater degree than if performed by a girl. In addition, similar behavior of a boy and of a girl is often met with scorn for the boy and acceptance for the girl. Finally, the concept that only men must achieve and be aggressive is a prime cause of boys' suffering.

(2) Society expects boys, more than girls, to overcome their innate biological characteristics. If it is true that the central nervous system differs between males and females, then it should cause differences in the behavior of male and female children. There should be differences in behavioral patterns even before the force of cultural environment takes hold on the two sexes.

(3) Such evidence of differences does in fact exist, based on six-month old infants. The reason for using six-month olders is that it is difficult to conduct a study of young infants under six months of age because of their lack of body control and inability to communicate effectively. Therefore, the study subjects must be at least six months old in order to perform a relevant study.

(4) One such investigation of six month old infants, which was conducted by J. Kagan and M. Lewis (1965), produced the following results of innate differences.

6 months

Male	Female
1) "Greatest cardiac deceleration, (a measure of attention) to an intermittent tone."	"Greater cardiac deceleration to complex jazz music."

13 months

Male	Female
2) "Preference for the low complexity stimuli."	"Preference for high complexity stimuli."
3) "Slower language development."	"Earlier language development."

(5) <u>This study indicates that</u> girls mature faster than boys even though society expects the opposite. This enables girls to conform to the cultural standards of behavior as well as avoid the stress that accompanies conflict with cultural standards. <u>However</u>, since culture views infantile behavior as feminine, boys are pressured to abandon their innate behavior and to conform to the assigned masculine role. The high percentage of males with psychological problems reinforces the claim that men suffer more than women because boys are forced to change their behavioral patterns which creates physical and mental stress. Culture does not force girls out of their infantile behavior because culture views it as feminine. Therefore, girls seldom experience the stress of altering their role. <u>Pressured to transcend their innately slower rate of maturation, boys also experience greater disapproval than girls do for opposite-sex behavior</u>. <u>For example</u>, a tomboy is barely noticed by others, but a boy who is reserved and passive is branded as a sissy by his peers. I have a tomboy and a passive boy on my bus route. After transporting her home, she often climbs a tree on her yard in order to show off for the others on the bus. The students on the bus do not respond with any negative reactions. <u>However</u>, the boy is often ridiculed as being a girl for an insignificant act such as not being able to open his window....

Certainly there are still flaws in the essay. One of this student's primary writing problems, however, was his failure to provide transitions, a fault that obscured for the reader the actual logic of the student's organization. A teacher who helps students command that particular skill does them a great service.

Chapter Eight

Style

We generally label style problems "clumsiness" or "awkwardness" or "poor word choice." They may be so acute that we want to work with them just as soon as the basic focus of a student's paper is clear. For example, here is a passage in which the student predicts Jessica Mitford's probable reaction to a proposal for more pleasant and sanitary prisons:

```
Mitford asked for reform or abolishion.  In abolishion she
wanted all prisoners out of jails now and put the hard-core on farms
or cities by themselves.  She was for abolishion so better prison
conditions would not go along here except when she wanted the
hard-core people on better, easyer land.
```

You'll want fairly quickly to attack style problems—in diction, sentence construction, wordiness. In this chapter I suggest ways in which you can identify the various problems that contribute to the clumsiness of the passage and talk with students about them.

At another level, you will find the student whose writing is well organized, clearly conceived, and free of mechanical errors. There are likely to be some slightly awkward passages, but you may be so glad to see a prince emerge from the mass of frogs that you don't feel like quibbling over whether his hair is combed or his posture straight. Or maybe you don't feel confident about giving him guidance on the finer points. But it's too bad to let him go out into the world with tousled hair or slumped shoulders when he has so much to start with. Yet that's what often happens in schools: poor writers get help in becoming competent writers, but competent writers get no help in honing their skills toward excellence. A student gets back a paper with an A or a B, the word "good" written across the top, and a few checks indicating minor mechanical errors, but not a single specific comment about where and why the writing style is successful or where it could be improved. So the teacher has not helped that student learn anything about good writing.

Or maybe the teacher has written "awkward" beside a paragraph or two. A sophisticated student may get the message, and it's better than no comment at all, but sometimes a student has no idea how to amend awkwardness, except to try reworking the passage, hoping to hit on something that will please the teacher. We can help students develop a smooth, precise, and crafted style if we as teachers learn and practice some ways of giving specific, detailed criticism about the finer points of writing.

But I know you're thinking at this point, especially if you've glanced ahead through this chapter, "That's all very nice, but if I tried to analyze in detail every paragraph and sentence my students write, I'd never finish." True, you wouldn't. So do as much as possible.

You often needn't, and in fact shouldn't, do a detailed critique of every paragraph in a student's paper. Usually a better teaching method is to explain the basic principle of parallelism or economy, illustrate how that principle could be applied to one or two paragraphs of the student's paper, and then ask the student independently to apply that principle to the rest of the paper.

We all know, however, that analyzing the finer points of writing style does take time, especially if you haven't had much practice at it. Nevertheless, if you can devote, say, ten minutes to each paper, you may have to spend that time, with some students, working on the focus of the entire paper or on sentence fragments, but with another you can concentrate on economy or word choice in a paragraph or two. Or, if you can't work on style with all your students, do it for just one class each semester, or for a few students from each class, or for everyone who gets a certain grade, or for those whose papers you think you would be able to analyze most skillfully. But do give some attention to those students who, with guidance and encouragement, could move from competent writers to really good writers.

The rest of this chapter offers suggestions about how you can learn to recognize stylistic successes and failures, describe them in specific and accurate terms, talk about them to students, and help students improve.

The four principles of style I discuss, though by no means a comprehensive list, should cover most of the problems we see as teachers:

- Good writing clearly indicates the *relative importance* of ideas.
- Good writing accurately reflects the *relation* among ideas.
- Good writing is *economical.*
- Good writing is *concrete, precise, simple,* and *vivid.*

Indicating Relative Importance

When reading a student's writing, ask whether the paper accurately reflects the relative importance of various ideas. There are two main ways of indicating relative importance.

1. By the *position* of words and phrases in the sentence or paragraph. Minor ideas are relegated to subordinate clauses, to modifiers, or to unobtrusive places in the sentence or paragraph. The most important words or ideas appear in spots that receive most attention—main clauses and at the beginnings and endings of sentences and paragraphs.
2. By the type of *structure* in which an idea appears. Important ideas are usually treated in a main clause; the writer avoids making a whole sentence out of a subsidiary idea that should be merely a modifying word or phrase.

The following, from a paper on the influences that shape men's roles in our society, illustrates both methods of indicating relative importance:

```
    (1) The masculine role is developed at an early age.
(2) Parents shape this role to a large degree.  (3) This is evident
by the different way parents treat their children.  (4) Fathers tend
to play rougher with boys, while mothers nurse, handle, and
verbalize less with boys.  (5) This was found in a recent study.
```

The student is writing about the masculine role—its origins and effects. In this sample paragraph, he is beginning a section on how the masculine role is shaped, first by parents and then by the media and the schools. Thus his first sentence in this paragraph appropriately states the thesis for this whole section. The next sentence also does its job well: it indicates that the writer is now about to discuss the parental influence. But though the paper as a whole and this paragraph as a part of it show a definite organizational plan, the writing is clumsy. In working toward a remedy, the instructor would do well to analyze the causes of the awkwardness. In this instance, the problem lies partly in the way the student has indicated the relative importance of various ideas. The most striking fault is that "This was found in a recent study" is not important enough to merit a full sentence or to deserve that climactic spot at the end of the paragraph. It offends in both position and structure. The fact should instead be presented in a subordinate phrase relegated to an unobtrusive place as in this example:

```
(4) Fathers, according to a recent study, tend to play rougher with
boys, while mothers nurse, handle, and verbalize less with boys.
```

There is another point in this paragraph at which the writer could better indicate the relative importance of two ideas. The beginnings and ends of sentences or paragraphs tend to be prominent. In sentence 2 the writer has not properly used these spots to distribute emphasis.

```
(2) Parents shape this role to a large degree.
```

Ask the student which of the two marked phrases is more important or forms the basis for further development later in the paragraph. The answer is "shape this role," since the rest of this paragraph and several succeeding paragraphs tell how parents shape children's roles. If "to a large degree" were the main idea developed by the rest of the paragraph, then the placement of "to a large degree" at the end of the sentence might be justified. Such a paragraph might look like this:

```
Parents shape this role to a large degree.  Lesser influence,
however, is also exerted by the schools.  Television has its impact,
too, as does magazine advertising.
```

The student's paragraph, however, does not develop the "to a large degree" idea but rather the "shape" idea. Therefore, "shape this role" could better have the prominent place at the end of the sentence. The revised version would thus read:

```
(2) Parents, to a large degree, shape this role.
```

As this example illustrates, the whole question of where to insert clauses, phrases, and modifiers needs to engage the attention of the writer. The first instinct of most beginning writers is to state the subject and the verb and then to stick modifiers on at the end. Though this structure can be effective, it also can produce sentences that trail off into confusion or trivia or that waste the climactic end spot on a relatively unimportant idea. Many beginning writers need to be reminded that sentence elements, like railroad cars, have couplings. One can often detach an element and insert it in a different spot. Phrases, clauses, and one-word modifiers can frequently be slipped into any one of several positions in the sentence, and the skillful writer makes a conscious choice on the basis of where the emphasis should fall. Further examples appear later in this chapter. But meanwhile, let us consider another, closely related aspect of writing.

Establishing Clear Relations

Good writing style depends a great deal on clearly indicating the relations among ideas and words. The writer has three important means of pinpointing these relations:

1. By the *position* of words, phrases, or sentences.

2. By *words and phrases* that accurately specify the relations between ideas.
3. By *grammatical construction.*

Position

Look again at the paragraph about how parents shape their children's gender roles. The paragraph improved after the student made two changes to clarify the relative importance of ideas. But more possible improvements become apparent when we ask whether or not the writer has clarified the relations among ideas. The altered paragraph reads like this:

```
    (1) The masculine role is developed at an early age.
(2) Parents, to a large degree, shape this role.  (3) This is
evident by the different way parents treat their children.   (4)
Fathers, according to a recent study, tend to play rougher with boys,
while mothers nurse, handle and verbalize less with boys.
```

One problem with this paragraph is that some ideas are placed where their relations to other elements are unclear or ambiguous. One example is sentence 4.

```
(4) Fathers, according to a recent study, tend to play rougher
with boys, while mothers nurse, handle, and verbalize less with boys.
```

When the word "less" appears, readers must go back and change their initial understanding of the beginning of the "mothers nurse ..." clause. When a student has made you retrace your steps through a passage of writing, you should feel gypped, take your complaint straight back to the writer, explain as clearly as you can why you had to backtrack, and ask that the problem be solved. One way to show the student how this sentence has set the reader up for misunderstanding is to read the sentence aloud to the student, modulating your voice or supplying elliptical phrases so as to emphasize the misreading that can occur: " 'mothers nurse boys, handle boys, and verbalize less ...' oops! Now I see that it should be 'mothers nurse boys less, handle boys less,' and so forth." If you are making written comments, jot down in the margin the misreading to which the reader is vulnerable, or ask a question that will allow the student to recognize the possible misreading: "Do mothers nurse boys or nurse boys less? Let me know early in the sentence."

Sometimes a problem of this sort will need merely the insertion of a comma, but often, as here, the remedy calls for a rearrangement of words or groups of words in the sentence. A revision of this sentence might read this way:

(4) Fathers, according to a recent study, tend to play rougher
with boys, while mothers less frequently nurse, handle, or verbalize
with boys.

The problem of ambiguous placement also emerges in sentence 3 of
the paragraph, where imprecise diction compounds the difficulty:

(3) This is evident by the different way parents treat their
children.

The position of the word "different" and the use of the word "children"
make the reader unsure whether parents treat their own children differently from other peoples' children or whether they treat some of their
own children differently from others of their own children or whether
different parents treat their children in certain ways. Thus the reader is
forced to go back and puzzle out the meaning. The teacher should again
read or explain the sentence so that the student sees the reader's possible
confusion. Then the student should revise until the result is something
like this:

(3) This is evident by the way parents treat their boys differently
from their girls.

Words and Phrases

Though sentence 3 is now better, it is still not quite right. It reflects
another common problem: relations between two ideas cannot be accurately expressed in inaccurate words or phrases. For example, the phrase
"this is evident by" does not really indicate the true relationship between
the two ideas it connects:

Idea 2	*Idea 3*
Parents . . . shape this role.	. . . parents treat their boys differently from their girls.

In working with the student, try writing these two ideas in separate columns, leaving a space between them, as above. Then ask the student to
tell you the relation between the two ideas and to write that in the middle. Or ask what the writer means by the phrase "This is evident by." Either of these exercises should help the student see that the phrase "is
evident by" is not accurate. What the writer really wants to say is that
parents shape roles *by means of* their different treatment of sons and
daughters. Thus a revision of the sentence might look like this:

(2,3) Parents to a large degree shape this role <u>by</u> treating their
boys differently from their girls.

Getting words and phrases right may require not only substituting better choices but also adding words or phrases for clarity. The paragraph with which we are working might be improved by the insertion of a transitional phrase such as "for example" between sentences 3 and 4 so that the reader realizes immediately that the recent study about mothers and fathers is an example of how parents shape gender roles by treating their sons and daughters differently. Here is a revision:

```
(2,3) Parents to a large degree shape this role by treating their
boys differently from their girls.  For example, fathers, according
to a recent study . . .
```

The final improved version of the entire paragraph now looks like this:

Original	*Revision*
The masculine role is developed at an early age. Parents shape this role to a large degree. This is evident by the different way parents treat their children. Fathers tend to play rougher with boys, while mothers nurse, handle, and verbalize less with boys. This was found in a recent study.	The masculine role is developed at an early age. Parents to a large degree shape this role by treating their boys differently from their girls. For example, fathers, according to a recent study, tend to play rougher with boys, while mothers less frequently nurse, handle, and verbalize with boys.

The paragraph could probably be further improved by substituting the simple phrase "talk to" for the more academic "verbalize with." But regardless of the remaining faults, the paragraph has been greatly improved by a more accurate indication of (1) the relative importance of ideas and (2) the exact relations between those ideas.

This discussion of clarifying relations between ideas by choosing appropriate words and phrases would not be complete without a mention of the ubiquitous "and," so often used as a connector when the writer needs a more accurate word. For example, one student writes:

```
Most activities in the rehabilitation center take place in the
blue room, and one large group is conducted twice a week in an
adjoining room.
```

This sentence illustrates a common failing: the "and" indicates that the two activities are parallel, but they are not; the second is an exception to the first. Ask the student to explain the relationship between the statement that most activities take place in the blue room and the statement that one large group meets in an adjoining room. If you can provoke the recognition that the second is an exception to the first, then the writer can choose a connecting word that specifically conveys the concept of exception—a word like "however," "but," or "although." A revision might read:

```
Most activities in the rehabilitation center take place in the
blue room, but one large group is conducted twice a week in an
adjoining room.
```

Grammatical Construction

The third way to show connections is through grammatical construction. An idea may be embodied in a main clause or merely in a single adjective. Sometimes the ubiquitous "and" needs this remedy; one of the statements linked by the inaccurate "and" should be changed to a dependent clause, a phrase, or a single word to more accurately indicate the relationship between a main idea and a dependent or subordinate idea. In the following example, the words in question are underlined:

Original	*Revision*
The catfish's mouth is surrounded by sensitive barbels, and these help in orientation and food gathering.	The catfish's mouth is surrounded by sensitive barbels that help in orientation and food gathering.
Chavez met with the grape workers and he decided to send six organizers to help them.	After meeting with the grape workers, Chavez decided to send six organizers to help them.
The sea turtle has flipper limbs and with these it rows itself along.	The sea turtle has flipper limbs with which it rows itself along.

In the examples above, relationships are indicated by the use of subordinate structures. Parallel ideas are often revealed by parallel grammatical construction—a technique with which students often need help. The principle is this (and you can write it this way on student papers): parallel ideas should be expressed in similar forms. Successful writers may modify this principle, but it is a useful guideline for amateurs. Its clearest application is in lists, where equal elements should be stated in similar forms. For example:

Original	*Revision*
My hypothesis was that rat #9 would dominate, be inclined to a high level of activity, and always getting into fights.	My hypothesis was that rat #9 would be dominant, highly active, and combative. *[Every element in the list is an adjective.]*

When working on something larger than a short list, the writer also can express relations through parallel grammatical construction. When students are faced with a number of elements or statements, you might urge them to break sentences or passages into individual units and then try to line them up. For example, here is one student's sentence:

In 1918, sixty percent of House members supported the measure, but it was opposed by sixty percent of them in 1919.

A way to work with the student on a sentence like this is to identify the "fulcrum" of the sentence (in this case the word "but") and then identify the elements on each side.

date	*percent*	*verb*
In 1918	sixty percent of House members	supported the measure

fulcrum: but

verb	*percent*	*date*
it was opposed	by sixty percent of them	in 1919.

By arranging the units in columns, the students can recognize departures from parallel form and can then revise. In this example, probably the best plan is to arrange the units in exactly the same order on both sides of the fulcrum, in the order date, percent, verb:

Original

date, percent, verb	In 1918, sixty percent of House members supported the
fulcrum	measure, but
verb, percent, date	it was opposed by sixty percent of them in 1919.

Revision

date, percent, verb	In 1918, sixty percent of House members supported the
fulcrum	measure, but
date, percent, verb	by 1919 sixty percent of them opposed it.

Here is another example of writing that lacks parallel structure (the superscript numbers in the writing samples refer to end notes in the students' papers):

```
                          A statistic that speaks most favorably
                          for Patuxent is its recidivist rate.
total                     A study showed that out of 210,
percent, who, verb        80% of the repeaters had been released from Patuxent
by whom, fulcrum          by the court while
who, verb, by whom        those who had been released by the staff of
                          Patuxent (who considered them ready)
                                                                        16
percent, total            made up only 20% of the 210 recidivists.
```

In this example the elements labeled "total" and "who" need not be repeated because they do not change. We can simplify this passage by gathering common elements in one spot—at the beginning: "A study showed that out of 210 repeaters. . . ." Now the writer can line up the contrasting elements in parallel order:

```
                          A study showed that out of 210 repeaters,
percent, verb             80% had been released from Patuxent
by whom                   by the court,
fulcrum                   while
percent, verb             20% had been released
by whom                   by Patuxent staff (who considered them ready).
```

The comment you make to help the student move from the first to the second version might simply be the phrase "parallel structure," if your students understand the term. If they need a longer explanation, you might say, "This is hard to follow. Use the same order for the elements on each side of 'while.'"

A related error is the misplaced sentence element, which can cause either confusion or a ludicrous misreading. We've all chuckled over some of these:

```
Reform school staff created much antiprogressive thought in the
public's minds by telling stories of policies and case decisions
which documented the permissive and chaotic state of administration
to the press and magnifying them.
```

Like many such student sentences, this one starts out just fine. In this case it's the modifying clauses and phrases tacked to the end of the sentence that cause the trouble. I frequently handle this kind of problem by circling the offending element and writing simply "place," if my class understands that comment, or "Is this placed correctly in the sentence?" In this sample I would circle both "to the press" and "magnifying them." Here is the resulting revision:

Reform school staff created much antiprogressive thought in the
public's minds by telling and magnifying, to the press, stories
of policies and case decisions which documented the permissive
and chaotic state of administration.

Here's a slightly different problem. This student is discussing her
response to a stage presentation of *Cat on a Hot Tin Roof*:

There are so many opportunities for Maggie to express her
"cattiness" on stage that I simply did not picture when I read
the play.

The "so" and "that" in this sentence may be misread at first as the
familiar "so many . . . that" construction, in which "that" introduces a
consequence of "so many" (e.g., "There are so many opportunities that I
don't know which to choose"). The latter structure is so common that
readers are likely to expect it here and then have to go back and reread
the sentence. The remedy is to change the sentence order beginning with
what is now the last clause and making the "that" clause into a main
clause. It's also helpful, of course, to delete the weak intensive "so":

When I read the play, I simply did not picture the many opportunities
for Maggie to express her "cattiness" on stage.

In the next example, the ambiguity of the last phrase can be remedied by inserting a word or two to clarify the relation of the phrase "rather than the Japanese" to the rest of the sentence.

Because of the Communist group, the Allies were constantly faced
with the problem of restraining Chiang from using the aid sent to
him against the Communists, rather than the Japanese.

Here, the first step is to add "against" so that the relationship of the last
phrase becomes clear:

using the aid sent to him against the Communists, rather than
against the Japanese.

If you want to do something about the slightly clumsy placement of "sent
to him," you might suggest substituting "their" or moving the idea to an
earlier part of the sentence:

Because of the Communist group, the Allies were constantly faced
with the problem of restraining Chiang from using their aid against
the Communists, rather than against the Japanese.

or

```
Because of the Communist group, the Allies, who sent aid to Chiang,
were constantly faced with the problem of restraining him from
using it against the Communists, rather than against the Japanese.
```
[14]

In the next example, the run-on sentence results from insecurity about handling a long parallel construction.

```
The Japanese were unpredictable, at times staying away from their
prisoners completely, then at other times they would descend on the
men, shouting orders and violently attacking them.  At other times,
they would share their cigarettes and food with the men and act in
a civil manner.
```
[13]

I would not mark this "run-on." Instead, I would say something like "Put these three parallel ideas in similar form, separated by commas." The revision might read:

```
The Japanese were unpredictable, at times staying away from their
prisoners completely, at times descending on the men, shouting
orders and violently attacking them, and at other times sharing
their cigarettes and food with the men and acting in a civil
manner.
```
[13]

You may want to urge a dash instead of the first comma, or you may decide that the sentence is too long and that it should be broken up.

Because the problems I've just been discussing are so often intermingled, I've preferred to hold off most examples until now, when I can analyze sample student pieces that demonstrate several stylistic faults in indicating the relative importance and relatedness of ideas. The first example illustrates the need for parallel structure as well as the usefulness of a connecting word more accurate than "and." The writer is comparing several experiments to determine the prey preferences of hawks. Experiment 1 showed that, when offered two prey animals of equal size and weight, the hawk preferred the more active. Experiment 3, however, showed that, when offered a small, active animal and a large, inactive one, the hawk preferred the inactive prey. Here is the student's conclusion (I have underlined the "and"):

```
Comparing the data in experiment 1, showing a strong preference for
the more active prey, with the third where the larger prey was less
active and still preferred, may have demonstrated a tendency in the
hawk to choose the apparently more profitable prey item in terms of
relative biomass.
```

In working with this student, you might first try to find a more accurate connective than "and." The writer might come up with something like "the larger prey was less active, *though* still preferred." Next, suggest that the student use parallel structure in describing the two experiments. The revision might look like this:

```
Comparing the data in the first experiment, showing a strong
preference for the more active prey, with the third, showing a
preference for the larger though less active prey, may have
demonstrated a tendency in the hawk to choose the apparently more
profitable prey item in terms of relative biomass.
```

You and the writer might judge this sentence too complicated for maximum ease of reading, because the subject "comparing" is so far away from the verb "may have demonstrated." If so, the student might clarify the subject-verb relationship by revising the sentence to read:

```
Experiment 1 showed a strong preference for the more active prey,
while experiment 3 showed preference for the less active though
larger prey.  In comparison, the two experiments may have
demonstrated a tendency in the hawk to choose the apparently more
profitable prey item in terms of relative biomass.
```

This revision, which holds closely to the student's own wording, still is not as precise as it could be, since it is not the comparison itself that demonstrates the hawk's tendency, but the third experiment in the light of the first. Thus the student might place the emphasis on the third experiment by making it the subject of the second, and most important, sentence:

```
Experiment 1 established the hawk's preference for more active prey.
Experiment 3, by showing the hawk's preference for the less active
though larger prey, may have demonstrated a tendency in the hawk to
choose the apparently more profitable prey item in terms of relative
biomass.
```

In the next example, the writer wastes the final sentence—a high-emphasis spot—on a subsidiary idea that should have been integrated earlier as a subordinate clause or phrase.

```
Another person who feels the program is too extensive is
Antonio G. Olivieri, a democrat from the upper east side of
Manhattan and a leader of campaigns to end solitary confinement
in juvenile prisons and halt the incarceration of neglected and
abandoned children and other nondelinquent children who merely need
```

```
supervision.  He thought that abolishing all juvenile institutions
was too radical for New York.  "Realistically there's no chance of
doing that," he said.  "We need some closed detention facilities."
He is in favor of shutting down the state juvenile training
schools.³¹
```

In analyzing this paragraph, I would focus on the final sentence, asking the student whether the information it contained should be given that late in the paragraph and whether that information deserves the climactic ending spot. Clearly the answer is no, so the student now moves the information to an earlier point, indicating its relative unimportance by making it a subordinate clause and clarifying its relationship to the rest of the sentence by adding "although." (A problem that remains in the paragraph, of course, is the switch from present to past tense.)

```
Another person who feels the program is too extensive is
Antonio G. Olivieri, a democrat from the upper east side of
Manhattan and a leader of campaigns to end solitary confinement in
juvenile prisons and halt the incarceration of neglected and
abandoned children and other nondelinquent children who merely need
supervision.  Though he favors shutting down the state juvenile
training schools, he thought that abolishing all juvenile
institutions was too radical for New York.  "Realistically there's
no chance of doing that," he said.  "We need some closed detention
facilities."³¹
```

The next example is from a report on hermaphrodites: what the types of hermaphrodites are, how they are identified at birth, how they are raised, and what can be done medically to help them adjust. At the end of the paper, the student uses this information to offer an opinion on the case of a hermaphrodite she had personally known.

```
In conclusion, I would like to express my learning of this to
my experience of growing up with my classmate.  I would have to say
that she would have been a lot happier if she would have been
brought up as a male rather than a female.  Her height would not
have been so put down if she was a male, her breasts are not fully
developed, and she had to have an operation.  The doctors, I feel,
made the wrong decision and should have consultanted specialists.
```

While I would discuss the problems in diction in this essay—particularly "express my learning of this," "put down," and perhaps "a lot"—and the confusion about verb tenses, I would first address the student's problem in indicating relations among ideas—a problem that could be remedied by correcting a false parallelism. The writer strings together three clauses with commas—the clauses about height, about breasts, and about the operation. Yet they are not parallel results of being raised female, as the first part of the sentence leads the reader to expect. So I would ask for a fuller explanation of what each clause means and then suggest that that explanation be the basis for the revision of the paragraph. The result might look like this:

```
    In conclusion, I would like to relate my investigations to
my experience of growing up with my classmate.  I would have to say
that she would have been much happier if she had been brought up as
a male rather than as a female.  Her height would not have been
ridiculed, the incomplete development of her breasts would not have
mattered, and her operation would have been simpler.  The doctors,
I feel, made the wrong decision and should have consulted
specialists.
```

The next sample shows how placement of elements in a paragraph can create a false emphasis, or focus, and mask the true meaning. The student is discussing the maturation of Esther in Sylvia Plath's novel *The Bell Jar.* To be consonant with the rest of the essay, this paragraph, though it summarizes part of the story, must focus not on the plot but on Esther's struggle to become independent of others' expectations. Despite this imperative, the paragraph gives too much emphasis to the chronology of the events and too little to their meaning.

```
    (1) After returning to the suburb and learning that she did
not make the writing course Esther decides instead to learn
shorthand and write a novel.  (2) By learning shorthand Esther
would still be clinging to the need of meeting others' expectations
(that of her mother); however we see that she is making progress
when she gives it up.  (3) After one day she decides to put off
writing the novel until she has been to Europe and had a lover
feeling that she has had no experiences worth writing about.  (4) And
in a different sense from this, because Esther has always merely met
others' expectations, she has no true experiences to write about.
```

I would begin by praising sentence 4 because the student has used a sophisticated sentence structure, inserting the "because" clause before the main subject and verb, thus effectively saving the main idea for the last, climactic spot in the paragraph. I would urge revision of sentences 1 and 3 because they place primary emphasis on chronology. I would suggest that in sentence 2 the writer reconsider the order of the last two elements: "she is making progress" and "when she gives it up." It would perhaps be more effective to hold the "progress" for the last place in the sentence or otherwise to emphasize that idea more prominently. Also in sentence 2, clumsiness results from having three prepositional phrases in succession: (1) "to the need" (2) "of meeting others' expectations" (3) "of her mother." When puzzled about a clumsy passage, check the number of prepositional phrases; I find that method often explains clumsiness that I otherwise can't quite put my finger on. Working on the basis of these three suggestions and remedying as well the unnecessary "from this" and the verb-tense problem in sentence 1, where "has not made the writing course" would be a better choice, the student might revise the paragraph in this fashion:

```
    Still struggling with her need to meet others' expectations,
Esther, after returning to the suburb and learning that she has not
made the writing course, decides to learn shorthand and write a
novel.  When she gives up her mother's expectation--shorthand--we
see she is progressing toward maturity.  After one day on the novel,
she decides to put it off until she has been to Europe and had a
lover, feeling she has had no experiences worth writing about.  And
in a different sense, because Esther has always merely met others'
expectations, she has no true experiences to write about.
```

Now the paragraph establishes a focus in accord with the paper's thesis, and it structures and arranges its sentences so as to develop that focus.

Economy

Economy in writing means that every word should pull its weight. In some contexts, extra words may heighten emphasis, clarity, or vividness or even contribute to a baroque richness necessary to the particular author's purpose; such passages are economical, even though their ideas could be presented in fewer words. Beyond what serves good purpose, however, all ideas should be expressed as briefly as possible.

The economy of the paper as a whole is closely tied to organization: the writer must eliminate or condense irrelevant, repetitious, or inflated subtopics. Once the overall focus of the paper is clear, the student must strive for economy in each paragraph and sentence. The best way for writers to achieve economical prose is to express accurately the relations among sentence elements, as discussed earlier, and to "write with nouns and verbs," as I explain in the next section, "Concreteness, Precision, Simplicity, and Vividness." In addition, when you are analyzing a student's prose, you can look for three enemies of economy: inflation, repetition, and the passive voice.

Inflation

Easiest to spot is the inflation that results when a student uses filler words that can simply be omitted. One learns, after awhile, to spot those most common to student writing: "the fact that," "in order to," "proceeded to," "the one who," "in the case of." In the examples below, the revision appears in parentheses.

The governor went to the flooded area in order to observe the damage that existed.
(The governor went to the flooded area to observe the damage.)

It seemed to me that the new holes were larger.
(The new holes seemed larger.)

One of the biggest points of difference between the two organizations is in the matter of structure.
(One of the biggest differences between the two organizations is their structure./The two organizations differ markedly in structure.)

In comparison with the rat study, many things evident in that study were also observed with mice.
(Many things evident in the rat study were also observed with mice./The mice reacted in much the same way as the rats.)

In other instances, the writer uses roundabout or attenuated grammatical constructions. Here are two of the most common:

The verb "to be":

subject +	verb "to be" or synonym	+ predicate adjective or predicate noun
The room	is	a cheerful place.

Try changing this to a noun plus an adjective: "the cheerful room."

The room is a cheerful place and encourages creative activities.
(The cheerful room encourages creative activities.)

Clauses beginning with words like "that," "who," or "which": A writer may use a clause beginning with "that," "who," or some similar word when an adjective would suffice. In the following examples the revisions are shown in parentheses:

An experiment which was successful. . . .
(A successful experiment. . . .)

The authors also discuss briefly the later chapters and what they will contain.
(The authors also discuss briefly the contents of the later chapters.)

His attitude was one that conveyed hostility.
(His attitude was hostile./He was hostile.)

Repetition

Sometimes a student will repeat one word—or a word and its syn-onyms—several times in a sentence or paragraph. The teacher can mark or list all the words that express a single idea. Then the student should re-vise the passage so that fewer repetitions appear. For example:

```
I have been working with (mice) and the effects of
crowding on (their) behavior.

(I have been working with the effects of crowding
on the behavior of mice.)

Of all (the hunter's) articles of equipment that (he)
uses, (his) rifle is most important to (him.)

(Of all the hunter's equipment, a rifle is most
important.)
```

Passive Voice

Often the use of the passive voice adds unnecessary words and makes the passage indirect and muted. There are at times very good rea-sons for choosing the passive, but students universally overuse it, so you'll often have to urge them to switch to the active voice.

In helping a student, you'll usually find that before you can warn students about the passive voice, you'll have to teach them to recognize it. If the student can pick out the subject and verb in a sentence, your task will be easy. Simply say that in the active voice the subject of the sen-tence *does the acting*: "The girl threw the ball." In the passive voice, the subject of the sentence *is acted upon*: "The ball was thrown by the girl." The ball does not do the throwing; therefore the verb is passive. Ask your students to go through their papers and label all the verbs passive or ac-tive. Next, they should try to justify all passive voice verbs. If they can't, they should change them to active.

The passive voice appears extensively in scientific writing, though even there its popularity is fading. In the next example, while the style is a bit wordy and clumsy, the student logically and legitimately employs the passive to impart objectivity to his writing and to avoid ascribing a cause or an actor to some action described in a verb.

```
The next part of the information gathering will be a compiling
of records on the individual students.  Height and body weight will
be recorded for each student.  These will be accompanied by a
```

subjective description of each individual concerning their general
physical appearance and condition. The attendance records of each
child for his past years in school will be recorded. The teacher of
each child will be asked to evaluate each child participating in the
study. This evaluation will consist of academic, behavioral, and
attitude ratings.

In contrast to the straight scientific use of the passive illustrated
above, this student uses the passive unnecessarily in describing the process of detasseling corn plants:

When the area supervisor decides to start detasseling, the
main office is informed to start lining up contractors to meet at
the field. At this meeting 2 or 3 contract supervisors and
contractors assemble. Supervisors distribute contract forms and
contract lists, while contractors are asked how many contracts they
want. Contractors are informed of the size of the contract and are
allowed to read the contract. If the contract is satisfactory it is
signed by the contractor and the contractor is also shown the plot.
At this time the contractor is also shown how to properly pull
tassels, and directed on the use of the fruit jars. This process is
repeated until all contracts are filled.

The use of passive voice here depends on purpose. If this essay is
attempting to describe the interesting process of corn detasseling for a
general audience, then most of these verbs should be put into the active
voice. Any passive verbs that remain might serve to retain the emphasis
on the *contractors'* experience—*their* view of the corn-detasseling process.
This was in fact the aim of the student who wrote the paragraph, but it
proved possible to eliminate most of the passive verbs and at the same
time enhance the paragraph's vividness and its emphasis on the contractors' experiences.

Contractors first hear about the advent of detasseling time
when, at the area supervisor's instigation, the main office starts
lining up contractors to meet at the field. At this meeting,
contractors assemble with 2 or 3 contract supervisors. Supervisors
distribute contract forms and contract lists. Contractors decide
how many contracts they want. They learn the size of the contract
and have a chance to read it. If the contract is satisfactory the
contractor signs it and then views the plot. At this time the
contractor also learns how to pull tassels properly and how to use
the fruit jars. This process is repeated until all contracts are
filled.

In writing papers students often use the passive voice awkwardly in affecting a pseudoacademic or an obtuse style. Here is an example:

> The creation of new alternatives was approached by the department by having therapeutic and humane homes instead of the custodial institutions. The use of small community-based programs instead of large institutions, and the purchase of services from private community groups rather that state-operated programs were also incorporated into the reform.

The revision makes "department" the subject all the way through the paragraph—an appropriate choice, since the department was in fact the instigator and since the essay emphasizes its role in changing juvenile services.

> As new alternative, the department created therapeutic and humane homes instead of custodial institutions. It instigated small community-based programs in place of large institutions, and it purchased services from private community groups instead of using state-operated programs.

Coaching the Verbose Student

Whether verbiage results from overuse of the passive voice, repetition, or inflation, it is one area in which teachers can legitimately suggest alternative wording. When a student's writing is verbose, I have found it helpful to write out the condensed version of the sentence or paragraph, to illustrate how it can be tightened. This is often an eye-opener that enables the student to practice economy throughout the rest of the paper. Here is a paragraph I chose from a longer paper as an example of the student's wordy style; I condensed it into an economical version and then asked the student to do the same for the rest of the paper:

> Toni's Restaurant owned and operated by Anthony Rocco is an example of a firm which did not design a marketing strategy plan. This plan consists of two guidelines: selecting a target market and developing the most appropriate marketing mix for the target market. Anthony Rocco failed to follow these guidelines and as a result it took several months for his business to become profitable.

The ¶ is wordy. It could read: "Toni's Restaurant, owned and operated by Anthony Rocco, took several months to become profitable because the owner did not design a marketing strategy based on two guidelines: selecting a target market and developing...mix." Can you revise the rest of the paper in the same way?

A teacher can sometimes achieve the same effect by editing:

> Toni's Restaurant owned and operated by Anthony Rocco
> ~~because the owner~~
> ~~is an example of a firm which~~ did not design a marketing
> ~~based on~~
> strategy ~~plan. This plan consists of~~ two guidelines:
> selecting a target market and developing the most
> appropriate marketing mix for the target market. ~~Anthony Rocco~~
> ~~failed to follow these guidelines and as a result it~~
> took several months for his business to become profitable.

Another method is to mark repetitions in some special way, using a different color ink or distinctive circles or boxes. Then you can ask the student to compose a second version, eliminating some of the repetition.

> Toni's Restaurant owned and operated by
> Anthony Rocco is an example of a firm which did not
> *deadwood*
> design a marketing strategy plan. This plan consists
> of two guidelines: selecting a target market and
> developing the most appropriate marketing mix for the
> target market. Anthony Rocco failed to follow these
> guidelines, and as a result it took several months for
> his business to become profitable.
>
> *can you eliminate the repetitions and deadwood?*

If a student needs more explanation and drill, you might suggest that he or she study a pertinent chapter in a writing text.

Concreteness, Precision, Simplicity, Vividness

One of the best ways for students to produce concrete, precise, simple, vivid prose is to "write with nouns and verbs." Most students think that when you get fancy, when you really spend time over your writing, you add more adjectives. Not so. If you build a fence and the posts aren't solid enough, the wood not hard enough, or the holes not deep enough, you're going to have to prop the fence up with extra boards. Students often build their sentences that way. It's important to get them to use strong, vivid nouns and verbs rather than weak or abstract words that then need the support of modifiers. A student, for example, will sink that vague verb "went" into a shallow hole and then prop it up with "slowly" instead of using "shuffled" or "dragged" or "meandered" or some other verb more precise, concrete, and vivid.

To see what makes for a bland paragraph, try reading just the verbs, then just the nouns. Are there many vague nouns like "thing"? Are there instances where "beast" or "carnivore" or "dog" would be better than "animal"? In scientific writing are all terms as specific as they can be? Are there catchall verbs such as "go," "run," "do," and "is" where more specific terms would be more accurate or livelier?

In teaching students about this aspect of writing, you can talk about the ladder of abstraction. Take a word like "mutt" and go both up and down with it. More abstract are "dog," "carnivore," "animal." More concrete is "Fido." When you find overgeneralized writing, circle the offending words and ask students to find more specific alternatives. Here is an example:

```
The car went down the hill.
(The Fiat whizzed down the hill.)

You don't lose your own culture when you come into a new one.
(You don't lose your own culture when you enter a new one.)

Her statement about U.S. TV programs is that there is too much
emphasis on violence and not enough on creativity.
(Her criticism of U.S. TV programs. . . .)

Maddox said, . . .
(Maddox argued, . . . )
```

In addition to substituting words lower on the abstraction ladder for words higher up, writers can achieve concreteness and vividness by using an example in place of the general term:

```
A veterinarian must be ready to handle any kind of animal.
(A veterinarian must be ready to handle everything from a cat's torn
ear to a mare in breech birth.)

In Cuba Mrs. Rio was able to make friends in all areas of her daily
life.
(In Cuba Mrs. Rio was able to make friends at the grocery store or
outside while working in the yard or waiting for a bus.)

My teacher can tell you something about almost all fields of
knowledge.
(My teacher can tell you about the Crusades, binomial theorems, and
chemistry equations.)
```

The following example illustrates the fuzziness of meaning that results, in scientific writing, from inaccurate use of words. Reporting his observation of nesting behavior, the student writes:

Two chicks remained in both of those and one of the suddenly
abandoned nests.

The remedy is to substitute the word "each" for "both" and to add
the word "in" to clarify the place of "one of the suddenly abandoned
nests" in the total sentence structure:

Two chicks remained in each of those and in one suddenly abandoned
nest.

The next example suffers from imprecise diction as well as from
several of the other problems we have discussed:

wordy — find one word for all this

The porifera seem to provide a paradox to observers in the
word choice way a current of water is able to move through them, ~~seemingly~~
in one direction. This study, ~~made~~ by Vogel, seeks to show
evidence for ~~some type of~~ valve system ~~to be present~~ in sponges
which prevents two-way flow.

Vogel si~~t~~es earlier information supporting the idea of a
one-way channel through sponges, water entering through ostia *word choice*
and exiting through osculum. He also connects this flow to the
word choice current of the water surrounding the sponge. It is here where
he tried to connect the seeming need for valves since the ostia
facing downcurrent cover a bigger surface area than the osculum;
thus the flow from a reduction of pressure should encourage more
water to exit through these ostia than through the osculum. *this is clearly stated*

Vogel outlines two experimental *word* set-ups, one with a
mechanical model and one with live sponges. His results
support the idea *word* of some type of built-in valve system located
in the dermal membrane and probably associated with the ostia,
yet the particular valve-like structure has yet to be found.

Still another technique for achieving precision and concreteness is
particularly applicable to papers that describe a complicated object or an
involved process. The writer can help by providing comparisons with objects or processes already familiar to the reader:

I divided the box into two parallel rows of six nests each, for
a total of twelve nests.
(I divided the box, like an egg carton, into twelve nests.)

The cornea and the lens help focus the image of an object on the
retina.
(The cornea and the lens help focus the image of an object on the
retina, much as a camera lens focuses light on film.)

You can encourage your students to use more precise and concrete language. You can have them read vivid language, or you can read it to them. Select a paper or a paragraph that uses definite, sharp words and read it in class. It may be a descriptive passage or a piece of scientific writing that simply uses great precision in its word choices, to make the meaning absolutely clear. Your goal in the reading is to make your students live for a moment surrounded by bright colors so that they will be dissatisfied with their own pastels. A related technique is to praise the specific language in a student's own writing. You can even mention the more generalized or vague word the student might have used, just so the writer becomes conscious of the choices available and can repeat the success. Your comment might read: "I'm glad you chose this word instead of a more vague noun like 'statement.'"

Another method for increasing precision is to circle generalized, vague, or inaccurate words and write some message you're sure the student will comprehend, like "word choice" or "Be more precise."

This student's journal entry illustrates some of the techniques the teacher can use:

> Our guest speaker today was Mrs. Rio who
> was originally from Cuba. One thing that she said *word*
> *word* that really stood out was that you don't lose your
> own culture when you enter a new one. *good choice* After listening
> to her talk, I am inclined to agree with her. Proof *agreement*
> of her statement are: 1) Mrs. Rio comes from a country
> where intelligence is stressed more than physical
> *word* ability (and) she feels that too much emphasis is put
> on sports in the U.S. schools. 2) Though the T.V. *this sentence*
> programs in Cuba are all politically orientated, they *structure*
> *good* have something of artistic value to offer. Her *works well*
> *word* criticism of U.S. programs is that there is too
> much emphasis on violence and not enough on
> creativity and 3) She feels that it is very hard to
> make friends her age in the U.S. because Americans
> are so busy all the time with their family and jobs
> leaving little time to be social. In Cuba Mrs. Rio
> was able to make friends at a grocery store, or outside) *good detail*
> while working in the yard or waiting for a bus. To
> her, Americans appear to always be in too big of *word*
> a hurry to stop and be friendly.
> I don't see Americans as time centered as *Good ending —*
> Mrs. Rio does but she compares it to a past that is *links to your*
> evidently still a part of her. *1st sentences*

One major barrier to simplicity and concreteness for some students is their assumption that, in writing for a teacher, they have to adopt a formal, academic tone. Their misconceptions about that tone cause them to write padded, phony, pseudointellectual prose that spurns simple language, eschews concrete or lively detail, and loses touch with their own natural voices. One student labeled this type of writing "Engfish."[1] Sadly, students are not the only culprits: teachers sometimes encourage such prose, and scholars sometimes write it. Robert Kesling has some fun with the constructions of the "sciensch" found in professional journals.[2]

"Sciensch"	*English Translation*
Our research, designed to test the fatal effects of XXX on dogs, was carried out by intravenously introducing the drug. In the experiments, a relatively small quantity, 3 cubic centimeters, was administered to each animal. In each case, XXX proved to be fatal, all dogs expiring before a lapse of five minutes after the injection.	The intravenous injection of only 3 cc. of XXX kills a dog within five minutes.
A method, which was found to be expedient and not very difficult to accomplish and which possessed a high degree of accuracy in its results, was devised whereby. . . .	An easy, accurate way to. . . .

"Sciensch" and "Engfish" ignore a number of principles discussed in this book, primarily those of economy and concreteness. Those who use it want to sound imposing, to achieve an academic tone. Thus in working with students who have this fault, you can in general urge them to write in a more natural and simple voice.

To illustrate, here are the responses of two college freshmen who were asked to tell how their own future lives might differ from those of their parents. The topic is personal, but these writers, seated row by row in a large college auditorium during orientation week, knew they were writing for a group of English teachers they'd never seen, who would place them in writing classes according to the quality of their essays. As a result, one student tried to sound academic and produced a vague, stilted essay that is boring because it lacks specific detail. The reader gets no sense of the writer's own personal style or experience:

As I grow up I learn many of my ideas from the world around me.
Earlier in my life I learned things from my parents. My life will
probably be different from my parents, but it will also be common
to theirs. I'll be living in a different time period, but will
probably use many of their thoughts on my reactions to things.

The differences that will occur is because I'm growing up in a
different period of time than they did. Many things that are
accetable now weren't then. Such as women going to collage and
getting a career instead of becoming only a houseweif. In society
now they put more stress on a higher education than before and it's
easier to obtain now. So I'm going to college where as my parents
went to collage much later in their life. By doing this I will
probably start with a more professional career for my first stable
job, than my parents did.

In contrast, another student adopted a natural, folksy tone and produced an essay far more lively and interesting.

College, that is one big difference between my folks and me.
Although I may not think of it as a privilege now, thirty or fourty
years ago it was a big opportunity. My dad for instance had to walk
2 1/2 miles to school everyday. And they didn't have schools like
we have today. Nope, the schools then were very crude and taught
only the basics. Work was more important than going to school, at
least for a young man. Dad had to give up school at the tenth grade,
because it was corn picking time and the crops came first.

When students like the author of the first essay gain more sophisticated vocabularies and learn to manipulate more complex sentence structures, their "Engfish" constructs even bigger superhighways to get from
the cabin to the outhouse. For example, this student is writing to the governor of her state, urging the construction of a certain type of prison. She
begins her paper in this way:

The following pages contain my comments on whether we should
construct a penal facility along the same guidelines as the
Patuxent facility. I believe that the policies represent a
maximum effort that has successfully provided proper penal
rehabilitation for the offender and thus has been beneficial to the
state's people.

If she had pictured the governor as she wrote, she would have re-
membered that the politician is not an expert in the jargon of penology
and will probably pick up her position paper late at night after a long
day's work on a host of other issues. Her wordy letter will be hard to

read. Appropriate diction for this situation would be simpler, more direct, more crisp:

```
    I believe we should construct a prison like Patuxent because
it has successfully rehabilitated prisoners and thus has helped
everyone in the state.
```

To help students toward concrete, precise, simple vivid writing, drive them back to their own speech. Though speech is not directly translatable into good writing (because of its tendency to be elliptical and repetitious), at least it often has the virtues of directness and simplicity. Students can learn to practice those virtues when they write. You may help some students by suggesting that they talk through their topics—with peers, to themselves, or to tape recorders—and later use their tapes or their notes as a basis for their written pieces. Or divide your class into small groups and have the students tell one another what they are writing about. That way they can listen to themselves and to the others, get in touch with the authenticity of speech, and capture that directness in their writing.

Part Two

GRAMMAR, USAGE, PUNCTUATION, AND SPELLING

Chapter Nine

Basic Concepts in Teaching Mechanics

Because definitions differ, I will explain the meaning I attach to each term in the title of Part II:

- *Grammar:* the grammatical forms of the language, especially verbs, pronouns, plural nouns, possessive nouns, subject-verb agreement, pronoun-antecedent agreement, and rules for word order
- *Usage:* the use of words and combinations of words according to accepted conventions (For example, should a phrase read "in respect of" or "in respect to"?)
- *Punctuation:* any mark that is not a letter—for example, colon, apostrophe, quotation marks—plus capitalization
- *Spelling:* the common meaning we all understand

I am not interested so much in classifying or defining the terms as in explaining the pedagogical methods by which we may help our students learn the rules subsumed under all four words. Needing a single word to express the whole gaggle of related skills, I use "mechanics." What we faculty commonly term "mechanics" is the bane of our lives, the subject on which we can always get up a conversation with another teacher, the weakness that often offends us most and on which we expend the most red ink.

When faced with a paper whose mechanics are deplorable, one is tempted to pick up the red pen, almost in anger and certainly in exasperation, and stab each of its errors with some kind of cryptic symbol. But before doing that, in fact before marking any mechanical errors at all, the teacher should make some careful decisions: At what point in the student's learning process, or at what stage in the evolution of this particular paper, is it worthwhile to expend energy on mechanics rather than paragraph construction or other concerns? What may keep a student from embodying in a paper the knowledge of punctuation or grammar that he or she already possesses? How can a teacher most effectively communicate with students about problems in mechanics? What teaching methods are most successful in helping students with mechanics, and which of them best suit the teacher of economics or engineering?

This part of the book offers some guidelines for helping students control mechanics. After I lay the groundwork by describing the concepts underlying a successful approach to mechanics, I discuss ways to reduce both "performance-based error"—made by students who know the rule but do not follow it—and "knowledge-based error"—made by students who need to learn more about the rules that govern written language.

The Place of Mechanics
in the Writing Process

In the first stages of the writing process, concern for one's audience takes the form of imagining the readers' expectations; deciding on the appropriate voice, tone, and organization; and then choosing words, sentence structure, and detail accordingly. Also shaped to the readers' needs will be any explanation of unfamiliar terms or support for debatable points. In the later stages of the process, the writer shows solicitude for readers by providing transitions where ideas clearly linked in the writer's thought may not be so obviously connected in the minds of the audience and by carefully checking spelling, making pronouns agree with antecedents, smoothing out ambiguous or awkward sentences, and tinkering with verb tenses. In other words, though some aspects of mechanics may be the object of conscious deliberation throughout the writing process, the writer usually directly attends to such problems at the very end, much as the chef, who has earlier worried about the freshness of the eggs and the temperature of the pan, now, just before sending the dinner out to the gourmand, arranges the omelette attractively on the plate and adds a sprig of parsley. Teachers, though, are often guilty of paying first, not last, attention to mechanics, or of behaving as though that's all there is. Sometimes, especially with poorer students, problems of thought are so closely twined with problems of grammar, usage, and punctuation that they must be approached as one from the start. Sometimes, however, we attack only mechanical problems because they're easier to correct than poor paragraph structure or unfortunate arrangement of subtopics. Or perhaps the errors are so numerous that they form an all too obvious projection on which our exasperation lights.

If we do little more than mark mechanical errors, we are unwisely and unnecessarily limiting our function: we have become editors of the product rather than coaches of the writing process, pouncers on mistakes rather than supporters of the students' growth in the full range of writing skills.

A teacher who gives help throughout the writing process may find that mechanical problems can best be solved in a polishing session near the end. When students invest effort and interest in their papers and revise them a number of times for other aspects, they often eliminate some mechanical problems along the way.

When you first read a draft, even if you are not giving major attention to mechanics, you may want to indicate several problems that seem especially troublesome for that student. The writer then gives those problems as much attention as he or she can spare, while continuing to work mainly on organization, tone, and paragraph structure. At the end, finally, the student goes after those wretched apostrophes or sentence fragments, and, with help as needed from teacher or tutor, cleans out the last of the varmints.

Sometimes it pays to attack mechanical problems head on at the beginning, especially when the basic conventions of the written language are so totally out of the student's control that they form a barrier to any sort of effective communication. Ironically, you may find yourself concentrating less on correcting errors than on helping students to relax, to find something to say, and to let their ideas flow. Then some of the troublesome punctuation and grammar problems may diminish or disappear. Sometimes, however, an intensive, well-planned, lengthy campaign of instruction and drill is needed. In fact, some students are so frustrated by their lack of control and so uptight about their errors that a head-on battle is what they desperately want. All the student's teachers should join such an effort; a learning center staff or a specialist in basic writing could also help. More about specific battle plans later.

The point is that you should resist the urge to attack every mechanical problem in a paper; instead, you should formulate a conscious strategy that takes into account the needs or anxieties of your student, the possibility that errors may result from nervousness or carelessness rather than from lack of knowledge, and the place of editing in the writing process.

Accepting Changing Conventions

Linguists have learned that all languages change all the time and that changes do not cause the language to decay. Thus we have no better reason to force students to follow the rules we learned in grammar school, if they have become obsolete, than we have to force them to use Chaucer's English.

Because conventions change, you and your students need worry only about those aspects of mechanics that bother today's readers. Even if you are dismayed by split infinitives, by "try and succeed," or by "I've got three apples," you should recognize that in these days most American readers, even educated ones, are not much distracted by those uses and that in a hundred years the "correct" forms of those words may have changed. Meanwhile, if your daily reading tells you that a certain rule you've always followed is now changing, let it go. Just as in 1975 the last Japanese soldier quit fighting World War II and emerged from the jungle on some isolated Pacific island, so at some point in the twenty-first century the last academic holdout for "shall" and "will" or for the unsplit infinitive will emerge, blinking sheepishly, from some citadel of learning. Neither Japan nor the English language was destroyed by the changes of the 1940s, and the tough, sinewy giant that is our language will not in any case be pegged down by our lilliputian efforts.

The Purpose of Rules and Conventions

One can teach a child to cross on the green light or to place the fork on the left side of the plate, but the youngster is much more likely to follow such rules if he or she understands their function in preventing traffic accidents or promoting graceful dining. Students who have serious problems with the conventions of written English often view these rules as mere nuisances imposed by English teachers or as a tangle of arbitrary and abstract injunctions whose only function is to make writers' lives miserable. Impatient to be on with the business of expressing their thoughts, students resist acknowledging the importance of such small marks as the comma and the period, or they blithely assume that it is the reader's responsibility to meet the writer three quarters of the way, puzzling out the meaning despite missing or misused punctuation.

The best way to change such an attitude is to explain that in the delicate balance between writer and reader it is the writer's obligation to make the reader's path through the text free of blind alleys, cul-de-sacs, stones, and bumps so that the reader can without difficulty follow where the author leads. In other words, the reader should never have to double back and reread a sentence in order to comprehend the writer's meaning. Read a paper aloud in front of the writer, mirroring in your responses any confusion or irritation that the prose causes you as a reader. Or ask another student to read aloud a passage that lacks conventional punctuation. Let the writer hear the derailments, hesitations, and frustration. In discussing a specific problem in a paper, emphasize the reader's confusion rather than merely the rule. For example, faced with a sentence fragment, you could say, "I had to read this twice because your punctuation confused me."

Errors interfere with smooth reading; they may also shape the reader's opinion of the writer. This consideration, too, can be a basis for your comments. Instead of marking "thier" merely as a spelling error, you may say that when you saw that word you began to suspect that the student either was an inept writer or didn't care enough about the writing to make sure that words were spelled in ways that readers would expect.

Motivation for the immense effort some students have to exert to control the conventions of written English probably will come, not from a driving ambition to follow the rules, but from the recognition that such control is necessary if they are to communicate effectively and establish their credibility and intelligence. If your assignments are imaginative and compelling enough to engage your students' keen interest, you will probably find fewer errors in mechanics and more effort expended to produce writing that follows the conventions.

Because rules are made for readers, you and your students need worry only about those aspects of mechanics that bother the intended readers of a certain paper. You can formulate a hierarchy of concerns, based on their "disturbance quotient" for readers. Some of the most important rules in any such hierarchy will be these:

1. Write in complete sentences. In some contexts, both sentence fragments and comma splices are becoming more and more acceptable. Many of us remember being shocked by sentence fragments when they first appeared in places like the Volkswagen ads of about ten years ago, but now a review of any magazine will show how common sentence fragments have become. We can probably expect the tendency to seep into more formal and academic writing as well. There are, however, still contexts in which sentence fragments, run-ons, and comma splices disturb readers.
2. Use quotation marks accurately to set off another author's words (but never mind, for now, whether the comma appears inside or outside).
3. Control the syntax so that sentences are readable, so that they "track" in ways that the reader expects.
4. Avoid glaring spelling errors. For example, "recieve" is a common error, less distracting to a reader than "doter" for "daughter." If you have a poor speller, consider beginning with the most disturbing words.
5. Use the proper verb forms. Constructions such as "If she was here" or "He would of asked" are less startling than "It relieve the problem," unless that audience is familiar with, and can appropriately be addressed in, the forms of black English vernacular, of which this is one.

Later in this chapter I discuss strategies for helping students in these and other areas. The point for now is that, in dealing with mechanics, you should foster the student's awareness that rules are made to serve readers. You might ask yourself which two or three kinds of revision would best serve to make this writer's prose less distracting to readers.

Modern Approaches to Teaching Grammar

Though you often still hear—from students, teachers, and parents, not to mention editorial writers—that what this country needs is a back-to-grammar approach, few truths have been more securely established in recent years than the certainty that formal grammar instruction does not by itself improve students' writing or punctuation (Haynes, pp. 84–85). So *do* participate as usual in your faculty council's annual hand-wringing session about student writing, but don't be among those who propose a required "grammar" course for every student.

"Knowing" grammar is much more complex than it seems on the surface. All normal persons past age five use the basic grammatical structures of their language every time they speak. In that sense they "know" grammar, and educators are trying to isolate and describe the factors at work in producing writing that conforms in punctuation, grammar, and usage to what readers expect. Some researchers are attempting to identify the perceptual and manual skills or the right brain–left brain cooperation that may be involved. Others are trying more accurately to define what "knowing" grammar means and why it is that students do not produce in their writing the grammatical forms they do in some sense "know" and can perhaps manipulate in speech. The differences between speech and writing are a third subject for investigation by those who surmise that such contrasts may hold the key to some of the so-called grammatical errors we see in student writing. Still others are experimenting with ways to teach not only narrow grammatical "correctness" but a wide variety of related skills, such as the ability to form various kinds of phrases and clauses, the awareness of options for expressing any single idea in writing, and a writer's sense of the possibilities afforded by the grammatical structures of the language—a sense that may or may not be separate from a person's ability to identify or label grammatical parts.

One modern method called "sentence combining" is gaining in popularity in classrooms from first grade to college. Sometimes called the Christensen method, the approach is based on the work of Frances Christensen, who, along with John Mellon, Frank O'Hare, and others, defined in a new way how parts of the sentence and the paragraph are generated and how they interact, thus laying the basis for a new way to develop students' skills in writing.[1]

The method tries to help writers learn to use various sentence structures in a mature and skillful way. There is some debate about whether immature writers of college age actually *do not know* how to form complex sentences or whether they *do* know how but just don't *use* such sentences appropriately in writing. In any case, it is clear that writers—lacking the possibilities of gesture, silence, and eye contact present in a conversation and working in a medium that is meant to be shaped and revised—need to use more intricate and accurate language structures than they do in speaking, in order to indicate precisely the various relations among their ideas. It is also clear that the writer who knows how to construct, control, and appropriately use a multiplicity of sentence structures can write a fully orchestrated piece—unlike informal speakers and poor writers, who often limit themselves to the simple subject-verb unit and depend on "and" to string together ideas.

To help students master complex sentence forms, the sentence-combining method has them, like toddlers with blocks, both build towers and break them down. In the hands of a skilled teacher, these exercises can also produce a toddlerlike glee. In a professional demonstration of the sentence-combining method, I once watched a pretty, lively woman delight her sixth graders by dancing up and down the aisles of the classroom while blowing soap bubbles. Chuckling, the students bent to write the basic sentence: "Mrs. Johnson blew bubbles." Then they began to add:

```
Wearing her red dress, Mrs. Johnson blew bubbles.
Mrs. Johnson, running up and down the aisles, blew bubbles
    at the students.
Mrs. Johnson was laughing as she blew shimmery bubbles at the
    students.
Mrs. Johnson blew bubbles that skipped and dipped around the heads
    of the students.
```

Taking a single idea, the youngsters devised various ways of embedding it in the main sentence:

```
Laughing, Mrs. Johnson blew bubbles.
Mrs. Johnson laughingly blew bubbles.
Mrs. Johnson laughed as she blew bubbles.
```

Having built their towers, students practiced breaking them down into their components:

```
The lovely, laughing Mrs. Johnson, in her red dress, ran up and
    down the aisles blowing shimmery bubbles at the students.
```

This turreted castle comes apart as:

```
Mrs. Johnson was lovely.
Mrs. Johnson was laughing.
Mrs. Johnson wore a red dress.
Mrs. Johnson ran up and down the aisles.
```

```
Mrs. Johnson blew bubbles.
The bubbles were shimmery.
She blew bubbles at the students.
```

Given a set of short blocks like these, the pupils could again erect a single sentence that combined them all.

In the high school or college classroom, the English teacher or the skills center tutor may not blow bubbles, but the sentence-combining exercises will be much the same. In the coming years you can expect to encounter increasing numbers of students who have been trained in sentence combining. Some schemes have a set of terms to describe the various ways of embedding ideas in a sentence; other systems use little terminology. Don't expect students to identify the parts of speech or the methods of embedding by the names you were taught. But you can expect them to have developed facility in building and altering sentences, identifying separate sentence components, distinguishing the kernel of the sentence, and sensing the presence of an incipient sentence in an adjective or a prepositional phrase. In the rest of this book I suggest at times how you or your writing specialist may employ sentence-combining techniques to help your students overcome certain problems with mechanics or to build their stylistic repertoire.

The Writing, Learning, or Tutoring Center

Skills centers are becoming more and more numerous. They may offer drop-in services or handle students only through structured tutorials or courses. Some concentrate only on writing problems; others offer a wider range of subject-area tutoring. They may be attached to an academic department, like English or education, or they may be part of student services. They may be funded by grants or by what people employed in such centers reverently refer to as "hard money."

Whatever its location, type, or status, your learning center probably can be of great use to you and your students. In the center I founded and directed at a midwestern college in the 1970s, we discovered that more students came at the suggestion of faculty members than for any other reason. So you can be fairly sure that both the center and the students will benefit from your referrals and encouragement.

But keep in touch with the center yourself. The research on how students can best master writing skills points not in the direction of hiring more grammar teachers, and not even solely in the direction of hiring more learning center staff, but rather in the direction of enlisting *you.* We hear more and more about the importance of constant and continuous practice in writing in all the students' courses and in all their school years. More and more we see the necessity of making a team effort to nourish literacy, rather than accepting the isolated effort of one unit such as the required English course or the skills center. In such a center your students can receive intensive help with mechanics, help that you may not have time or training to provide. Nevertheless the results are better when the teacher and the center cooperate than when the teacher merely passes the problem on to the center staff.

If you are very short of time, if you think you are not skilled enough to deal with mechanical problems, or if you have a number of students with serious difficulties, you may wish to let the skills center carry the ball for mechanics and spend your own time on other kinds of writing and learning problems. This approach can work if you take three steps:

1. Early in the semester, give a writing assignment that will allow you to identify students with problems in mechanics. Get the referral process going immediately.
2. Strongly and personally encourage students to attend the center. Let them know that you want and expect them to go.
3. Become at least generally aware of how your skills center works with students, what its basic philosophy is, and what goals it sets for students in your class. Then continue to back up the center's efforts as you evaluate each student's writing.

Dialect Influence

When dealing with a student who forms verbs, possessives, pronouns, or plurals inappropriately, ask this basic question: What influence may dialect be exerting in this case? An understanding of how dialect affects writing is essential in handling students' grammar and usage problems. Some initial information about language acquisition may help.

By five years of age, all normal children have learned most of the grammatical patterns of the language(s) they have heard.[2] For some native English speakers, however, dialect that they learned as tots and that they continue to use in the neighborhood store and at home is not always one that teachers and employers consider "correct." In American society, those whose colloquial speech differs most sharply from standard English are the ethnic minorities and the poor. To paraphrase an old Afro-American saying, if lions had power in our society, roaring would be correct English. But since middle-class whites are the advantaged group, their grammar and usage are regarded as standard.

The lions are therefore at a disadvantage. But that is not to say they are culturally or linguistically "disadvantaged" or "deprived" in the way some misguided philanthropists, educators, and government officials have used the terms. Black students from an urban ghetto are not necessarily linguistically or culturally deprived at all; they belong to an extremely rich culture, whose dialect is vivid, tough, and graceful. Linguistic research has shown conclusively that there is no inherent connection between language competency and race and that every dialect and variety of language is equally capable of serving its purposes (Langacker, pp. 98–99). Thus the dialect spoken by a ghetto black child from Boston or by a backwoods youngster from Arkansas is just as complex, just as precisely rulebound, and just as useful a tool of communication, in its own setting, as the so-called standard English spoken by a white Scarsdale banker's child.

Though all languages and dialects are in some ways equal, a particular student who writes for your class may have a greater or smaller vocabulary than others, may be more or less skilled in using the nuances of the language, or may manipulate the complexities of the language with more or less facility. Part of this student's difficulty may be a result of limited mental or verbal capacity. Part may stem from the home environment. Children may grow up speaking in what linguists call a "restricted code," in which language is sparsely functional, or an "elaborated code," in which language is rich and full. These codes may depend partly on class and culture, but wide variations in language skills and habits can be found in students of all cultures and socioeconomic classes.

Furthermore, you can't always tell how linguistically adept a student is. You can perhaps judge with some accuracy the language competency of a student from a background similar to your own: it is, however, much harder to determine the language competency of a student whose dialect and culture differ from yours and whose behavior may be influenced by cultural tensions and perhaps overt discrimination in school. Judgment is further hampered if you misinterpret the habits of stance, eye contact, or response to authority figures customary in the student's native culture. For example, in some American cultures it is considered cheeky for a child or young person to make eye contact with an authority figure. So in a conference with the teacher, the student will politely stare at the floor, and the white middle-class instructor, unable to get the student to meet his or her eye, may conclude that the student is sly, shy, sullen, or stupid. Thus by the time such students come under your tutelage, their language ability may be obscured by feelings of inadequacy, self-consciousness, and frustration developed during years of struggling with the school system.

That dialects can influence even those students whose school writing does not have identifiable dialect characteristics further illustrates the complexity of the dialect problem. One test of college freshmen who showed no recognizable dialect forms in their writing but who were judged to need remedial work for other reasons showed that a high number of them *knew* dialect forms.[3] So it appears that even when you have no overt features to guide you, you must realize that a particular student who has for years spoken some dialect has lacked practice in the constructions of standard written English, or what linguistics call Edited

American English (EAE).

So how does this information about language affect you as you evaluate a batch of student papers? First of all, especially if your own spoken language is close to EAE, you will want to watch for grammar and usage that may look wrong to you but that are acceptable in the student's own dialect. Of course, students' writing also contains many examples of grammar and usage that don't belong to any language, that would readily be identified simply as "goofs" by the students themselves, or that are due to causes other than dialect. If you're not sure whether a particular form might be dialect-related, it helps to know that dialects of English differ most markedly in their verb forms, pronouns, plurals, and possessives.

Let's say that a black student in your class has written "I work" where EAE would demand "I worked." You recognize this as a dialect form. Now what? It is important that all your subsequent dialogue with the student proceed from your own recognition that the other person is not writing "incorrectly" and is not "leaving off the *-ed* ending of the verbs." Rather, the writer is recording the "correct" form of the past tense as heard and learned from childhood. In communicating with the student, you will want to do your best to avoid words like "wrong" or "incorrect" and instead employ words that communicate the concept of "appropriateness" or "dialect choice" or "level of formality." You will also want to avoid making any subtle assumptions that such students are culturally deprived or that their race or socioeconomic class has caused them to be linguistically less sophisticated or less able than other students.

The white middle-class teacher should also be careful not to take a patronizing attitude toward "those people." Again, linguistic studies show that people learn to command an astonishing variety of dialects and levels of formality. To assume that a student who does not yet command EAE will not be able to do so is a form of discrimination.

Recognize also that dialect features are a matter of class, culture, and other factors, not solely of race. Some studies show that black, Hispanic, and white students in a given college course will all produce many of the nonstandard writing forms we associate with dialects.[4]

Although the dialect issue is full of complexities, you should not simply leave the writer alone. The choice of dialect and the level of formality should be the subject of conscious and thoughtful deliberation for every writer, and those aspects of a writer's work are appropriate topics for student-teacher dialogue. Therefore you will want to talk with the student who, in an academic paper, uses "I work" as the past tense. You will want to speak in terms that transmit your respect for the student's own language and your recognition that the problem is one of appropriateness, not of correctness. The discussion will result in some kind of decision about dialect forms and level of formality in the paper.

Such a decision is usually a matter of degree and consistency. Even if you and the student decide that certain dialect forms differing from EAE are appropriate to a particular paper, the student will often not have used those dialect forms consistently but will have mixed them in with EAE forms, since the writing of many dialect-speaking students is already, by the time a teacher sees it, a mixture of their own dialects and forms they think will be acceptable to the teacher. Thus you must decide not only whether dialect or informal language is appropriate, but which forms, to what extent, and at what points in the paper.

In making the decision, you may take one of several positions. The student may strongly wish to master EAE. Most students realize that if they wish to earn degrees, get good jobs, and enjoy a number of society's other cookies and gumdrops, they will have to be able to speak and write EAE. Thus many students are happy to have a sympathetic teacher help them learn it.

You may choose to help students learn and write EAE without letting their skill in this area affect their grades. That way the students are not penalized by grade while they are still struggling to master EAE.

Another possible position is to accept only EAE and grade down for use of other dialects. Some teachers justify this stand by saying that, since other teachers and employers will demand EAE, the teacher who cares about students ought to show them graphically what it's like out in the world, where they will be required to use EAE.

Other teachers, though they know that students will be forced to use EAE in other situations, refuse to become part of "the system." Such a teacher can, however, make clear to the student the penalties suffered in American society by one who does not speak or write EAE and can stand ready to help the students master EAE if they wish.[5]

Inexperience in Writing

In addition to mastering the grammar and usage that are appropriate to various types of writing and that may differ markedly from the grammar and usage students use in ordinary speech, those who would become good writers must cross a second Jordan: they must learn the rules that govern written English. They must spell words in universally accepted ways and use marks of punctuation according to established codes. As speakers they need not be concerned with either spelling or punctuation; only in writing must they stop to deliberate: Should I use a comma or a period here? Should I spell this word "effect" or "affect"? Thus even gifted and practiced speakers may, if they've not had much practice in writing, be astonishingly clumsy and unknowing about written codes. Such lack of exposure may be a matter of culture, ethnic background, socioeconomic class, or home and school environment. Within a particular race or class, children may differ greatly in the amount of writing they have been exposed to in their homes. Schools also vary in the amount of reading and writing they ask students to do. According to one estimate, compared with the 1,000 words a week that a British secondary student is likely to write, American middle-class high school students average 350 words a week, and many of our students, especially those from schools in poor or ethnic neighborhoods, may be asked to write only 350 words a semester.[6]

Most of us who became teachers learned early, through lots of exposure and practice, the eye-hand coordination, the techniques of memory, and the punctuation and spelling rules needed to transcribe written language. It is hard for us to imagine ourselves without those abilities. If the bump on your third finger, which comes from holding a pen, has been there as long as you can remember, then it is easy to think that both it and the writing skills whose long practice put it there must be part of everybody's natural equipment. But watching, for example, a four-year-old try to spread peanut butter on a slice of bread makes you aware of the complex series of skills required for an act that you perform unthinkingly. Mina Shaughnessy, who taught writing under the open-admissions policy at City University of New York, made a seminal contribution to the teaching of writing when she helped teachers look with new eyes at those students who, as writers, are still at the peanut-butter stage. She describes the feeling of such a writer, coming to the academic enterprise without the manual skills, the ability to notice punctuation, the habits of mind and eye that practiced writers take for granted. For such a learner, Shaughnessy reminds us,

> academic writing is a trap, not a way of saying something to someone. The spoken language, looping back and forth between speakers, offering chances for groping and backing up and even hiding, leaving room for the language of hands and faces, of pitch and pauses, is generous and inviting. Next to this rich orchestration, writing is but a line that moves haltingly across the page, exposing as it goes all that the writer doesn't know, then passing into the hands of a stranger who reads it with a lawyer's eyes, searching for flaws. (p. 7)

It is important to the progress of such students that teachers understand the difficulties writing presents for them and view them as toddlers in the writing process, not as congenital failures lacking some natural human equipment.

Analyzing Patterns of Error

It may be difficult to classify problems in the writing of a student who is highly unskilled in written English. Shaughnessy, however, shows that a teacher can learn to pick out patterns even when the writing at first seems hopelessly tangled. Viewed from the air, the numerous, winding country roads of my part of Iowa have logic: they flow through valleys, they follow section lines, they head toward rivers, they avoid rough terrain. Even in the densest mass of errors, keep in mind that what you are seeing is not a random fistful of mistakes that dropped accidentally from the sky but the path of a student trying to master the forms of written English. Mistakes are likely to be logical: they are extensions of things learned in other contexts, they are the result of rules misunderstood or misapplied, they are stages in the process of mastery, or they are the student's own habits and patterns fashioned out of the confusing tangle of life rafts and dock ropes thrown out by various teachers throughout the years of education. The more clearly you are able to identify, classify, group, and analyze errors, the better you will be able to help your students. The next chapter includes such diagnostic hints, as I discuss ways to remedy both performance-based error and knowledge-based error. Chapter 11 describes the methods for identifying patterns of error.

Chapter Ten

Eliminating Performance-Based and Knowledge-Based Errors

The two problems of not knowing the rules and of not applying them blur into each other at the middle but are still sufficiently distinct to be usefully separated by the teacher working with mechanics. I have often burdened a student with a long explanation of a mechanical error only to find that the pupil knew the governing rule all along. Or I have wrung my hands over a paper full of mechanical errors only to find that the same writer, when really interested in a topic, turned in a paper with almost no mechanical problems. I once taught in an English department where the standard policy was that student papers must be written in complete sentences. Any paper with a run-on sentence, comma splice, or sentence fragment (except fragments used with good reason) would automatically receive an F. While this method has some disadvantages—it may, for example, make writers so afraid of committing an unforgivable sin that they have no energy left for free and joyous expression—it did show me how many such errors are errors of performance, not knowledge, and it illustrated that, if sufficiently motivated—even by abject fear—students are capable of eliminating many performance-based errors without direct instruction. So it's wise to ask yourself, in dealing with problems in any area of mechanics, "Do I merely have to get students to fish the rule out of some dark pool in their minds, or do I have to stock the stream?"

Helping Students Practice What They Already Know

If you suspect the lunkers are already in there, you have several ways to find out. One method is to hand the paper back unmarked, say that there are a number of mechanical problems, and ask the student to sit down alone with the paper for fifteen minutes and find as many mechanical errors on the first page as possible. A second method is to administer one of the pretests that come with many programmed English texts. Look for a book that has a pretest for each unit, if you want to test knowledge of one area only; find a book with a general pretest to get an overall view of the student's strengths.

Another way is to watch the level of error in papers you know the student cared about and spent time and passion on. Or create a pressure-free writing situation by asking the student to write on something he or she cares about and knows well. Under these circumstances some students will be able to put into practice the knowledge of mechanics that eludes them in tense or demanding situations. Or listen closely to the student's speech: aspects of EAE grammar and usage that appear incorrectly in writing may appear correctly in conversation.

The purpose of these techniques and any similar ones you can think of is to identify rules that students know, even though they may not consistently embody these rules in their writing. Every student has a smaller or larger body of such unapplied or inconsistently applied knowledge. How can you coax it forward into performance?

Giving Encouragement and Removing Threat

Talk with your students about past language and writing experiences. Are they anxious about writing, afraid of making errors? Does writing ever seem rewarding and important, or is it in every situation the forced and feared fulfillment of someone else's assignment? Can they identify some rules that they know but do not always follow? Can they suggest ways in which you could create a situation in which writing could be less error-ridden?

Think of ways to encourage students to take pride in their writing. A teenage boy knows perfectly well how to comb, brush, pick, or braid his hair, but he'll be sloppy about it until some young woman lets him know she's interested in him. Are there ways in which you can apply the courtship syndrome to students' writing? For example, is there a format, however informal, for "publication" of student writing, in preparation for which students might comb and pick their papers? Is there a place where good-looking student essays, spiffy and error-free, can be displayed?

Teaching Students to Proofread

Proofreading is a skill that requires a mind-set and eye different from those one employs when reading for meaning. Trying to grasp the writer's ideas, one minimizes distractions—supplying missing parts, correcting mistakes, automatically gliding over rough or misleading language. We do a Rorschach every time we read. When it comes to proofreading our own writing, however, we combat not only the Rorschach syndrome but also the "beam in your own eye" phenomenon recorded by one authoritative source long before Rorschach was born. It's harder to see flaws in your own prose than in someone else's.

For any beginning writer, but especially for those unaccustomed to dealing with the written word or unfamiliar with the way in which good writers read their work over and over, strengthening the skill and habit of proofreading may be important in eliminating errors. To help students develop this ability, suggest that they read their writing aloud or listen as someone else reads it. Another strategy is to follow the words one by one with a pen point, viewing each singly, marking it out for scrutiny, making it justify its grammatical form, its place in the sentence, its spelling, and its punctuation. If students find themselves hopelessly scanning the jungle of their prose with glazed eyes, they can try scouting for only one beast at a time, going through the paper first for sentence fragments, then for apostrophe use, and so on. Or have the student make a list of the half-dozen most common errors he or she has made in the past, and then check each line, each phrase, each word of the new piece to eliminate those mistakes.

Did you ever see an eight-by-ten photo of a grasshopper's leg? You notice lots of things you never saw before. Sometimes a student's proofreading is sharpened by changing the visual image. Seeing the paper typed rather than handwritten often helps greatly. Or try putting the paper on an opaque projector.

Be alert for poor eyesight—a possibility sometimes overlooked, perhaps just because it's so obvious an explanation of why a student can't see errors.

If a student cannot accurately transcribe aspects of the language that he or she uses properly in speech or cannot proofread for individual letters or parts of a word, a program of perceptual training may be useful. Perceptual training is what's involved when your musician friend attends a concert with you and, while you thoroughly enjoy the music, cringes because she hears that the second violins are slightly off-key. There are ways to train not only the listener's ear but also the writer's eye.[1] Students lacking writing skills sometimes benefit from practice in noticing and copying various written marks, just as you and I would need to practice identifying the tiny differences that distinguish one Chinese character from another.

Helping Students Learn to Copy Accurately

Some students make a different set of mistakes every time they copy over their papers; others have trouble copying a quotation accurately. Again, be alert for possible visual problems. If eyesight's not involved you might find a book that will help. Some programmed texts contain (usually at the very beginning) a unit on accurate copying. If you can't locate a text, incorporate copying in just your own exercises by asking the student to copy first short passages and then longer ones, simply striving for accuracy in copying.

Watching for Special Problems

If a copying problem persists, especially if the student is reversing letters like ("tired" for "tried" or "gril" for "girl"), there may be a learning disability. According to some estimates, ten percent of the population is afflicted to some degree. Even at the college level you should by no means discount the possibility that you may encounter, for example, a dyslexic student whose problem has never been diagnosed. If you suspect such a problem, try to find someone trained in learning disabilities to evaluate the student.

Be careful about slapping the label "learning disabled" or "dyslexic" on any student. These are fad words; identification is sometimes fuzzy, and social and emotional factors are involved. Further, given the benefits for some handicapped students of "mainstreaming," the specialists at your school, even if their evaluation of a student's reading has revealed such problems, may not want the student labeled dyslexic by teachers and peers.

They say that Samuel Taylor Coleridge wrote some of his best poetry while under the influence of opium, and Virginia Woolf, though plagued by emotional instability, wrote brilliant novels and essays. Students with similar problems, however, are not likely to pull off similar successes. Their writing is more likely to resemble the performance of a Bowery bum trying to fly an airplane. It's futile to keep repeating the rules of flying when what the bum really needs is somehow to be shoved or loved back into sobriety and stability.

Helping Students Learn the Rules

So far this chapter has emphasized that, whether you are dealing with dialect-related language or with other types of errors, students actually may know, or partly know, the rules governing EAE grammar, usage, spelling, and punctuation. Giving them love and encouragement, teaching them to proofread, and helping them learn to copy accurately will enable many students to improve their mastery of the mechanics of formal writing, always assuming, of course, that there are no serious emotional problems or learning disabilities.

Some students, however, need to learn the rules governing punctuation, grammar, usage, and spelling. What can teachers do who have little or no class time and precious little outside time and who, though they follow the rules in their own writing, have not necessarily been trained to teach those rules to students? What can teachers do when two, or five, or fifteen students in a class, even after everything has been done to eliminate performance errors, still need, not just to fill in some gaps about whether commas go inside or outside the quotation marks, but to learn the most basic rules governing written English? Sometimes it may seem that students need only master a simple rule about avoiding sentence fragments, but that rule turns out, when tugged at, to have a massive underground root system of grammatical principles that the students must also comprehend before they can really overcome the problem.

Using the Skills Center

The answer for most of us is to get students who need basic training into a writing class or a skills center and then back up the staff's efforts. Chances are the center will place the student in some program of learning and drill—either one that staff members have developed themselves or one of the printed, taped, televised, or computerized instructional aids currently on the market.

Using the Never-Again Notebook

The one method I can recommend for use either alone or in conjunction with another instructional program is the never-again notebook. Students purchase standard spiral or loose-leaf notebooks. On each student's paper the teacher marks the two or three most frequent or most disturbing mechanical problems: for example, errors in apostrophe use or subject-verb agreement. Then students must learn to apply the pertinent rules. The explanation may come from the teacher, an assistant, a skills-center tutor, a handbook, or a slide-tape. Once the rule is clear, students copy in their notebooks all the mistakes they made in those areas, including the way they corrected each mistake and the rule that applies. Then students drill themselves every day on just those rules. In succeeding papers they try never again to make those particular mistakes. Once they master the first goals, the teacher picks one or two new rules for them to work on or lets them make the choice.

The never-again notebook works well alone if the student needs merely to fill in the gaps of a basically sound knowledge of mechanics. For example, the fine points of writing quotations (does the comma go inside or outside? when does one use a comma?) are easily handled in this way, and the explanation can come from any standard handbook on English punctuation. Students with more extensive or basic problems can use the never-again notebook along with a more systematized program of instruction. The problems chosen for the notebook will then be those that appear in the student's papers and that have already been covered in the program. The notebook thus serves to bridge the gap between correctly completing all the exercises in some book and actually eliminating a certain kind of mistake from one's own writing.

You can, if you wish, connect your grading to the type of incremental progress made in the never-again notebook. For example, you may say to the student, "If your next paper has none of the mistakes we've so far put in your never-again notebook, I will give it a B." When the student achieves that goal, you can raise the ante: next time the student must add one more mistake to those included in the notebook and banished from papers.

The beauty of the never-again notebook is that it focuses directly on students' actual, current problems and provides drill based on their own writing mistakes. Once you've explained the system and had students obtain notebooks, you need only mark in your own records what never-again writing mistakes each student is working on. Then you can read their papers only to check those aspects and, if appropriate, to pick the next entries for the notebooks. If you wish, you can call in the notebooks along with the papers.

Using Self-Instructional Programs

The never-again notebook assumes that the explanation of the rules comes from some source other than yourself. For explanations, and for drill and practice in applying the rules, students may turn to a number of self-instruction programs.

If you are working with a skills center, the following discussion should give you a nodding familiarity with its methods and help you understand and support its efforts; if you do not have such services available, this overview should enable you to make a reasonably intelligent choice of a self-instructional program for your students and to supplement that program with appropriate analysis and backup.

The student's motivation, interest, and desire are probably more important than the material used to teach mechanics. There are many materials on the market; some I believe to be better than others, but it may not make much difference which you choose, provided its method is consonant with the basic facts about language and the basic approaches outlined earlier in this chapter.

The availability of certain materials may influence your decision. Find out what's in your college bookstore or learning center. Also check with the offices of grant-funded programs such as Special Services, Upward Bound, or Title IV. Often such programs purchase learning materials.

The students who have to "learn" the rules may be in several different situations. Some may already have a good grasp of the grammatical structure of the language, so that they can comprehend and put into practice most rules stated in the technical terms of grammar. They may have some gaps in an otherwise solid foundation and simply need to add a few missing stones, such as the use of the colon and the use of commas on both sides of an interjected phrase. For these sorts of problems a standard English handbook is a good tool. I use Edward Corbett's *Little English Handbook*, but others are equally good.[2] Find out what your bookstore or library has, or ask what is required in your school's beginning composition classes and thus is likely to be available secondhand. The student looks up the rule in question, examines or completes examples or drills, and then, with the aid of the never-again notebook, learns to apply the rule in writing assignments.

Some students are not sufficiently familiar with the parts of speech to comprehend or apply a handbook's rules of punctuation and usage, especially rules that require a substantial knowledge of grammar. A handbook is not the answer for such students because it does not provide the extensive explanation of grammar and the extensive drill required. Instead, they can use self-instructional aids of various kinds in conjunction with the never-again notebook. See if your school owns programmed texts, explanatory texts with workbooks, or programs using filmstrips, slides and tapes, or computers.

Self-instructional programmed texts break down the learning task into small units and give the student the correct answer at once. Such books are set up in "frames." Each frame presents a bit of information and then asks a question about it. The student answers the question and immediately checks it in the answer column. If it is wrong, some books have the student go back over the same frame; some provide alternative explanations or more drill. Once the student has mastered the information in one frame, he or she goes on to the next.

The strengths of the programmed text are that it breaks down the job of learning a rule into its smallest components and presents a task from which much of the fright has been removed. The novice doesn't say, "This book asks me to walk to California, and I can't do that," because all the book asks is that the student put one foot in front of the other. After each step the book says, "Great! You took that step just fine. Now here's another step to take."

Computerized learning programs work on the same principle, but instead of uncovering the answer or turning the page to find it, the student learns it from the computer.

The self-instructional texts called "workbooks" usually contain explanations (longer than the frame in programmed texts), followed by exercises and drill. Answers may be in a separate booklet, at the back of the workbook itself, or at the ends of chapters.

Slide-tape or filmstrip programs are useful for students who have difficulty reading or who benefit from the audible reinforcement. Sometimes such a program is used along with a workbook.

Teachers have one common complaint about these instructional methods, however. Some students complete every step of the text and perform beautifully on all the exercises, yet fail to avoid the same errors in their papers. Such students need either more drill to set the rules or more help in solving problems of proofreading, copying, and motivation.

Another common concern is that while texts and workbooks may be ever so sound pedagogically, walking to California is tedious, boring, and exasperating, even when broken down into easy steps. Lots of pioneers, you know, gave up and settled in Nebraska. And your students are not pioneers. They're just trying to make it through school with as little sweat and pain as possible. So you may have to love, harry, and browbeat them through the pages of the text or the reels of the tape.

In choosing a text, workbook, or media program for your students, watch for the extent to which the text depends on mastery of the elements of traditional grammar. In grammar-oriented texts many questions call for grammatical terms as their answers. The table of contents and the foreword will also reveal an emphasis on grammar. Another type of text teaches as little grammar as possible. It typically begins, not with basic grammatical analysis of sentences, but with the areas in which unskilled writers make the most errors: spelling, complete sentences, agreement of subject and verb, formation of verb tenses. Attempting to eliminate the student's most frequent mistakes, these texts teach only as much grammar as absolutely necessary and avoid grammatical terminology wherever possible. This kind of text is probably best for the student who has no previous knowledge of traditional grammar or who is afraid of it. The more traditional text works for the student who has some grasp of grammar or who seems to master that type of material quickly and with pleasure. Whatever you do, be sure that the text does more than teach students to identify parts of speech; it must focus on using that knowledge to teach punctuation and other skills that students need to improve their writing.

Texts and audiovisual programs differ in vocabulary and reading levels. If you have a student whose vocabulary is limited or who is a poor reader, make sure you use a simple enough text.

Texts differ, too, in their separability. Some are composed of entirely discrete units, so that the student can easily cut from the herd the section that explains apostrophe use and deal with that beast all by itself. Other texts require the student to go through the entire sequence, perhaps omitting those parts for which a pretest shows efficient mastery of the material, but otherwise following a systematic approach. Again, your choice depends on the needs of the particular student.

Aids for Dialect Speakers and Speakers of English as a Second Language

For the dialect speaker there are special self-instructional programs that borrow many techniques from foreign language instruction. For example, they have drills in which the student compares dialect forms with EAE forms or translates back and forth from one to the other. An important characteristic of such texts—and one you will want to look for in other programs—is their avoidance of the phrase "correct English." They talk instead about choice of dialects or levels of formality. Such books use words like "error" and "correctness" only in clear reference to correctness *for EAE.* (In matters of spelling and punctuation, which are not features of dialect, the concept of correctness is, of course, more appropriate.) Special texts are also available for students learning English as a second language (ESL).

For dialect and ESL speakers, the most obvious teaching method, in addition to workbooks, and the one you will use unconsciously anyway, is the same method by which students learn any language—exposure and practice. All the reading and listening that you can work into your classroom activities will join with the listening and reading provided in other classes to give students valuable exposure. Beyond that, you can borrow ideas from foreign language teachers. You can also find out how much exposure to EAE your students are getting outside class. Students who socialize primarily with those who speak their own dialect or language might benefit from pairing up each day for lunch with a student who speaks something close to EAE. Sometimes a class in teaching methods for high school English or teaching English as a second language will provide tutors. Perhaps psychologically the best pairing is one in which the EAE speaker also tries to learn the other's dialect or language, so that the sessions involve exchanges between students rather than one-way tutoring. Or move to the written medium: have the student write, in EAE, a page a day about anything at all; then ask another student familiar with EAE to pick out the variant forms. In other words, do anything you can to approximate the kind of language teaching that takes place at the nightly French dinner, the French House, or the French Club. Imitate the ways in which your school goes about helping English students learn another tongue.

The methods for dealing with mechanics suggested earlier will enable you to work more intelligently at the problem, either in conjunction with your school's writing staff or on your own. Remember that, instead of spending your time marking every mistake on all student papers, you might better formulate a thoughtful approach to mechanics, geared to the needs and capabilities of each student. Concentrate first on the mistake or two or the pattern of error that each has the most trouble with. Concentrate first on eliminating performance-based errors. When you get down to the rules that a student needs to learn, you can suggest self-instructional materials. More important than the specific program you choose is the encouragement you provide, the motivation you foster, and the priority you assign to students' control over written English. Crucial, too, I believe, is the never-again notebook, which sets priorities for each student and helps him or her eliminate errors in an individualized, systematic way.

Chapter Eleven

Finding and Amending
Patterns of Error

You may be looking at rough drafts to spot problems that students should eliminate in their final papers; you may be looking at short pieces assigned early in the semester to help you discover which students will need the most help; you may be perusing final papers that, to your consternation, are still nests of errors—whatever kind of writing you're looking at, your first step is to ask, What sorts of errors do we have here?

Reading a paper, you may quickly see that a student's difficulties are concentrated in one or two of the areas I discuss, later in this chapter, in roughly descending order of importance. At other times, when you face a maze of mistakes, try to place at least some of them in one or the other of the six categories, and then choose one category for primary emphasis. Or scan the paper for errors in one category and, if you find some, stop right there and decide to concentrate on them. You needn't slow your pursuit of a tiger just because there are also leopards and lions in the jungle. When a paper is dense with error, it is better to give priority to one cluster of problems than to mark every transgression in the paper with no attempt to categorize the mistakes or indicate their relative importance.

The second step in reading for mechanical problems is to distinguish between performance errors and errors that result from ignorance. Because this distinction is an integral part of the diagnosis and remediation of mechanical problems, the following pages stress the importance of looking for performance errors and suggest ways of integrating performance considerations with the techniques I recommend. I rely, however, on the previous discussion of such errors to give you an idea what to do about them. My greatest concern in this section is to show you how to analyze errors of knowledge and help students avoid them.

My discussion draws heavily from the work of Mina Shaughnessy, who analyzed thousands of papers written by inexperienced students and categorized the errors they made. I have adapted her discussion to apply to more sophisticated writers as well, to be useful to the content-area teacher, and to simplify the more technical aspects of her book, which is aimed at writing teachers and tutors.

Finding Time

This analysis of papers may seem like a great deal of work. And it is, especially when you're not used to it. To a great extent, however, it eliminates the need to mark every mechanical error on every paper. Instead, you spend some time diagnosing the problems and deciding what weakness you can help the student overcome during the relatively short span of your course. Then you get the student started on some plan of remediation. In subsequent papers, tests, or exercises, you may do nothing with mechanics except look for errors in the one area of priority and guide the use of the never-again notebook. In addition, you try to provide motivation for the student to continue through the self-instructional program, to attend the lab, or to keep coming to class and handing in writing assignments. It may be that you have time to do this kind of careful work with one problem and also to mark all others; however, if you don't, consider concentrating on one problem as an alternative to marking all mechanics errors.

Sentence Faults

In learning to write complete sentences, students must come to recognize and avoid sentence fragments, run-ons, and comma splices.

1. A sentence fragment is a group of words that is not a complete sentence but that is punctuated like one. For example:

```
That the first of the patients had been treated even though several
    in the later group remained without help.

When the discovery had been made and the news of it had generally
    been communicated to scientists.
```

2. A run-on sentence results when two sentences are joined with no punctuation whatsoever. For example:

```
The senate voted the bill was passed.
```

3. A comma splice (sometimes included under the label "run-on") occurs when sentences are separated by a comma.

```
The other type of diabetes is maturity onset diabetes, it has
insulin circulating in the blood stream and responds more
satisfactorily to oral hypoglycemic drugs.
```

Many students try to avoid fragments or run-ons either by writing only short, simple sentences or by stringing sentences together with a familiar connective word such as "and." When you see a strangely abbreviated prose style, or a strangely attenuated one, it is worth finding out how great a factor anxiety about fragments and run-ons has been. Short, simple sentences are the most common means of avoiding sentence errors. Here's an example, taken from a student nurse's report to her supervisor:

```
At the onset of the patient's pregnancy she was diagnosed as
having Diabetes Mellitus.  Later in the pregnancy the patient
developed toxemia.  The patient was put on a diet to counteract
the toxemia and then the diabetes.  The patient had a sugar level of
four plus.  The patient was also suffering from anxiety.  The patient
feared that she was pregnant because of amenorrehea for four weeks.
The patient's husband had a vasectomy two months earlier.  The
patient stated that the doctor told her husband that his sperm count
was negative.  The nurse first relieve the patient's anxiety.
```

In speech, this student is in control of more complex sentence patterns than she uses here. The trick is to find out what is causing this choppy style. Possibly, it is fear of making mistakes in punctuating longer sentences.

Appreciate Students' Problems

Whether you are seeing run-ons, fragments or an awkward style that comes from avoiding them, ponder the problems students face in writing complete sentences. One barrier is that complete sentences punctuated with periods and capital letters on the written page are not the same as the "sentences" used in conversation. The latter are clusters of words, not necessarily complete sentences, separated by pauses or by the pitch of the speaker's voice. Fragments and ellisions are rife in conversational speech. Discrete units may have boundaries quite different from the boundaries of a written sentence. The difference between a spoken "sentence" and a written sentence is nowhere so clearly shown as in the writing of those students who try to punctuate according to the way they breathe or pause in conversational speech. That method doesn't always work. To punctuate the written sentence successfully, one must know how to recognize, not a spoken "sentence," but a written sentence—one that has a subject and a predicate and can stand alone. This identification is difficult for those inexperienced in writing or unsure about how to find the subject and predicate.

Second, writing complete sentences is difficult because the rules are currently relaxing. More and more fragments appear in print, and we are beginning also to see comma splices. Given these devilish waterings, it is little wonder that fragments and run-ons flourish in some of your students' writing.

Identify Performance-Based Problems

If you identify problems in writing complete sentences and decide to concentrate on them, here's what to do. First, find out to what extent the problems are performance-based. Techniques for doing this, along with methods for ameliorating the problems, are discussed on pages 169–72.

Once you get down to difficulties that are knowledge-based, you can begin to diagnose the problem and try to teach the students what they do not know. At this point you may refer the students to a skills center, with instructions to work toward eliminating sentence fragments, run-ons, or a "scared style." Or you might recommend a self-instructional text with a section on punctuating sentences, or on run-ons and fragments, or on embedding, subordinating, and coordinating. Labels like the last one often indicate a chapter that tries to help the students not only to avoid fragments and run-ons but to compose and manipulate various kinds of clauses and phrases and to punctuate them appropriately. This approach and sentence combining are probably more useful in the long run and more effective, especially with inexperienced and unskilled writers.

Make a More Specific Diagnosis

To refer students to a learning program at this point, however, is to do so before you really understand the nature of their problem. Consequently you run the danger of applying a misdirected or vague remedy— like using an all-purpose garden spray that contains eleven poisons, just because you haven't taken the time to identify the kind of bug that's eating your roses.

You can be much more accurate and effective if you take another step or two before making that referral to the skills center or to the self-instructional program. This discussion will outline the next diagnostic steps you can take, or the steps your skills center is likely to take if you leave the diagnosis to its staff. Begin with a careful analysis of the writing and then have an individual conference with the student. Your goals are to discover the feelings, attitudes, and rules that guide the student's punctuation practices; to check once again whether some error is performance-based, and to determine what knowledge the student needs to acquire.

Before the conference, take a close, analytical look at the student's paper. Sometimes you can see patterns that reveal where the problem is. For example, you may discover that the student uses commas to separate sentences closely connected in content and periods to separate sentences more distantly related. The student is punctuating according to logical units—a rhetorical sensitivity that you can sincerely praise. For example, here is a paper in which all sentences are punctuated correctly except two that are similar in content.

```
    If I was to go through high school again, I think that I would
take more math & english.  I didn't take anymore math after nineth
grade algebra, because I had to work hard to get a "C."  A "C" to me
in algebra was a "A."
    I really didn't know how important english was until I was a
senior in high school, thats when I wished that I would of payed
more attention in english class & that I should of taken more
classes in composition.
    English is gonna be a hard subject for me in college because I
didn't prepare myself right for it in high school, but I'm willing
to learn it because I know that if I study it hard that I'll do
good in it.
```

Such a student is already making distinctions between discrete sentences and pairs of sentences closely related. The job is to learn when to replace that comma with a semicolon or a conjunction. This student's use of the dash may be questionable, but the dash is clearly an advance over the comma that many students would have been tempted to use.

```
    In the first place, I haven't had to struggle as hard my dad
did just to get to college.  As he was raised during the Great
Depression, times were very hard, and his mom and dad didn't have  .
the money to send him to college--they barely had enough to eat
with as it was.
```

Here is a student who has almost mastered the use of the semicolon, except he's using it incorrectly with a connective:

```
    My life will proable be a lot different because they (my
parents) like small towns and simple thing; but, I like th bigger
cities such as Des Moines.
```

This writer illustrates another common near hit on the way to mastery of the semicolon:

```
    The colonists were extremely angry, however; no riots erupted
that day.
```

To sum up, one common cluster of error centers around the student's sense that some pairs of sentences are closely related and should be separated by something less final than a period. Often, however, the use of the semicolon is unfamiliar to such a student; consequently, you may see the comma as a connective, or you may see the semicolon used incorrectly. The remedy for both errors is to offer practice in using the semicolon, so that students can turn to it with confidence when they feel that two sentences are too close for a period. An appropriate textbook chapter might be entitled "Avoiding Comma Splices," "Avoiding Run-ons," or "Coordinating." Some students—especially if they're reversing the semicolon and the comma, as in the last example above, or if they're using a semicolon with conjunctions, as in the earlier example—could simply consult a handbook that explains the uses of the semicolon.

A second common pattern you're likely to find occurs when students write in sentence fragments. See whether you can define the kinds of fragments that they mistake for complete sentences. Often, their fragments are groups of words before or after which the voice would drop significantly in speech. Sometimes they are certain grammatical constructions, such as clauses beginning with "that" or "who" or "what" or "after" or "because." For example, one student writes:

```
In conducting this survey I had two basic concepts in mind. What
4th and 5th graders considered male and female jobs and togetherness
in play.
```

The next student makes a common mistake by starting a rather involved construction and then seeming to forget that it requires another clause. This student starts with an "In" phrase, adds a "that" clause, and then forgets that these structures, though they've taken up a good deal of space, are not complete in themselves.

```
In Greers statement that, while women are different, they are not
inferior, and are in fact "neighbors."  To me this sentence says an
awful lot.
```

This kind of error is sometimes due merely to the complexity of the structures. Try simplifying the wording to see whether the student can punctuate it. Then, in the never-again notebook, have the student practice simple structures in this pattern, gradually building up greater complexity. For example, the student would write in the notebook:

```
In Greer's statement there is much to ponder.
In Greer's statement that women are different there is much to
    ponder.
In Greer's statement that, while women are different, they are not
    inferior, and are in fact "neighbors," there is much to ponder.
```

The complexity of this final version may lead the student to fashion this sentence in a different way in the final paper, but in the never-again notebook, the writer can practice holding to the sense of the sentence through a number of distracting structures.

Sometimes the student will be thrown off by the appearance of a gerund, participle, or infinitive that looks like the verb of a sentence. In the following examples the misleading words are italicized:

```
They worked all night.  Sharing their bread and coffee.
```

```
She wants a place where the prisoner could come and go as he pleases.
Be a part of the community he is near.
```

The student may need only to learn the difference between verbals and true verbs. A textbook chapter on sentence fragments usually covers this problem.

In summary, then, certain common patterns appear in the writing of students who are composing run-on sentences or sentence fragments. If you recognize these patterns, you can help, especially when the problems are limited to an area or two.

Sometimes, however, a student has several kinds of difficulty or makes errors that form no defined or limited pattern. For example, several kinds of sentence problems appear in this long report of a survey the student did in the school where he was an aide. The purpose of the survey was to discover what the children thought on two issues: what adult jobs were appropriate for each sex and what rules should apply when boys and girls play together.

```
1       In conducting this survey I had two basic concepts in mind.
    What 4th and 5th graders considered male and female jobs and
    togetherness in play.  With male and female jobs I incorporated
    the question about smartness.  A common stereotype is the one
5   that deal with intelligence.  Since boys are told there're
    smarter than girls they aspire the better jobs.  For girls its
    just the opposite.  When told constintly you can't do something
    sooner or later you'll tend to believe it.  The other questions
    can be linked with question 7 and togetherness.
10      With the jobs question, every other one was favorable to
    males and the other female; except for questions 10 and 12 which
    are for both.  Over 80% of the boys and girls believe they have
    equal intelligence.  I was expecting to see some females select jobs
    that would be heavily populated by men, but this didnt happen.
15  Except for one girl who chose carpentry, all the other girls
    choose jobs that are strongly populated by women.  Boys also chose
    those jobs that are male oriented except for elementary teacher.
    The vast majority of the students believed boys and girls have the
```

same intelligence. My expectation of applying this to the job
20 question didn't take place. Another interesting fact that came
about was, the 47 boys that answered they all either believed
boys were smarter or that neither group was. In turn, of the 41
girls that answered they either believed girls were smarter or that
neither group was. As far as self esteem goes girls hold a high
25 one along with boys, through intelligence they get this. I suppose
not seeing many females in certain occupations the girls probably
thought those were the jobs women couldnt or shouldn't do. Questions
10 and 12 girls and boys were suppose to select. With the popularity
of women tennis and Iowa High School girls basketball and the
30 coverage the media has given both were some of the reasons why
they were choosen.

Togetherness in play pertaining to elementary kids, had one
major must. The opposent sex must be able to complete at the level
of the others. Boys played games that were considered for girls
35 and girls played games that were considered for boys. Battle ball,
kick ball and four square were 3 of the most popular games in both
groups. I asked each class I visited if they played the games with
their own sex or together. Only 2 boys in 48 said girls and boys
should never play the games together, whereas no girls said this.
40 Of the boys 14 said they should always play them together. There
were 9 girls with the same response.

Some of the games are required activities such as battle ball
or square dancing while others like four square or tether ball are
usually played at recess. I inquired about all the games and activities
45 in general; to see how they felt about them. Large majorities
of both boys and girls believed they should play games only
sometimes. The kids didnt mind having someone of the opposent sex
playing with them except when they were inferior.

In just about any game played on a playground there will be
50 either fights, tests of bravery, determination of whos better, and
the kid who releases his frustration through crying. Most kids believe
fighting (all types) is wrong. Many of the kids believed
physical fighting between the sexes is a taboo. In the games
they play they would certainly argue but not necessarily hit one
55 another. Both sexes were consistent with their responses. The
majority in both cases answered boys and girls should never fight,
while the rest said sometimes.

Both the boys and girls believe by wide margins that bravery,
regardless where its at is equal. The games the kids play believe
60 it takes the same bravery for a girl to catch a ball someone has
thrown as it does for a boy. As far as pride in determining who's
better or who crys more, say after a lose, the girls answered
with large majorities saying both the same. The boys on the other

Sentence Faults

hand say either they are better or both are the same when it comes
65 to bravery. Boys tend to believe that girls cry more or both the same.
      The large majority of boys believe either girls cry more or
both do the same.
      With the help of teachers and parents kids arent brought up
or told one sex is better than another. The trend is to judge
70 people indivigually rather than in groups. With most jobs,
intelligence or knowledge of subject is needed, the kids showed
that both sexes are capable of suceeding or failing. There is
still a sterotype of the type of jobs that are male dominant or
female dominant. The kids basicaly upheld the myths that only
75 men are firemen or busimen, While girls did the same with jobs
of a nurse of secretary. In the area of play boys and girls both
enjoyed the same games. The vast majority of both sexes agreeed
they should get together in play. Again both sexes have the
thoughts towards fighting and bravery. Boys then deviate from the
80 girls when crying and sports come in the picture. The majority
of the girls believe that both are the same.
      This survey showed me that the attitude boys have of girls
has improve over the years. But the results from questions 4 and
5 definitely tell me that there is still work to be done.

I chose this long paper because it illustrates the situation all of us
often face in handling sentence problems: we often find other significant
problems in punctuation, grammar, and syntax, as well as poor organization and clumsy or inept handling of the subject. Certainly you will want
to work with this student on techniques for organizing a survey of this
nature, and you will want to push for greater clarity. Beyond that, a number of mechanical problems need attention. I believe, however, that it
would be counterproductive to spend your time marking every mechanical problem. Instead, you might focus on sentence errors, since they are
serious and since the report contains several of them.

This paper has one sentence fragment (l. 2) and two comma splices
(ll. 25 and 71). In addition, an analysis of the student's sentence-punctu-
ating habits must take into account the two misuses of the semicolon (ll.
11, 45). This mark is properly used when it separates closely connected
sentences, and in this paper its absence in some cases and its inappropriate appearance elsewhere are part of the same problem. Note that in line
11 the student uses the semicolon to connect closely related clauses.
Though its use here is incorrect, the student does have some notion of the
purpose of the semicolon. The other semicolon appears where the succeeding group of words somewhat resembles the "except" clause in line
11. Thus emerges the pattern: the student has the beginnings of a notion

about how to use the semicolon, but he is not sure what sorts of clauses it should precede.

The comma splices vary. The first (l. 25) may have come about because the words "through intelligence" may sound like the sort of phrase that would continue a sentence rather than begin a new one. The second comma splice (l. 71) may be due simply to the accidental omission of the word "where" before "intelligence." The sentence would read correctly if that were inserted: "With most jobs, *where* intelligence or knowledge of subject is needed, the kids showed that both sexes are capable of succeeding or failing."

The sentence fragment may stem from a common problem: students often mistake a "what" clause for a sentence. Later (ll. 39 and 57), however, the writer again uses such clauses, this time starting with "whereas" and "while," and these are correctly joined to the preceding sentence with a comma. Thus it may be that this fragment, especially since it is the only one, resulted from the student's incorrect use of a period in place of a colon. If we insert a colon, the fragment disappears: "In conducting this survey I had two basic concepts in mind: what 4th and 5th graders considered male and female jobs and togetherness in play." The student may have had only a shadowy acquaintance with the colon—or none at all. When he sensed a need for some kind of punctuation in this first sentence, he fell back on the familiar but inappropriate period.

Remediation for this student thus can focus on two main issues: (1) where to use the semicolon instead of the comma between clauses and (2) how to use a colon to introduce a list. A careful look at the paper has prevented the teacher from taking the first sentence fragment as the key problem and sending the student off to have his fragments fixed, when in fact they are not the central difficulty. Analysis has also allowed the teacher—instead of marking several different corrections such as "semicolon," "comma splice," or simply "punctuation"—to see a number of the paper's problems as one and to identify what the student really needs to learn. The teacher can verify that understanding and amplify in a conference with the student. The next step would be either an instructional text or a referral to the skills center, together with the never-again notebook. The teacher's careful analysis has provided an accurate focus for whatever remedial steps are taken.

Let's look at another diagnostic problem. The following example illustrates a basic and thorough confusion about sentence boundaries and punctuation:

```
The main point of this topic is that the Children an College
students aren't learning how to read and write for that they will
used later in life.  I don't believe society has prepared me for
```

Sentence Faults

```
the work I want to do that.  is in education speaking, that my
main point in being here,  If this isn't a essay.  of a thousand
word's that because I don't have much to say. for it has been four
year since I last wrote one, and by the time I am finish here I hope
to be able to write an number of essay.
```

Even in this passage, Shaughnessy, who quotes it, finds pattern: the inclination to use the comma as a period and to employ the period to mark subordinate structures (p. 14). Note the word "inclination," which Shaughnessy uses. Especially in the work of basic writers such as this, one finds not so much consistent rules as tendencies and inclinations. To a trained observer, however, the tendencies indicate a direction for remediation.

The best guidance for such a student's efforts comes from a teacher or tutor trained in remediation. If your school has no such resource, however, you can use a self-instructional program that offers not only rules of punctuation but also practice in constructing various sentence patterns. The text must begin with the basic sentence, with identification of subject and predicate, and with practice in forming the various constructions that amplify the basic subject-verb unit. The text should be written very simply.

Whatever text students use at this level, you will undoubtedly want to provide a great deal of support and encouragement, for such students have a long, discouraging route to travel before they achieve academic excellence, or even competence. In your course, ask such students to write often but in short units. Have the student use the never-again notebook to record not only errors but daily responses to class lectures and readings. Any format that encourages fluidity and relaxation will be helpful. You can also use the never-again notebook for sentence-pattern drill. Have students write a series of sentences according to various patterns, starting with the most basic subject-verb units and advancing to more complex patterns. You might begin, for example, by asking the student to write, "This isn't an essay of a thousand words." Then go to other simple subject-verb units following the same pattern. Next the student writes, "If this isn't an essay of a thousand words, that's because I don't have much to say." Then request other sentences that begin with "if" or similar words. Finally, the students might practice adding units: "If this isn't an essay of a thousand words, that's because I don't have much to say, for it has been four years since I last wrote one, but by the time I am finished here I hope to be able to write a number of essays." The three graduated steps of this exercise may roughly match the student's progress through a printed text that works first with simple subject-verb units, then with sentences beginning with "if" and similar adverbial clauses, and finally with sentences that tack on additional units by means of a comma plus a connective such as "for," "but," or "and." Try to make the never-again notebook a bridge between the stages of a student's progress through the printed text and the sentences that actually appear in the student's written assignments. Use it also to provide simple practice in putting pen to paper. Remember that a significant part of such a students' dilemma is likely to be that he or she has done very little writing, ever.

In the writing of students who are not sure how to identify or punctuate sentences you will find much puzzling punctuation. You can assume, however, that there is some pattern that you cannot immediately see. It is worthwhile, if you have the time, to try to decipher patterns of error, so that you can suggest specific and useful remedies.

Identify Where Knowledge Ends

After a careful look at what a paper itself reveals, schedule a conference with the student. The first goal of such a conference is to learn what feelings and attitudes the student brings to the learning task. Does the writer feel highly nervous about correctness? What rules for sentence punctuation does the writer already know? Has this student been criticized by teachers in the past for using run-ons and fragments? If so, what feelings or behavior resulted? What attempts have been or are being made to remedy the problems? The answers to these questions may uncover fears, avoidance patterns, and misunderstood or misapplied rules, and they may also establish open communication on which you can build a well-motivated learning effort.

Second, in the conference, you will want to probe the extent of the student's present knowledge. Most particularly, you will want to find out how much the student knows about identifying complete sentences—the basic skill that will make correct punctuation possible. More specifically, the writer should know:

1. *How to identify subjects and predicates and how to tell whether a group of words has both a subject and a predicate.* The student's greatest difficulty is often in distinguishing true verbs from verblike constructions such as "being only a youngster" or "attached to the rock" or "to operate complicated machinery." Finding the subject is also difficult when it is a noun clause or a verbal phrase such as *"Giving to the church* was a normal part of living for people in Provincetown." Finally, subjects are sometimes hard to ferret out among other nouns and pronouns in the sentence: "Although I was aghast at the prospect, nevertheless, with the encouragement of my teacher, *I* went ahead."

2. *How to tell a sentence from a nonsentence.* Once students have learned accurately to identify the true subject and predicate, then they must distinguish "incomplete" groups of words containing both a subject and predicate from true sentences. The greatest difficulty comes with clauses that have a subject and a predicate but are not complete sentences be-

cause they possess some additional factor that makes them, in traditional grammatical terms, dependent rather than independent clauses. A clause always has a subject and predicate; what makes it dependent (that is, what makes it a nonsentence) is an introductory word like "when," "because," "after," or "although" (i.e., an adverbial conjunction). A clause is also dependent when it has as its subject a relative pronoun such as "who," "what," or "that." For example, here are some dependent clauses of the type students often punctuate as complete sentences:

```
Because the earlier measures had failed to produce any changes
     in the patient's pain level.

When I went to the legislature to work for the summer.

He referred me to the curator.  Who was in charge of the extensive
     collection of guns in the museum.
```

3. *What punctuation to use between independent clauses if one does not want to use a period.* I frequently ask students what three alternatives they have for linking independent clauses. If they don't know, and if they recognize an independent clause, I tell them the three—it's a fairly simple list, and I find that some students appreciate having the three options pulled together and presented to them this way. Either no one has done that for them before, or they haven't been ready to hear it before.

a. Semicolon: The first bill passed easily; it dealt only with administrative structures for the program.

b. Comma plus a conjunction such as "and," "but," "for" or "or": The first bill passed easily, but it dealt only with administrative structures for the program.

c. Semicolon, plus a word like "however," "nevertheless," or "therefore," followed by a comma: The first bill passed easily; however, it dealt only with administrative structures for the program.

4. *How to integrate an idea into a sentence as a dependent element and how to punctuate the resulting structure, or how to make a sentence fragment into a complete sentence.* For example, when the student, proofreading, finds a fragment or a run-on, he or she must know how to work that fragment into the surrounding discourse, how to make it a complete sentence, or how to recast the whole group of words into a more effective structure. This fourth skill perhaps should be placed first in the list, because when a student is having serious problems in writing complete sentences, the teacher should not only deal with specific punctuation mistakes but try to build the student's confidence and facility in handling various structures of written discourse.

Your object in this interview is to discover how much of the above information the student already knows. You can get a rough idea by simply pointing to several groups of words in the student's paper and asking whether the word groups are complete sentences. Pick some phrases, some clauses, and some true sentences. Ask how the student identifies groups of words as complete sentences. If answers to these questions are fuzzy, then drop back a step. Pick a complete sentence and ask the student to identify the subject and predicate. Then select a fragment or a dependent clause and ask how the student could add it to the sentence before or after it, or ask how it might be transformed into a complete sentence.

In addition to, or instead of, using this approach, you may want to give some students a diagnostic test from some remedial text or workbook. Remember, when students are faced with questions in a testlike situation, they may become so nervous that the words swim in front of their eyes and their knowledge fails to show. Second, the style of the test sentences may be different from the students' own writing style. Correcting the run-ons and fragments in a book differs from writing in complete sentences. Reduce tension as much as you can, and work as closely as possible with the student's own writing.

Summary of Methods

To summarize, here are three steps you can take to help students with the punctuation of sentences:

1. Establish that the student is having a problem writing in complete sentences or is restricting his or her prose style for fear of writing run-ons or fragments.
2. Take a careful look at the writing to further identify patterns of error.
3. Hold a conference with the student to discuss feelings and attitudes about the problem, to discover how much the student knows, and to establish trust and motivation.

Throughout these three steps, be alert to distinguishing performance-based errors from knowledge-based errors. After any of these three steps, depending on your own time limits, you may refer the student to a skills center or recommend a self-instructional program. In either case, you can support learning by asking the student to keep a never-again notebook.

Quotation and Documentation

We can divide the area of quoting and documenting into two levels of importance, and I will treat only the first here, near the top of the "capital offense" list. I stress citation because of the wide use of quotation and documentation in academic writing and because ignorance of such conventions may lead students to be accused of plagiarism.

The first rule is that writers must put quotation marks around all material copied directly from a source and must identify—in a note or in parentheses in the text—the source of all information and ideas, whether quoted directly or paraphrased. In some ways this rule is easier to teach than sentence punctuation because it does not depend on an understanding of grammar.

In looking at any paper containing documentation or quotations, consider first whether problems show up as errors or as patterns of avoidance. Some students, for example, never quote directly because they are unsure how to use quotation marks. Others quote everything because they don't know whether paraphrasing requires quotation marks or a footnote.

In a conference, ask the student what kind of material should be documented and discuss the uses of quotation marks, footnotes, and parenthetical documentation. Students having trouble in this area sometimes need only to be made aware that the liberties they took in their high school work are no longer permissible.

Some students need practice in recognizing differences among direct quotation, indirect quotation, and paraphrase. Here are some common patterns (a note number would be required after each of these sentences):

- He said, "My investigations have revealed that the bureau is a thicket of deceit."
- He said that his investigations had revealed the bureau to be "a thicket of deceit."
- He said that his investigations had revealed widespread dishonesty in the bureau.
- There is widespread dishonesty in the bureau, reports Maxwell.

Some self-instructional texts give explanation and drill in punctuating all kinds of quotation and paraphrase. Or you can give students a short passage from a research source, as well as the sentences above to serve as models, and you can ask them to compose sentences using the quotation in different ways.

A related problem, also in the "serious" category, is the use of direct quotation where paraphrase or summary would be better. Sometimes this is part of a larger problem, the student's failure to establish an individual thesis and direction. Sometimes, however, a student has a good focus but simply makes wrong choices about how much quoting to do. Give out the general rule: "Quote directly only when the exact words of the source are important for some special reason." In getting students to follow this rule, you will have to combat their tendency to quote because they think that the prose style of the original is better than anything they could write, or because they don't understand the quotation well enough to paraphrase it, or because it's just easier to copy than to state an idea in their own words. Talk to your students about these poor reasons for quoting; you'll see by their guilty grins that you've tapped the underground currents that shape their papers.

Other problems that arise with quotations and documentation are discussed on page 217 because I consider them part of a myriad of punctuation problems of a less serious order.

It is sometimes wise to give the whole class, orally or in writing, all your advice on quoting. Here, for example, is a first-day handout adapted from one developed by Jack Breihan for his Loyola College history students. Feel free to copy or adapt it for your own students.

Guidelines for Use of Research Material

1. Whenever you use another writer's exact words, or state another author's idea in your own words, or use facts from a source (unless these facts are so common as to be part of the generally accepted store of knowledge in the field), you must give credit to that other author and tell the reader where the information or idea came from. Note that I said you must give credit even when you use your own words. This may be contrary to some habits you've developed in high school, but it is very important, because not to do so is plagiarism, which has serious consequences. It is a kind of stealing—stealing someone's idea or the data someone has collected, without giving that person credit.

2. In the humanities, the basic forms used to give credit to another author and to tell the reader where the information came from are the footnote and the bibliography. (In the sciences and some other fields, somewhat different forms are used, so check with your instructor before you use footnotes in those disciplines.)

3. It is easy to get "captured" by another author's words or organization and to end up using too much quoted material, or too many ideas from other authors, in a paper. To avoid this problem, you must establish your own purpose, your own plan or outline, and your own point of view. You must also be sure about who your audience is. Then search for the facts or ideas you need to support your own goals. That way, material from sources will *fit into* your own plan, not *be* your plan. If you need more help doing initial reading and establishing a plan for your paper, consult the first few chapters of James Lester, *Writing Research Papers,* which is available in the college bookstore. It's required in freshman composition at this school, so you may be able to borrow a copy from another student. It's also on reserve at the library.

4. When sources contradict one another, or when there are several places from which to get information or ideas, you must evaluate the worth of the sources and use the most reliable. Consider such factors as the date of the material, the reliability of the person or journal or newspa-

per reporting it, the likelihood of a person's being knowledgeable about, or present at, a reported event, and so on. The least reliable sources are encyclopedias, secondary compilations of documents, quotations of quotations, prefaces, introductory surveys, or chapters in broad, general texts. More reliable, as a rule, are original documents, firsthand accounts, the work of original researchers or thinkers or compilers who first printed an idea or a research report or a statistical table, and people who are experts in a specialized field, not writers of some compilation such as an introductory textbook or a popular magazine account. Common sense will often help you decide which sources to use (whom would you call as witness in a trial—the person who saw the accident or the person who only heard about it?). If you need help evaluating the worth of a book, check the *Book Review Digest* to see how others have viewed it. If you need help selecting from several possible sources, see whether there is a recently published selected bibliography. The word "selected" tells you that someone who knows the field more or less well has selected from many possible books and articles the ones he or she considers best for a certain purpose (make sure you know what that purpose was; if it was different from yours, that person's choice may not be useful to you). If you are unsure how to evaluate the worth of a written source, ask for help at the desk of the reference librarian. That desk is near the reference section; it has a sign saying "Please disturb." The librarians mean it: don't be afraid to ask for help.

5. Many students quote too much. The guide is this: use a direct quotation only when the precise words of the author are needed to justify your interpretation, or when those words are too exquisite to be missed. Avoid long, dull quotations. Consider paraphrasing (saying in your own words) most of a long passage, even if you do want to quote some of it.

6. When you use material from a source, whether you quote it directly or not, you must footnote it. Footnote numbers appear at the end of quotations or citations, or, if the cited material is more than a paragraph, at the end of each paragraph (so the reader doesn't get lost). If you need help with footnote form, consult Lester's book, cited above.

7. When you quote material directly, you have an additional responsibility besides the footnote. If the quotation is shorter than four lines, use quotation marks and just include it right in your paragraph, making sure that it fits in smoothly. Remember to include both sets of quotation marks, at the beginning and at the end of the quote. If it is longer than four lines, then use no quotation marks. Instead, indent the whole thing five spaces and single-space it. The spacing serves instead of quotation marks to tell the reader that the passage is quoted; the indentation and single spacing make it easier for the reader to identify and read long quotations. If you need more help with this aspect, consult Lester.

Syntax

"Syntax" refers to the way words are arranged in phrases, clauses, and sentences. Faulty syntax is the mishandling of a group of words that should proceed according to a standard pattern. For example:

```
It turned out to be more than a task than an easy preliminary gesture.
```

```
I might even would want to try it someday.
```

```
Playing rugby has put my worries to ease about my physical fitness.
```

Few rules apply across the board to problems of syntax because the language contains thousands of different formulas. Once you begin a pattern, you must know what words or formulations are consistent with it. Syntax problems are vocabulary problems, really, since they arise because the student does not know the constraints surrounding the word used or the patterns that can follow or precede it.

Sometimes, as in this paper, syntax is a striking and dominant problem throughout the student's writing. I have italicized the problem spots.

```
     Now that I am at college, and have been given an opportunity
to meet new people and see different life styles, I have been able
to recognize a great difference in what the world has to offer me,
than what the world offered to my parents.
     To start out with, education, my father was only able to
complete eight years of school, because he was expected to help
earn a living.  My mother who because of marriage was only able
to obtain a high school education.
```

[A sentence fragment, but in this context probably best recognized as a part of the student's larger problem of shaping sentences according to expected syntactical patterns.]

```
                    She was married at an early age and was
unable to, so called, "play the field" as I am able.
     Out side presures, such as inner family and socoial presures,
influenced their decesions as to what to buy and what not to buy,
and people see and people not to be seen with.
     I find that there is not so much emphasis on "what" or "who"
in my life.  I know that there are many changes in life style which
I will have to make, but I'm willing to make them without worry of
what people think.
```

Faulty syntax results either from the student's unfamiliarity with a certain pattern—perhaps because that pattern is used much more in writing than in speech—or from the student's inability to keep track of a pattern begun earlier in the sentence, especially if additional words or phrases have intervened. The remedy, on a large scale, is to increase students' reading, so that they become more familiar with common syntactical patterns found in written discourse; you should also have them write frequently, so that they develop the short-term memory necessary for controlling syntactical patterns.

In diagnosing syntax problems, try to find out whether students produce the patterns accurately in relaxed speech. Often the nervousness or strangeness of the writing situation will cause students to misuse formulas that they can employ correctly in conversation. In these cases, they are usually able to hear mistakes. Simply ask the students to read the offending sentences aloud, or read them yourself, and ask the students to recast them.

If they cannot hear syntactical errors, then possibly they are dealing with patterns they do not use in speech or that are unfamiliar to their ears. You can then either suggest substitute patterns or provide corrections. You'll want to discourage the use of syntactical patterns that are pseudoacademic or too complicated and precious for their context. But sometimes the use of an unfamiliar pattern represents a laudable attempt to learn the more intricate and precise words and patterns that distinguish good writing from conversational speech and that allow writing to be tighter and more accurate than speech. Try not to discourage such attempts. When you find syntax problems, isolate one or several and offer drill in forming the proper pattern. You may have to give some advice about the use of a thesaurus. That reference is well used if it reminds writers of words they already know and structures they can firmly control, but it may suggest words and constructions only half familiar, inviting syntactical problems. To help students control the syntactical patterns that appear incorrectly in their writing, use the never-again notebook to offer practice in those forms. You'll find that errors fall roughly into two categories: the first is primarily a vocabulary problem; the student uses a word without knowing which other words fit with it. For example,

```
Playing rugby has put my worries to ease about my physical fitness.
```

If the writer does not hear the mistaken word choice in that sentence, then ask him or her to write in the notebook:

```
Playing rugby has put my mind at ease about my physical fitness.
Playing rugby has put my worries to rest about my physical fitness.
```

Then have the student compose, in the notebook, other sentences using the same patterns:

```
Taking vitamins has put my mind at ease about my nutritional
    well-being.
```

```
Taking vitamins has put my worries to rest about my nutritional
    well-being.
```

The above example illustrates a vocabulary constraint, but sometimes a syntactical problem involves a structural pattern:

```
Greer realizes that men and women have totally different types of
minds, but she believes that in more ways than one that they are
equal.
```

The problem lies in handling the "that . . . they" formula in cases where another phrase, such as "in more ways than one," intervenes. In the never-again notebook, have the student write:

```
. . . she believes that they are equal.
. . . she believes that in more ways than one they are equal.
```

As I mentioned above, you may want to suggest that, when a syntactical problem seems to arise because of the complexity of the sentence, the student first write the simplest form of the pattern: "she believes that they are equal." Often the student will easily be able to manipulate the pattern in a simpler sentence. Then add the intervening words and phrases that have made the sentence more complex and caused the error: "she believes that in more ways than one they are equal." Then ask for other similar patterns:

```
She worried that he would be killed.
She worried that while riding in the rodeo he would be killed.

They thought that ten more lives had been lost.
They thought that, in the confusion of that scrambled rescue effort,
    ten more lives had been lost.
```

From the essay quoted earlier, on differences between the student and her parents, one might select several syntactical patterns for drill in the notebook (at this stage one hopes for progress toward mastering the problematic syntactical pattern and disregards the need for further revisions to improve the stylistic grace of the "corrections," shown in parentheses):

```
I have been able to recognize a great difference in what the world
has to offer me, than what the world offered to my parents.

(I have been able to recognize a great difference between what the
world has to offer me and what the world offered to my parents.)
```

```
My mother who because of marriage was only able to obtain a high
school education.  She was married at an early age and was unable
to, so called, "play the field" as I am able.
```

```
(My mother, who because of marriage was only able to obtain a high
school education, was married at an early age and was unable to
"play the field" as I can.)
```

```
I'm willing to make them without worry of what people think.
```

```
(I'm willing to make them without worrying what people think.)
```

Here is a sentence that ends in an unexpected way, illustrating another syntax problem. Part of the problem is that the reader pauses after the first "curriculum," only to learn that "required to move on to the next task" is a modifier for "curriculum," much as if the sentence had read, "The students are all going through the curriculum for the fourth grade in the same way as through the curriculum for the fifth grade." There is a second problem in the sentence: the word "those" has no clear antecedent.

```
The ungraded students are all going through the curriculum required
to move on to the next task in the same way as those in the graded
curriculum, but they move at their own pace.
```

One might simply reflect confusion in a comment to the student: "I can't understand this sentence." Or mark it this way:

```
The ungraded students are all going through the curriculum Who?
(required to move on to the next task) in the same way as (those) in
the graded curriculum, but they move at their own pace.
```

Hard to follow; find another way to describe the curriculum.

A revision might read:

```
The ungraded students are all going through the curriculum step by
step, in the same way as pupils in the graded curriculum, but the
ungraded students move at their own pace.
```

The best remedy for syntactical problems is this kind of individual drill, based on the mixups the student is actually producing. Some workbooks provide practice in correcting the syntactical errors that students most often make, but these may not be the same mistakes your student commits. In any case, the ultimate solution is simply plenty of practice in reading, hearing, and writing the patterns of English until they become so familiar that students can reproduce them accurately in their own compositions.

Inflection

Inflected words are words that change their form according to their role in the sentence—according to person, number, tense, and so on. Errors in inflection fall into four main categories:

1. Forms of verbs
2. Forms of pronouns
3. Possessive and plural forms of nouns
4. Negatives

Several factors make errors of inflection difficult to confront and correct. First, it is the inflected forms that are most likely to be influenced by dialects the students have spoken or heard. A related difficulty is that most of us slur or omit the endings of verbs and nouns, no matter what dialect we speak. For example, we don't say the first *s* in the phrase "Dave's sweatshirt" or the *ed* in the sentence "The dog lapped the milk." In addition, the rules that guide inflection in English are highly complex, with many irregularities. Also, attention to inflection is difficult for students because the change in form is often not necessary to establish meaning. For example, "She went to Mary house" makes amply clear whose house she went to; the apostrophe is not necessary for meaning. A final reason for students' difficulty with this cluster of errors is that applying the rules requires more background knowledge than may at first be apparent to the exasperated teacher who wonders why the student can't grasp the rule and follow it. The simple prescription that "a verb must agree with its subject" requires that a student be able to pick out the true subject and the true verb without being distracted by subjectlike or verblike structures or by modifiers. Take, for example, this sentence: "Each of the soldiers, after saluting the officers, steps back into line." Here the student must select "each" as the true subject without being swayed by the presence of "soldiers" or "officers." Then the student must identify "steps" as the verb that has to agree with "each"; the writer must not be distracted by "saluting." After picking out the subject and verb, the student must know whether the subject is singular or plural and how to construct the appropriate verb form. In the above sentence, for example, some writers might use "step," because they don't know that "each" is singular, because they think "soldiers" is the subject, or because they are not sure of the standard verb form. This could easily happen with a dialect speaker who is used to saying, "He step back into line."

Given all these difficulties, it is not surprising that errors of inflection are so numerous in our students' writing or that they persist tenaciously in the face of instruction and drill. It is an area in which the teacher must count the cost, decide which errors are strongly disturbing to readers, and set priorities.

In this section, I will treat the types of inflectional errors in turn.

Verb Forms

Of all the multitudes of problems that arise with inflection, difficulties with verbs are probably the most pernicious. Problems appear in three main areas:

1. Making the verb agree with its subject.
2. Choosing the appropriate verb form.
3. Deciding which tense, mood, and voice to use.

Making the Verb Agree with Its Subject

Even students who speak EAE have two problems with subject-verb agreement. First, they are sometimes distracted by intervening words and thus will form the verb to agree with some word other than the subject of the sentence. And second, they may not know whether certain subjects are singular or plural—especially collective nouns like "crowd" or pronouns such as "each" and "everyone." These students need information and drill on certain troublesome subjects, and they must practice ignoring distractions. For example, here is a sentence from a student paper in linguistics:

```
First, consider the group that have divergences occurring with
the addition of phonemes.
```

You can send such a student to a handbook or workbook with a section on collective nouns, or you can use the never-again notebook. For example, have the student write several sentences in the notebook:

```
The group has divergencies.
Consider the group that has divergencies.
First, consider the group that has divergencies occurring with the
     addition of phonemes.
```

Then ask the student to compose other sentences using words like "group," "crowd," and "team."

As this student's original sentence illustrates, sometimes a collective noun is not the best choice. A revision might read, "First, consider the words that have divergencies. . . ."

Here an intervening word group has distracted the student:

```
The advantages for women, as equals, except in the cases of equal
    pay for equal work, is very few.
```

In the notebook, this student would write:

```
The advantages are very few.
The advantages for women are very few.
The advantages for women as equals, except in the case of equal
    pay for equal work, are very few.

The opinions were negative.
The opinions of the senators were negative.
The opinions of the senators, except for five or six old-line
    conservatives, were negative.
```

For the student whose troubles are limited to mishandling collective nouns or being distracted by intervening elements, the use of the never-again notebook should be sufficient.

Sometimes, however, the troubles are more widespread. The "women as equals" sentence above, for example, actually is part of a longer passage that reveals the student's difficulties in handling plurals, both in subject-verb agreement and in noun-pronoun agreement. In addition, the student has a problem with the singular of "women." Here is the whole paragraph. You will recognize it as part of the women's liberation paper cited earlier. The paper has a number of problems with mechanics. It is obviously a rough draft, so some of the mechanical problems are undoubtedly performance-based and will straighten themselves out as the student hones his focus, becomes clearer about his real message, and revises his prose. If confusion about plurals persists in a final draft, however, you will want to help the student control plurality, as it affects subject-verb agreement, noun-pronoun agreement, and formation of plural nouns.

```
     The advantages for women, as equals, except in the cases of
equal pay for equal work, is very few.  I really can not see how
women could possibly be benefited, by wanting to come out of their
protective home, mother, housewife, shells, to work along side a
man in some kind of hard backbreaking job.  About the only logical
advantage that a women would have would be where equal work gets
```

```
equal pay.  If women are qualified and can perform the same work
that a man does, she should receive equal pay.
```

In this passage, you can praise the use of "shells," which, though separated widely from the plural noun "women" and from the plural pronoun "their," nevertheless remembers its plural antecedents. Many students would have written "shell." Thus the maintenance, in that sentence, of a consistent plural shows the student's ability to keep the plural concept in mind throughout a complex sentence. You will want to build on that base by suggesting that the student put himself through the appropriate sections of a programmed text, workbook, or media program; that he work in the never-again notebook; or that he do both. The appropriate sections of texts will be labeled "Subject-Verb Agreement," "Noun-Pronoun Agreement," or "Singular and Plural." In the never-again notebook, I would work on three issues. One is the distraction problem noted above. The next is the spelling of "woman" and "women." Have the student write both forms and then compose sentences using the singular and the plural.

```
Women are crazy.
A woman is crazy.

Some women do not want to become liberated.
Sometimes a woman does not want to become liberated.
```

The third step is to work on the last sentence in the paragraph. The problem is that the student, after correctly spelling the plural "women" and joining it with a plural verb "are," then shifts to a singular pronoun "she." Have him practice retaining the plurality through the pronoun, even when the pronoun comes way at the end.

```
If women are qualified and can perform the same work that a man does,
     they should receive equal pay.
If a woman is qualified and can perform the same work that a man does,
     she should receive equal pay.
When the plants begin to look scraggly, they should be brought out
     into the sun.
When a plant begins to look scraggly, it should be brought out
     into the sun.
```

Having students draw arrows, as above, sometimes helps in tracking singular and plural constructions.

Inflection—verbs

The problems of plurality in the women's liberation paragraph at first appear jumbled and hopeless. Careful analysis of the paragraph, however, reveals some signs of the student's consistency and effort. It also reveals that the difficulties are separable into three units, which can be attacked separately in the never-again notebook or broadly in a program that will give the student practice controlling plurality in general.

Forming Verbs

Sometimes, regardless of whether subject and verb agree, the verb forms themselves are not in accordance with the rules of EAE. Verb forms are strongly influenced by dialect. Here are the most common dialect-influenced errors in verb forms:

1. Omission of the *s* at the end of third-person-singular verbs, as in "he say."
2. Omission of the *ed* in forming the past tense, as in "Yesterday I walk."
3. Omission of the verb in certain constructions, as in "It heavy."
4. Changes in the form of the auxiliary, as in "My mother be working" or "It be's that way."

Though these are recognized characteristics of black English vernacular, the forms will appear also among members of other ethnic groups and among whites. For example, Chinese students might say, "It heavy," because their language allows a similar omission of the verb. Do not make the mistake of believing that dialect influence is limited to people of color. Many white students will show in writing the same variations from EAE verb forms, either because their everyday speech contains some dialect forms or because there is pressure, in every language and dialect, to erode inflections that are not necessary to meaning.

An additional eroding influence on inflectional endings is the context in which the word appears. If it is followed, in speech, by a similar consonant, the two may slide together so that one doesn't hear the ending at all. Since students don't hear it, they tend not to write it, or they write something that approximates the sound, as in "She would of gone."

Perception is undoubtedly a highly important factor as well. As every foreign language teacher knows, people differ greatly in ability to hear and reproduce small differences in sound or accent. Some students seem to have a difficult time learning the verb forms common to EAE, even if they hear or read them often.

In this unusually complex area your task is to discover how much of the problem is performance-based, whether or not the student needs to undertake a program that teaches, step by step, the forms of EAE verbs, and, if so, where such instruction should begin. Usually it is a matter of only partial ignorance or of unsteady control, since it is a rare speaker who has not been corrected or exposed to "standard" dialect, thereby gaining at least some notion of what the accepted EAE forms are.

When faced with the need to teach verb forms, try to determine whether the regular or irregular verbs give trouble and find out which forms students need to work on. If they are having difficulty with regular verbs (verbs whose different forms are created by adding *s* or *ed*), you might choose a self-instructional text that includes drill on regular verbs, or you could simply set up a series of patterns in the never-again notebook, practicing the *s* and *ed* forms of regular verbs. If you choose a text, avoid one that teaches all forms with equal ferocity, intent on covering the verb system in English. The task is not to learn all verb forms—as one might learn *amo, amas, amat,* out of equal ignorance of all three and with no substitute already in habitual use—but rather to recognize those points at which EAE forms differ from those the writer uses in speech and to learn to use the EAE verbs in writing. The most appropriate self-instructional texts are based on this recognition; they give the student practice in recognizing and changing the problematic forms. Often the drills help exercise perceptual and proofreading skills as well.

Irregular verbs are those that are inflected by changes in spelling rather than by adding *s* or *ed.* No one is guiltless of misusing these verbs. Aren't you still sometimes hesitant about "lie" and "lay"? So the task for students is to pick out those misformed irregular verbs that seem most disturbing for readers and then memorize them one by one, until the correct form comes easily to mind, even in hasty writing. From a student's paper select one or two misformed irregular verbs and have the student enter them in the never-again notebook in the following grid:

Today I (you, she, we, you, they) _____ .
[separate set of blanks for each pronoun].
Tomorrow I (etc.) will _____ .
Yesterday I (etc.)_____ .
Until now I (etc.) have _____ .
Until then I (etc.) had _____ .

In addition, offer drill in the specific form misused in the student's paper, whether the subjunctive, the verb with an auxiliary such as "have," the infinitive form, or the verb in a distracting context. Here, for example, is a student who does not correctly form the past tense of "forbid":

```
The Americans were stubborn, and although the guards often forbid
them to congregate, they arranged programs with songs and skits.
```

Instead of having this student turn to a workbook chapter on irregular verbs, you might concentrate on the particular verb the student is misus-

Inflection—verbs

ing. Just use the never-again notebook to drill the student on the form of "forbid" that's troublesome. Another student may need help with "may" or "to be" or "lie."

Deciding Which Tense to Use

The problem of tense has two aspects. The first involves deciding on a dominant tense—past or present. This is especially problematic for papers such as historical narratives, which might be handled in the past or in the historical present. It also becomes a problem when the student is recounting past events that still hold true, as in the paper on rape that follows shortly.

Once the dominant tense is decided on, the writer deals with the second aspect: aligning other verbs in a fashion consistent with that initial decision. Inconsistencies may result from the student's losing track of the original tense and slipping into another, or they may arise from insecurity in handling the tense called for, especially when it is a tense not frequently used in conversational speech, such as the past perfect (*"have had* to face").

This section of a paper on rape illustrates several interrelated aspects of the tense problem (superscript numbers refer to endnotes in the student's paper):

Rapists usually work alone and attack only lone women. In completed rapes ninety five percent of the victims were alone, and in attempted rapes ninety one percent of the victims were alone. About sixty percent of completed rapes and eighty percent of attempted were perpetrated alone so it is safe to say the majority of rapes involve one victim and one offender.[16]

The time and place of occurrence of rapes is very rarely the stereotype of a women being attacked in a dark alley. In contrast more than one-third of rapes occurr during the daytime (6 am to 6 pm). About one-half occur during the evening hours (6 pm to midnight) and one-sixth (midnight and 6 am). Through the evidence we can see that most rapes occurr during the evening hours.[17]

About one-fifth of all reported rapes occurr in the victims home, and an additional fourteen percent took place nearby. More than sixty five percent of rapes occurred in open outdoor places.[18]

Feelings women have after rape are disturbing because of the terrifying ordeal which they had to face.

This student must first decide on a dominant tense. The problem is connected to the student's doubt about whether the study being quoted can be assumed to support statements about rape in the present. The absence of any up-front discussion about the nature, date, or circumstances of the study, as well as the vacillation of verb tenses, is the student's way of hiding from this dilemma. Help the writer be forthright about the study. Then show her how to make the tenses consistent.

It may be that the last sentence illustrates not only the writer's doubt about which tense to make dominant but also her inexperience in handling the perfect tenses. If this is the explanation, turn to the section on the past perfect in a self-instructional text and/or use the never-again notebook to offer drill on use of this tense:

```
Feelings women have after rape are disturbing because of the
terrifying ordeal which they have had to face.

Feelings women had after rape were disturbing because of the
terrifying ordeal which they had had to face.
```

Revision of the diction in this sentence might offer a better basis for drill:

```
Feelings women experience after rape are disturbing because of the
terrifying ordeal they have had to face.
```

For additional practice in using the perfect tenses, have the student compose other pairs of sentences based on the same model.

Pronoun Forms

In pronouns you and your students again face a shifting scene. Not only are some distinctions fading, like the one between "who" and "whom," but the whole castle of pronoun usage has recently been assaulted by feminists and will certainly never be the same. In addition, the pronoun's position in the sentence is often sufficient to make the meaning clear; inflection is therefore a redundant clue and easy to skip over. For example, if a student writes the common black English vernacular form, "They lost they hats," the meaning will be made perfectly clear by the pronoun's place in the sentence; the inflection is not needed for meaning.

In helping students achieve accurate EAE pronoun choices, it is helpful to examine five categories in which students often make errors:

1. Knowing the EAE pronoun form.
2. Making the pronoun agree with its antecedent.
3. Avoiding ambiguous or nonexistent antecedents.
4. Avoiding redundant pronouns.
5. Choosing appropriate pronouns, especially "I," "you," and "one," and resolving the issue of sexist usage.

Knowing the EAE Pronoun Form

A pronoun derives some of its characteristics from its place in the sentence, and students' mistakes in this area are usually caused by a difference between the language of informal conversation and that of more formal writing. Three of the most common mistakes are:

1. Use of the nominative form (he, you, they) where EAE would require the possessive (his, your, their). For example:

```
Go back to the playground and get you bat.
She told the children to eat they dinner.
```

2. Use of the nominative form (I, he, they) where EAE would require the objective form (me, him, them), or vice versa. For example:

```
She gave the tapes to he and I.
He took a blood sample from Jerry and I.
Him and me went to the store.
```

3. Confusion among "who," "whom," and "whose."

The first problem involves a dialect form and needs the same kind of learning and practice as other dialect forms. The other two problems are common among all English speakers. Sometimes you can help the student by teaching a substitution trick: in a sentence where the writer is in doubt about whether to use "she" or "her," or "who" or "whom," have the student eliminate companion nouns and pronouns, substitute another pronoun, or change to regular subject-verb sentence order. Here's how these techniques work. A student writes:

```
The young woman who they had punished complained to the social
worker.
```

Teach students to make a simple subject-verb sentence out of the "who" clause and to substitute the appropriate pronoun form of "they" or "she." When they have done that, they will hear the correct form. The student thinks:

```
They had punished (she, her).
```

Now make clear that "her" equals "whom," and students can make the correct choice without grammar instruction on direct objects and the objective case.

The elimination of companion nouns and pronouns works this way. The student has written:

```
He took a blood sample from Jerry and I.
```

Inflection—pronouns

Ask the student to omit the companion noun "Jerry," so that the sentence reads:

```
He took a blood sample from I.
```

In this form the student will usually hear the mistake. Here are some more examples of the type you might show a student or have students enter in their never-again notebooks:

```
The baby who the doctors had operated on was again in trouble.
The doctors operated on (he, him).
The doctors operated on him.
The doctors operated on whom.
The baby whom the doctors had operated on was again in trouble.
```

Making Pronouns Agree with Their Antecedents

The same problems arise with pronoun-antecedent agreement as with subject-verb agreement: many students do not know whether certain nouns (such as "group" or "crowd") or certain noun phrases (such as "each of the apples") are singular or plural; therefore they do not know which pronoun to use to refer to these antecedents. This problem, when it appears in the work of students who are otherwise in control of EAE pronoun usage, simply requires developing a sense about certain collective nouns that are sometimes handled as singular and sometimes as plural. Here, for example, is a student who refers back to "Congress" with a singular verb and a plural pronoun:

```
In an article they wrote together Moe and Teel's feelings were that
since it is assumed that congress has lost influence and their role
more of legitimating and amending policies initiated by the executive
then at some prior time congressional influence must have been
greater.  Sometime in the past there must have been a "golden era."
Moe and Teel protest that there was never this "golden era."
```

The complex pattern of the sentence is consistent here, showing a certain linguistic sophistication, but the pattern chosen does not work well; it is too hard to follow. When the student revises to a simpler sentence pattern, the problem pronoun may disappear; however, since pronouns with group nouns like "Congress" are common, I would point out the error and offer practice in handling collective nouns.

In this example, the student erroneously uses a singular pronoun but maintains it with consistency.

Inflection—pronouns

```
Inmates must attend these therapy sessions and talk about himself,
his relationship to his parents, his past sins and learn what his
"problem" was.
```

For this slip, it is helpful to have the student draw arrows from each pronoun to the antecedent. Such a practice should result in correct pronoun choice, since the plurality of "inmates" is clear, and there are no particularly distracting sentence components in the way. Note also that this passage illustrates the student's unfamiliarity with the present perfect tense; the sentence would be improved if the last part read "learn what his 'problem' *has been*." The sentence could be further revised to remedy its faulty parallelism.

In the next example, the disparity between pronoun and antecedent occurs because the student begins a quotation and neglects to choose his own noun to agree with the pronoun "they" in the quoted material:

```
In Irenaeus, evil was started by Adam (man) in his eating of the
forbidden fruit.  Man "being newly created they were therefore
childish, and immature, and not yet fully trained for an adult
way of life."
```

The teacher here can emphasize that quotation marks must not distract the writer from lining up pronouns and antecedents.

Avoiding Ambiguous or Nonexistent Antecedents

A closely related problem is the pronoun without a clear antecedent. In the following example, the problem is caused by the two possible antecedents—"car" and "track"—and the sentence structure does not make clear which is the antecedent of "it." The word "which" suffers from a similar ambiguity:

```
To keep the car on the track it has a tiny peg that sticks out
the bottom which fits into the slit.
```

It is usually enough to circle the ambiguous pronouns and reflect the reader's question, "What has the peg?" or "What fits into the slit?"

In this example, an ambiguous pronoun occurs in a much more complicated passage that contains many nouns and pronouns. It may be the complexity that distracts the student, who seems to lose control at the paragraph's end. In a previous paragraph the student has explained that administrators of Patuxent have been criticized for treating the "defective delinquent" differently from others.

```
The administrators of Patuxent don't feel that these criticisms
are in any way valid.  They feel that the defective delinquent is a
```

very particular type of criminal. A court case was decided in their
favor on these grounds. The court held that the statutory definition
was clear enough to meet the requirements of the 14th Amendment.
The defective delinquent is one that acts on impulse, so political
and professional criminals are naturally excluded. They also are
very careful about their decisions by having a board composed of one
psychologist, one physician and one psychiatrist to make the
decision.

The paragraph falls apart in several ways after the fourth sentence.
The thread of reasoning is not clear; consequently the paragraph loses coherence. With the general weakening of control comes the pronoun problem. So in addition to remonstrances about pronoun references, the
remedial work would include recasting the paragraph so that the last two
sentences are better integrated.

The same paragraph illustrates another common problem: students
often use "that" where "who" would be more appropriate, since the reference is to a person, not a thing. This usage offends my own ears, as perhaps it does yours. It appears so commonly nowadays, however, that I
would categorize it as one of those distinctions that are disappearing from
the language, so I don't worry about it except in very formal papers or
with a student who has everything else under control.

A revision of the paragraph might read:

The administrators of Patuxent don't feel that these criticisms
are in any way valid because the defective delinquent is a very
particular type of criminal--one who acts on impulse. By this
definition, political and professional criminals are clearly
excluded. A court case in the administrators' favor held that the
statutory definition was clear enough to meet the requirements of
the 14th amendment. Administrators exercise additional caution:
all decisions are made by a board composed of one psychologist,
one physician and one psychiatrist.

One common characteristic of student writing is the use of "this" or
"it" with no clear antecedent. For example:

I feel a major supporter of the Chondrasekhor limit is the nova
T. Coronae Boreales whech keeps reoccurring. It seems to me that
this nova is trying to get under the limit and this explaens its
lack of intensety as the number of sightings grows. (It) also   *What?*
supports the limiting factor of a star and the continuous process
that proves that there is an infinite characteristic in the stars.
They will always be there but they will always be dieing and   *I'm*
being reborn.   *lost.*

Inflection—pronouns

In this paragraph the ambiguous "it" signals the breakdown of meaning; after that pronoun, the reader can no longer easily follow the writer's thought. I would mark the "it" and point out the general loss of coherence.

As you deal with pronoun-antecedent problems, you will suggest ways of amending problem sentences. This passage and its revised version illustrate the three primary ways in which students can be taught to remedy pronoun difficulties:

```
        Beck and his colleagues were against Hitler's
               , which, they believed,
policies believing that they might get Germany

into a conflict with another country.  Hitler had
                                          Austria-acts
already occupied the Rhineland and invaded Austria,

which were openly antagonistic on the part of

           The group was
Hitler.  They were also against his dictatorial

rule.
```

Avoiding Redundant Pronouns

Some dialects characteristically repeat the pronoun in places where EAE would omit it. For example:

```
The children who were waiting in the car, they began to scream.
My father he is an engineer on an oil tanker.
```

Remedy may include having the student go through the pertinent sections of some text, usually entitled broadly "Pronoun Usage." Or you can simply provide drill in the never-again notebook. In cases where the pronoun directly follows the noun, as in "My father he," you are probably dealing with a dialect form. Provide the student with practice in deleting the redundant pronoun. In cases where other sentence structures intervene between the noun and the redundant pronoun, practice simplifying the sentence. For example, suppose that a student has written this:

```
The company officials, after an investigation by the environmental
protection agency, they decided to install a costly precipitator.
```

In the notebook, this student should write:

```
The company officials decided to install. . . .
The company officials, after an investigation, decided to install. . . .
The company officials, after an investigation by the environmental
protection agency, decided to install. . . .
```

Making Choices about Pronoun Usage

Problems in using the appropriate pronoun fall into three subdivisions: the use of "I"; the choice between "you" and "one"; and the question of "sexist" pronouns.

"I." When I urge students to revise a sentence by using the pronoun "I," they often object, "But my teacher in high school told me never to use 'I.' " Teachers who give such advice are undoubtedly trying to eliminate the wordiness and inappropriateness of phrases like "I believe that . . ." and "I would like to state that . . ." in academic papers. A worthy aim. In fact, such verbiage *is* often best left out. Students, however, often mistakenly interpreted such strictures as prohibiting all use of "I" in school writing. So they write circles around it, or they resort to awkward phrases such as "this writer." Make clear to them that, while they will want to avoid self-conscious or wordy "I" statements in formal academic writing, the word "I" has a place in writing, even, in some cases, in formal academic writing.

"You" and "one." Another cluster of problems circle around the use of "you" and "one." Typical is the dilemma this student faces:

```
In Medieval literature the evils were in the forms of
temptations that were more physical, lust, greed, etc.  And in
Renaissance the evil was to aspire to be greater than you really
were. . . .  Everyman was evil because he did not live as he should
have to make his ascent to heaven easy.  But Everyman showed that
one could redeem one's self if one confessed and repented.
```

The first principle to enforce is that of consistency. The combination of "you" and "one" in this passage does not work. In deciding whether to change everything to the more informal "you" or to the more formal "one," your judgment and the student's maturing sense must be the guides. Sometimes it is possible to recast the whole passage to get rid of the pronoun and thus avoid the problem altogether. For example, this passage could be revised to read:

```
And in the Renaissance the evil was for a person to aspire to
be greater than he really was. . . . Everyman showed that a person
could redeem himself if he confessed and repented.
```

Inflection—pronouns

Sexist pronouns. This last example illustrates a problem more and more discussed: what, if anything, should be done about the issue of sex bias in pronoun usage and in related aspects of language. It is an area in which you or your students may have strong feelings. I do not intend to get into the issues here; I will merely indicate the three possible positions one can take in regard to pronouns.

1. *Use "he" in all instances* as the singular indefinite pronoun: "In the Renaissance the evil was for a person to aspire to be greater than he really was."

2. *Use "he" in instances where the meaning is obviously indefinite.* But where use of "he" might indicate bias, attempt to avoid it. For example, in the sentence above, "he" is quite obviously the indefinite pronoun. The following sentence, however, implies that all Romantic poets were men: "Both of these ideas were seen in the Romanticist's poetry as he witnessed poor people trying to improve themselves." You may want to avoid using "he" in such sentences.

3. *Avoid "he" as the indefinite pronoun.*

Students who want to avoid the controversial "he" can find alternatives. They may use several, as I have done in writing this book:

1. They can use the plural rather than the singular. Instead of "A chemist may seriously limit his career," they can write, "Chemists may seriously limit their careers."
2. When they think it will not offend the audience's sense of correctness, they can follow conversational rather than formal written codes and use "their" or "they" with a singular noun. Instead of "When someone contacts his legislator," they can write "When someone contacts their legislator."
3. They can omit the pronoun. Instead of "A chemist may seriously limit his career options," they can write, "A chemist may seriously limit career options." Instead of "A merchant, if he sells produce, must have a license," they can write, "A merchant who sells produce . . ." or "A merchant selling produce."
4. They can use a combination of masculine and feminine pronouns, like "he or she," "his or her," or "s/he." Since, however, these combinations trouble many readers, you may want students to adopt one of the first three practices to avoid the third-person singular pronoun to refer to someone of unspecified sex. When the singular cannot be avoided, the writer can choose (a) to use a combination or hybrid even though it sounds awkward; (b) to use the masculine

pronoun, perhaps with a disclaimer (some writers, like Maimon and
Shaughnessy, cited in Chapters 5 and 9, have said in their prefaces
that they know no graceful way of avoiding the masculine pronoun
and they want the reader to know that they use it to mean a person
of either sex); or (c) use the feminine pronoun, at least some of the
time, as the indefinite: "When a doctor lists her number with us, we
follow three special procedures." Faced with these alternatives, you
may establish your own policy and ask students to adhere to it, or
you may let students establish their own, provided that they base it
on a carefully considered and consistently applied rationale.

Possessive and Plural Nouns

In forming possessive and plural nouns students make errors in adding the apostrophe, in deciding whether the *s* or the apostrophe comes
first, and in forming the plural of nouns. Unlike other inflected forms, a
possessive noun has not only an audible component but also an inaudible
and scarcely visible punctuation mark. Apostrophes are probably the
most frequently omitted bits of punctuation left in the English language.
Most students know, or at least have a pretty good idea, where to put
them. They just have to be encouraged to get into the habit of going
through their papers and putting apostrophes in. If you find a student
who does not understand the concept of possessive case, self-instructional texts will help. Such books are also the best approach if students are
using the apostrophe and "s" but need to learn the rules that determine
which comes first.

Forming the plural of nouns is, for the most part, a matter of adding
an *s.* Occasionally, however, students will form the plural of a noun with
an apostrophe and an *s,* for example, "We ride the horse's each week."
Find out whether the student can distinguish the possessive use of a
noun. If so, emphasize that the apostrophe occurs with nouns only in the
possessive case, never in any other.

Plural forms of irregular nouns are also sometimes a problem. The
best remedy is drill in the never-again notebook, one noun at a time:
mouse, mice; goose, geese; addendum, addenda.

Negative Forms

Most problems in making negative statements come from carrying
over into formal writing the non-EAE forms found in conversational
speech, such as:

It don't matter.
I didn't have none.
He didn't have no reason.
We never said nothing, neither.

Inflection—possessive and plural nouns—negatives

Describe these forms to students as "too informal" or as "dialect choice." If you call the problem to their attention, you will find that many students know the EAE forms. If they do not, provide drill through the never-again notebook. Self-instructional texts go through the forms of negation in EAE, but the information may not "take" until the student works with it in the writing for your class.

Punctuation

I will not attempt to cover all the rules of punctuation in English. I leave that to the handbooks and the self-instructional texts. Instead I will complement those resources by offering a discussion of the punctuation problems students face in certain common writing situations. A given situation may involve several different rules, or several different sections of a handbook, so it is often more helpful for the student to focus on a writing situation and learn the punctuation it involves than to memorize all the uses of the comma.

Interrupting Sentence Elements

Students must learn to set off interrupting phrases with commas on both sides. For example, this student put in the first comma but not the second: "Mitford, since she wanted all prisoners out would like the idea." A remedy is to circle, or have the student circle, the entire interrupting element. Certain short elements of course do not need commas—for example, the "of course" in this sentence. There is a large area in the middle where the writer may choose.

A special concern is restrictive and nonrestrictive clauses—that is, the rule that a "who" or "which" clause *is* set off by commas when it is *not* necessary to the meaning of the noun but *is not* set off when it *is* necessary. For example, "The man who is sitting on the bench is my father." Other men are present. From all of them the speaker marks one by an identifying descriptive clause. If, however, there are only three women and a man at the bus stop, the speaker can say, "The man, who is sitting on the bench, is my father." The identification of the man would be clear without the "who" clause; the clause merely adds to the description of the man and thus requires commas.

Many self-instructional texts and handbooks explain this difference, or you can simply explain it to your students.

Along with teaching the use of commas to set off interrupting elements, help students develop a sense of when to use parentheses and dashes. Simply mark in their papers the punctuation you would suggest, or let them know when their choices do not strike you as right. It is, in any case, an area in which the writer has considerable personal choice.

Comma for Clarity

Commas are the most common mark writers can use to achieve clarity, especially in complex passages or in sentences that might be ambiguous without commas. For example, it is perfectly admissible to write this sentence with no commas: "After we ate supper we went to the game." In a possibly confusing situation, however, a comma would be advisable: "After we ate, supper was served to the others." Here the comma is necessary to prevent the reader from thinking that "After we ate supper" is an introductory clause to be followed by something like "we went to the game."

Encourage students to read with an eye for possible ambiguities. When you find them, point out the other possible reading with a comment or, if you think the student will grasp your meaning, mark the sentence "ambiguous."

Introductory or Concluding Elements

Sometimes, especially with introductory material, the comma is used to separate a phrase or clause from the main sentence: for example, "Since Buys's book was written before 1972, it does not reflect recent developments." Sometimes students leave out necessary commas in these cases. If so, you have to help build the habit of including the comma. Other times, the student substitutes a period, so that the introductory element becomes a sentence fragment. If this is the case, deal with it as a problem in writing complete sentences, discussed earlier.

Lists

One type of list is a sequence of two or more adjectives—for example, "The complex, lengthy document was read twice before the vote." Another type of list is the string of items presented as a list. Students have problems determining where and when to use a colon to precede a list. A colon, you can tell them, announces that a list or an explanation will follow, but it should not interrupt a simple sentence. In handling each of these problems, it is helpful to present both punctuation patterns. For example, a student has written:

```
The items on the menu that day were:  carrots, potatoes, salad
and pork.
```

In the never-again notebook, have this student write:

```
The items on the menu that day were carrots, potatoes, salad,
and pork.
The items on the menu that day were as follows:  carrots . . . .
```

Punctuation—clarity—introductory or concluding—lists

A related problem is whether to use commas or semicolons between items in a list. The rule is simple: use semicolons when individual members of the list contain commas; otherwise use commas. I find this one of the easiest rules to explain, and I usually just say it or write it directly to the student.

Quotations

Once you have helped students master basics of quoting, as described earlier, you're left with "Does the comma go inside or outside the quotation marks?" To give students a general guide, you can tell them, "Inside will hardly ever do you wrong." More varied are the rules governing use of capital letters in quoting. Further, the student must know how to alter a quoted passage, either by using points of ellipsis (dots) to indicate omissions or by using brackets to indicate insertions (students most often use parentheses instead of brackets for this purpose). Handbooks and self-instructional texts explain these rules, as do many handbooks on writing term papers.

Documentation

You may have to teach the students the form of documentation common to your field, whether footnotes or parenthetical insertions. Often students learn documentation methods in composition classes taught by instructors trained in literature, who usually teach their own methods, not necessarily those used in your field.

In both quotation and documentation, teaching students to use style handbooks is probably more important than teaching them the rules, since nobody remembers all the rules anyway. In fact, few of us could produce a professional article without consulting an appropriate style manual. If you are teaching the documentation methods for your field, ask students to obtain the appropriate style manual or make it known and available to them. Then teach them how to use it. Have them bring a copy to class, or ask them to Xerox the table of contents, the index, and selected passages and bring those instead. Illustrate how they can use the handbook to find answers to their dilemmas; demystify the book for them.

Dates, Numbers, and Proper Nouns

In trying to decide how to write dates, numbers, and proper nouns, even practiced authors thumb the handbook pages. You can focus on a specific rule or two and try to teach it through the never-again notebook. You can also concentrate, if you wish, on teaching students how to use handbooks efficiently (for example, some students need to be taught what a "proper noun" is so that they can look up answers to their questions about capitalizing and punctuating the names of places, persons, and institutions).

Spelling

A special word about spelling. Poor spellers are the students who are perhaps most likely to become discouraged, sometimes feeling like the only ones on the ward with an incurable disease. It takes forever for them to get their papers ready to hand in because they have to look up every other word in the dictionary, and occasionally they don't even know enough of the spelling to find the word. Tonics for poor spellers come in two basic types, and both taste awful; but there's no sugar-coated alternative that works. One approach is to have the student learn the rules that govern English spelling. Several workbooks and programmed texts take this approach, and for some students it is helpful. The problem is, of course, that there are so many exceptions to the rules that when you get done you may have as many chickens still running around the barnyard as you've managed to shut up in the coop.

A second approach is to rely primarily on memorization of the most frequently misspelled words and/or the misspelled words that are most likely to distract readers. Texts and workbooks that rely on this method present the two or three hundred most commonly misspelled words and ask the student simply to drill and memorize, with perhaps a little guidance from some obvious or simple rules, like "*i* before *e* except after *c*. . . ." Your student may or may not be misspelling the same two hundred words as the other students in the national sample, however, so a pretest might help.

The never-again notebook is an excellent tool for spelling because it allows students to concentrate on their own spelling errors, not just on the words in the workbook. Select five words for the notebook from the student's own writing. Once those are mastered, never to be misspelled again, choose five more. Base your choice on misspelled words you think would be most disturbing to readers.

Summary

If you've read this book straight through, you've been bogged down for a long time now in clauses and colons. But in the total view, my advice to those who want to help students write more effectively can be summarized in just three statements. First, writing is the yeast of the learning process, not merely the frosting. To integrate writing as a significant element in your course is to enrich students' learning, and the thoughtful teacher can increase the yield by careful attention to the types of writing students do, the purposes writing fulfills, and the way assignments are explained to students.

The second tenet of this book is that the teacher should become a coach of the student writer rather than merely a judge of the written product. Third, the wise instructor, instead of merely marking errors simply because they're there, analyzes the writing as a communication by a writer to a reader. In communicating to the student about a paper, the teacher should concentrate on the writing-learning process the student is following and should tailor the response to the individual student: what the student already knows, what the student is able to learn in the particular writing exercise, and what the student needs for optimum learning—praise as well as criticism, help in setting priorities, and so on.

If teachers practiced these three principles across the curriculum, I believe that we would significantly enhance the quality of writing—and, more broadly, the quality of learning—that takes place today in institutions of higher education.

Notes

Introduction

[1]C. G. Enke, "Scientific Writing: One Scientist's Perspective," *English Journal,* 67 (Apr. 1978), 40.

[2]Ann S. Bisconti and Lewis E. Solomon, *College Education on the Job: The Graduates' Viewpoint* (Bethlehem, Pa.: College Placement Council Foundation, 1976), pp. 36–37.

[3]Robert Gagne and Ernest Smith, "A Study of the Effects of Verbalization on Problem-Solving," in *Readings in the Psychology of Cognition,* ed. Richard C. Anderson and David P. Ansubel (New York: Holt, 1965), pp. 389–90.

[4]Robert H. Weiss and S. A. Walters, "Research on Writing and Learning: Some Effects of Learning-Centered Writing in Five Subject Areas," Session on Research in Composition, National Council of Teachers of English Convention, San Francisco, March 1979 (ERIC Ed 191 073).

[5]Janet Emig, "Writing as a Mode of Learning," *College Composition and Communication,* 28 (1977), 122–28.

[6]See Jeremy M. Anglin, ed., *Beyond the Information Given: Studies in the Psychology of Knowing* (New York: Norton, 1973). See also Jerome Bruner, R. P. Oliver, and P. M. Greenfield, *Studies in Cognitive Growth* (New York: Wiley, 1966).

[7]Andrea A. Lunsford, "Cognitive Development and the Basic Writer," *College English,* 41 (Sept. 1979), 38–46. See also Jean Piaget, *Six Psychological Studies* (New York: Random, 1967).

[8]Peter F. Woodford, "Sounder Thinking through Clearer Writing," *Science,* 156 (1967), 745.

Chapter One

[1]The studies are summarized by Elizabeth F. Haynes in "Using Research in Preparing to Teach Writing, " *English Journal,* 67 (Jan. 1978), 84–87.

[2]Gene Stanford and the Committee on Classroom Practices, *How to Handle the Paper Load: Classroom Practices in Teaching English, 1979–1980* (Urbana, Ill.: National Council of Teachers of English, 1979).

Chapter Two

[1]Janet Emig, *The Composing Processes of Twelfth Graders,* National Council of Teachers of English Research Report 13 (Urbana, Ill.: National Council of Teachers of English, 1971), pp. 22–25.

[2]Virginia Woolf, *A Writer's Diary,* ed. Leonard Woolf (New York: Harcourt, 1954), p. 21.

[3]Nancy Sommers, "Revision Strategies of Student Writers and Experienced Adult Writers," *College Composition and Communication,* 31 (Dec. 1980), 382–83.

[4]Charles K. Stallard, "An Analysis of the Writing Behavior of Good Student Writers," *Research in the Teaching of English,* 7 (Fall 1974), 211, 217.

[5]Donald Murray, *A Writer Teaches Writing* (Boston: Houghton, 1968).

Chapter Three

[1]Doris Clinard Weddington, "Taped Feedback—Have You Tried It?" *Journal of Developmental and Remedial Education,* 1 (1978), 10–11, 18.

[2]Donald Murray, "The Listening Eye: Reflections on the Writing Conference," *College English,* 41 (Sept. 1979), 13–18.

[3]Peter Elbow, *Writing without Teachers* (New York: Oxford Univ. Press, 1973).

Chapter Four

[1]James Britton, "The Composing Processes and the Functions of Writing," in *Research on Composing: Points of Departure,* ed. Charles R. Cooper and Lee Odell (Urbana, Ill.: National Council of Teachers of English, 1978), p. 15.

[2]Richard Lloyd-Jones, "Primary Trait Scoring," in *Evaluating Writing,* ed. Charles R. Cooper and Lee Odell (Urbana, Ill.: National Council of Teachers of English, 1977), pp. 33–66.

Chapter Five

[1]Judson Monroe, Carole Meredith, and Kathleen Fisher, *The Science of Scientific Writing* (Dubuque, Ia.: Kendall/Hunt, 1977).

[2]Richard L. Larson, "Problem-Solving, Composing and Liberal Education," *College English,* 33 (Mar. 1972), 628–35.

[3]Linda Flower, *Problem-Solving Strategies for Writing* (New York: Harcourt, 1981), pp. 35–48.

[4]Elaine Maimon et al., *Writing in the Arts and Sciences* (Cambridge, Mass.: Winthrop, 1981).

Chapter Six

[1]W. Ross Winterowd, *The Contemporary Writer: A Practical Rhetoric* (New York: Harcourt, 1975), pp. 98–101. In preparing his guide, Winterowd drew on Richard Young, Alton Becker, and Kenneth Pike, *Rhetoric: Discovery and Change* (New York: Harcourt, 1970), pp. 126–29.

[2]Linda Flower and John R. Hayes, "The Cognition of Discovery: Defining a Rhetorical Problem," *College Composition and Communication,* 31 (Feb. 1980), 21–32.

Chapter Eight

[1]Ken Macrorie, *Uptaught* (Rochelle Park, N.J.: Hayden, 1970), p. 18.

[2]Robert V. Kesling, "Crimes in Scientific Writing," *Turtox News,* 36 (Dec. 1958), 276.

Chapter Nine

[1]Frances Christensen, *Notes toward a New Rhetoric* (New York: Harper, 1967). Frank O'Hare, *Sentence-Combining: Improving Student Writing without Formal Grammar Instruction,* Research Report No. 15 (Urbana, Ill.: National Council of Teachers of English, 1973).

[2]Ronald W. Langacker, "An Initial Look at Language," in *Language and Cultural Diversity*

in American Education, ed. Roger Abrahams and Rudolph C. Troike (Englewood Cliffs, N.J.: Prentice-Hall, 1972), pp. 95–100.

[3]Daisy Crystal, "Dialect Mixture and Sorting Out the Concept of Freshman Remediation," *The Florida FL Reporter,* 10, No. 1–2 (Spring-Fall 1972), 43–46.

[4]These studies are summarized in Jenefer M. Giannasi, "Dialects and Composition," in *Teaching Composition: Ten Bibliographical Essays,* ed. Gary Tate (Fort Worth, Tex.: Texas Christian Univ. Press, 1976), pp. 282–83.

[5]For a discussion of these issues, see Giannasi, pp. 275–304. See also E. D. Hirsch, *The Philosophy of Composition* (Chicago: Univ. of Chicago Press, 1977), pp. 43–50.

[6]Mina Shaughnessy, *Errors and Expectations* (New York: Oxford Univ. Press, 1977), p. 14.

Chapter Ten

[1]For the steps in perceptual training, see Patricia Laurence's "Error's Endless Train," *Journal of Basic Writing* (Spring 1975), pp. 23–42.

[2]Edward P. J. Corbett, *The Little English Handbook* (New York: Wiley, 1973).

Suggested Reading

Britton, James, et al. *The Development of Writing Abilities (11–18)*. London: Macmillan, 1975.

Cooper, Charles R., and Lee Odell, eds. *Evaluating Writing: Describing, Measuring, Judging*. Urbana, Ill.: National Council of Teachers of English, 1977.

———. *Research on Composing: Points of Departure*. Urbana, Ill.: National Council of Teachers of English, 1978.

Crombag, H. F. M., J. L. De Wijkerlooth, and E. H. van Tuyl van Serooskerken. "On Solving Legal Problems." *Journal of Legal Education*, 27 (1975), 168–202.

Dickerson, Reed. "Legal Drafting: Writing as Thinking, or Talk-Back from Your Draft and How to Exploit It." *Journal of Legal Education*, 29 (1978), 373–79.

Diederich, Paul. *Measuring Growth in English*. Urbana, Ill.: National Council of Teachers of English, 1974.

Elbow, Peter. *Writing without Teachers*. New York: Oxford Univ. Press, 1975.

Emig, Janet. *The Composing Processes of Twelfth Graders*. Urbana, Ill.: National Council of Teachers of English, 1971.

Flower, Linda. *Problem-Solving Strategies for Writing*. New York: Harcourt, 1981.

Flower, Linda, and John R. Hayes. "The Cognition of Discovery: Defining a Rhetorical Problem." *College Composition and Communication*, 31 (Feb. 1980), 21–32.

Harrington, Elbert W. "Rhetoric and the Scientific Method of Inquiry." *Univ. of Colorado Studies*, Series in Language and Literature, 1 (Dec. 1948), 1–64.

Haynes, Elizabeth F. "Using Research in Preparing to Teach Writing." *English Journal*, 67 (Jan. 1978), 84–87.

Hirsch, E. D. *The Philosophy of Composition*. Chicago: Univ. of Chicago Press, 1977.

Kasden, Lawrence, and Daniel Hoeber, eds. *Basic Writing: Essays for Teachers, Researchers and Administrators*. Urbana, Ill.: National Council of Teachers of English, 1980.

Larson, Richard. "Bibliography of Research and Writing about the Teaching of Composition." Published each May in *College Composition and Communication*.

———. "Problem-Solving, Composing, and Liberal Education." *College English*, 33 (Mar. 1972), 628–35.

Martin, Nancy, et al. *Writing and Learning across the Curriculum 11–16*. Schools Council Publications. London: Ward Lock, 1976.

Mathes, J. C., and Dwight Stevenson. *Designing Technical Reports*. Indianapolis: Bobbs-Merrill, 1976.

Moffett, James. *Teaching the Universe of Discourse*. Boston: Houghton, 1968.

Monroe, James, Carole Meredith, and Kathleen Fisher. *The Science of Scientific Writing*. Dubuque, Iowa: Kendall Hunt, 1977.

Murdock, Michael L. *Effective Writing for Business and Government*. 2nd ed. Washington, D.C.: Transemantics, 1977.

Murray, Don. "The Listening Eye: Reflections on the Writing Conference." *College English*, 41 (Sept. 1979), 13–18.

————. *A Writer Teaches Writing*. Boston: Houghton, 1968.

Odell, Lee. "Piaget, Problem-Solving, and Freshman Composition." *College Composition and Communication,* 24 (Feb. 1973), 36–42.

Sawyer, Thomas M., ed. *Technical and Professional Communication.* Ann Arbor, Mich.: Professional Communication Press, 1977.

Shaughnessy, Mina P. *Errors and Expectations: A Guide for the Teacher of Basic Writing.* New York: Oxford Univ. Press, 1977.

Sommers, Nancy. "Revision Strategies of Student Writers and Experienced Adult Writers." *College Composition and Communication,* 30 (Dec. 1980), 378–88.

Stallard, Charles K. "An Analysis of the Writing Behavior of Good Student Writers." *Research in the Teaching of English,* 8 (Fall 1974), 211–17.

Stanford, Gene, et al. *How to Handle the Paper Load.* Urbana, Ill.: National Council of Teachers of English, 1979.

Strunk, William, Jr., and E. B. White. *The Elements of Style.* 2nd ed. New York: Macmillan, 1972.

Tate, Gary, ed. *Teaching Composition: Ten Bibliographical Essays.* Fort Worth, Tex.: Texas Christian Univ. Press, 1976.

Weddington, Doris Clinard. "Taped Feedback—Have You Tried It?" *Journal of Developmental and Remedial Education,* 1 (1978), 10–11, 18.

Winterowd, W. Ross. *Contemporary Rhetoric: A Conceptual Background with Readings.* New York: Harcourt, 1975.

————. *The Contemporary Writer.* New York: Harcourt, 1975.

Young, Richard, Alton Becker, and Kenneth Pike. *Rhetoric: Discovery and Change.* New York: Harcourt, 1970.

Index